DEADLY
SECRETS

M. WILLIAM PHELPS

PINNACLE BOOKS
Kensington Publishing Corp.
http://www.kensingtonbooks.com

KENSINGTON BOOKS are published by

Kensington Publishing Corp.
119 West 40th Street
New York, NY 10018

Copyright © 2009, 2014 by M. William Phelps

All Kensington Titles, Imprints, and Distributed Lines are available at special quantity discounts for bulk purchases for sales promotions, premiums, fund-raising, and educational or institutional use. Special book excerpts or customized printings can also be created to fit specific needs. For details, write or phone the office of the Kensington special sales manager: Kensington Publishing Corp., 119 West 40th Street, New York, NY 10018, attn: Special Sales Department, Phone: 1-800-221-2647.

Kensington and the K logo Reg. U.S. Pat. & TM Off.

ISBN-13: 978-0-7860-3549-6
ISBN-10: 0-7860-3549-8
First Mass Market Edition: February 2009

eISBN-13: 978-0-7860-3550-2
eISBN-10: 0-7860-3550-1
Kensington Electronic Edition: November 2014

10 9 8 7 6 5 4 3

Printed in the United States of America

For the day of vengeance was in my heart,
and the year of my redemption has come.

—Isaiah 63:4

PROLOGUE

On that morning, after she dragged herself out of bed, put on her large-framed glasses, lit that first cigarette of the day and looked out the window, she began to think about her life. The wooded area surrounding her house reminded her of how much she adored living in the Catskill Mountains. It was where she belonged. So secluded and pastoral. The air fresh and full of vitality. Almost too perfect a picture, really. This morning there was no wind. No snow. Temperatures in the high thirties, with just the right amount of punch in the air, reminding everyone that winter was soon coming. In fact, it occurred to her as she sat, smoked and sipped coffee that Halloween was just three days away. The kids would soon dress in plastic masks of former presidents, Power Rangers, Batman and Barbie, and walk up and down the neighborhood streets with pumpkin flashlights and toothless smiles.

The bliss. The splendor. The silence of the morning. *How had such a simple life,* she thought, *come down to this?*

As she sat and thought about it, the beauty of autumn and the innocence of living in the country meant little. She was in a terrible spot. Full of anxiety. Panic. Dismay. Her gun was in the drawer underneath her water bed, and whenever she walked by that area of the room, or sat down on the bed, it seemed to speak to her.

Finish the job.

Don't do it.

But he'll kill my son.

I must go through with it.

Indeed, there was one time not too long ago when she woke up in the middle of the night for no apparent reason and realized she was on the floor, staring at the open drawer, the gun sitting there atop her folded clothes, looking back at her. And yet, she had no idea how she had gotten there.

"Psychologically," she later explained, "it was working on me twenty-four/seven."

It seemed so darn simple when she tossed it around in her mind. The threats to her family, she later claimed, in one respect, terrified her, and in another, made it easier to think about actually going through with his plan. She had known him for twenty-plus years. "He had a reputation," she once said, "for being able to *make* bad things happen to people. Good people."

He had connections in town—or, rather, that's what he led people to believe.

"I believed he was as powerful as John Gotti," she later admitted.

"I know *people*," he had once told her. "I'm *connected*" was how he put it.

And that's how this entire idea of murder all began: a few idle threats and a seemingly routine telephone call with an invitation attached. "Come to my house," he said. "We need to talk about *things*."

He sounded serious and urgent—all at the same time—which he could accomplish with that almost mature natural inflection of his. His tone, she said, could be menacing and put fear in you, but without alarm. He could intimidate and bully in subtle ways, without raising his voice.

The master manipulator.

The man with the gun in his hand.

The puppeteer.

He was all of these.

And more.

Weeks before that October 28, 1999, morning, she drove the hour south from the Catskills, down into Pleasant Valley and onto Poughkeepsie, then into Hyde Park, where he had lived all his life.

His wife wasn't home when she arrived.

She never was.

"Come in," he said, answering the door. "Come. I want to show you something." He had a cocky smile on his face. He was up to something. She knew it.

Pulling into the driveway moments before, she had glanced over at the new garage out in back of his house. Nearly $500,000 worth of metal, wood, concrete and aluminum. *Where'd he get the money for that?* Moreover, she knew the inside of that garage as if it were her own home. She had been in there with him—and her—and the others. She later said she hated herself for doing it. But then, he had that kind of control over people. He had always made her do things she didn't want to do.

And she did them.

For him. It was *all* for him.

Or so she said.

Walking into his house, she looked toward the dining-room table, where he had a collection of photographs in a scattered pile, all spread out so she could see each one clearly. He encouraged her to take a closer look, saying, "Go ahead." Then, pointing to one in particular, "You see that one?"

At first, she was confused. Then horrified, she later

said: "My mom, my son, my sisters, my stepchildren, my in-laws, my husband, everybody that was close to me. These were pictures that captured each one of these people in a setting where they were by themselves in a lonely place."

Explaining further, she said there was a photograph of her aunt, for example, walking her dog. Just a casual stroll around the Catskill neighborhood where she lived with her husband. It was secluded and woodsy, where gunshots are a common occurrence. Someone had snapped an image of her aunt from afar, as if the photographer was conducting surveillance.

She picked it up off the table and pulled it closer. She couldn't believe it.

"It would be a real shame," he said as she lifted her glasses off the bridge of her nose to get a clearer view, staring intensely at the photo, "if there were a hit-and-run accident. That lady could get badly hurt."

She couldn't believe what he was implying. He had said it with that low monotone: a clever little caveat implicit in the nuance of his voice she knew all too well. He didn't need to make a direct threat. No doubt something he had perfected from his years of bossing people around as the water superintendent in nearby Poughkeepsie. He loved that: the control. To be able to tell people what to do. It made him feel like he was *somebody*. Being short in stature, many later said, he had that dreaded little people's chip on his shoulder: a Napoleon complex. Today, though, standing in his kitchen, with those photos spread across the table as she stood next to him and trembled, he was larger than life. Ten feet tall.

She winced. *Are you serious?*

"In addition to members of *your* family staying healthy," he added, "I'll exonerate that debt you owe me."

The photograph of her son hurt more than any of

them. Her son was standing on the dock of the building where he worked, smoking a cigarette, staring off into the distance.

Man, how she loved that kid, her only child.

To put it into context, she later said, "This building is out in the middle of nowhere."

He watched as she stared at that photo. He let her think about it some. Then he said, "It'd sure be a shame if there was a drive-by shooting and your son was hit. Out there, nobody would *ever* know. The noise of all those machines inside the building . . ."

He sort of laughed.

Standing, thinking about the photographs and his threats, she went through their life together. She remembered that his first wife had been terrified of him. During the divorce proceedings, he had hired someone to run her off the road. Then, apparently, she later heard, he hired a dump truck driver to swerve into her lane and hit her. It never happened, but the implication was always there that no one refused him when he wanted something.

If this man would do that to a woman he supposedly loved, she told herself, *what's he going to do to people he doesn't even know?*

Some friend. In so many different ways, she had believed that they *were* friends. She had known him for so long. Two decades and counting. She'd slept with him when no other woman would have him. Kept him company when his wives walked out. He'd even proposed marriage to her once, but she had turned him down. "Friends with benefits" was the deal between them. Nothing more. She could never love him *that* way. They had been through so much together. Births and deaths. Wives and husbands. Sure, she owed him a bundle, borrowing $300 here, $400 there, running a tab of close to—and again, this is her count—$5,000. But when she borrowed the money, he had always told her, "Don't worry about it. No need to pay me back."

Now she knew why. Now he wanted that money back—but in a different way. It was as if their lives together, and so-called "friendship," had led up to this *one* furtive, seminal moment that would help shape their future. He had been grooming her. She could wipe out her debt to him in one fatal moment, he suggested, and save her family from being hurt, at the same time.

It was her choice. Take it . . . or, of course, leave it.

But then, if she walked away, she'd have to live with the consequences, he insisted, which were sitting on the table in front of her.

She felt involved to a point where there was only one way out—or at least that's how she saw it. She *had* to do what he wanted. There was no other way. He would hurt her family. He would expose all of those nasty, salacious sexual acts she had been doing for him with those other men and that *other* woman, whom he now wanted dead—sexual acts he had on videotape. It would destroy her reputation. Ruin her marriage. She'd lose the respect of her son. Not to mention her job.

Was there any other choice?

CHAPTER 1

With a name like Byrd you'd almost expect your life to, at some point, revolve around flight. Although he lived in Pleasant Valley, Richard Byrd had been a Poughkeepsie police officer for going on three decades now, and a member of the Hudson Valley Balsa Busters (HVBB), a local radio-controlled model airplane club, for only the past two. "One of my favorite things is to fly radio-controlled model airplanes," Byrd said later.

Byrd was good friends with HVBB's president, sixty-year-old Fred Andros, who oversaw the club's twelve-hundred-foot-long, 280-foot-wide grass airstrip on some seventy-five acres the HVBB maintained just outside Poughkeepsie. Undergoing a revitalization project today, back in 1999, Poughkeepsie was nothing more than a run-down mill town on the banks of the Hudson River still trying to stake a claim to its reputation as a quintessential small town. Over the years the town has undergone its share of social blemishes and political scandals. But nothing can change the towering Catskill Mountains hovering over Poughkeepsie's shoulder, in the shadow of the famous Bardavon marquee on Main Street, a gold-and-white flashing sign that has, through many incarnations, marked New

York's oldest opera house for the past 130 years. Manhattan sits in its saddle of worldly celebrity about two hours south of Poughkeepsie. Some might say, Poughkeepsie, which bills itself as a "forward-thinking city with historic beginnings," is nothing more than a pit stop, a quick jaunt off the interstate to stop and fuel up, grab a bite to eat and use the restroom while en route from Manhattan to Albany, or vice versa. But men like Richard Byrd and Fred Andros have grown to love the city and its people, respecting the quiet repose residents often say drew them there in the first place.

Byrd had fallen deeply into his new passion: flying model airplanes. It had taken Byrd nearly a year to learn how to fly the planes by himself. But he stuck with it. "Kids are better with their hands," Byrd said later in court, "than us older fellows. And, roughly, a young fellow could probably learn how to fly within three or four months. Myself, it took me the better part of the summer and almost the next spring of the following year to learn."

Byrd, Andros and the rest of the HVBB group met at the United Methodist Church on Martin Road in Pleasant Valley. The comradeship in the group was important to Byrd. Flying the planes was a way to lose oneself in something, affording the plane operator a sense of empowerment, much like that all-encompassing authority of being a cop Byrd loved so much. Working on the airplanes and building them from scratch stimulated Byrd's itch to have a hobby. He was just about to move on to flying gasoline engine planes. Up until then, he said, "I had been flying glow engines. . . ." Ordering spare parts and waiting for them to arrive was all a part of the process, and he, much like his good friend Fred Andros, always anticipated the delivery of a new plane.

Byrd met and befriended Fred in 1997, when he was first indoctrinated into the group. At the time Fred had been Poughkeepsie's water superintendent, having worked for the town as a laborer and then rising up through the ranks the old-fashioned way over thirty-one years of service. The two men had become fast friends. Byrd understood Fred's authority and superiority over the planes—and even envied it in many ways. He wanted what "Freddy" had: that control. Fred was himself newly married for what he later told friends and associates was the third time (but was actually his fourth). He had a thirteen-year-old son, *Roger* (pseudonyms are italicized on first use), a heavyset kid from a previous marriage who had battled cancer and lived with Fred and his new wife, Diana. Roger was a model plane expert, performing feats with his ten-foot-span Piper J-3 Cub that the elders in the club simply shook their heads at and wondered how in heck the kid did it.

Fred adored the boy. He was proud of the way he could fly those planes and the fact that they held such a tight bond.

Byrd had a teenage son, too. The families hung out together on occasion.

Not everyone was fond of Fred, and Byrd knew it. Some later described Fred as hideous, a self-centered man of colossal moral and social ignorance who cared about nothing more than his own needs.

"I can't imagine why a woman was ever attracted to Fred," the mother of one of his lovers said of him. "This was even more puzzling when I actually *saw* him."

But Byrd was only concerned with how he viewed Fred. To him, Fred was an okay guy. A friend.

Late into the afternoon of October 28, 1999, Byrd called Fred. He had some great news. Something they had been waiting on for weeks had arrived.

"UPS was here," Byrd explained excitedly. "They delivered those parts."

"Come over tonight," Fred suggested, "I'll be home this evening."

Byrd had been waiting on several parts. He often hired Fred to help him build his planes. (Fred Andros did nothing for free. Whether you were his friend, relative or a stranger, there was always a price to pay for what Fred did for you.) Fred had grown up and lived in Hyde Park, a twelve-minute ride north of Poughkeepsie. The basement in his multistory gold Colonial was rigged to work on the model planes. He had drill presses and workbenches. Vises and tools of all sorts. He spent hours in the basement getting lost in his model planes.

"We'll be over about seven, seven-thirty," Byrd said. He was going to his parents' house for dinner first, and then he and the wife would stop by afterward.

"See you guys then."

Fred seemed fine on the telephone that night, Byrd later explained in court. "He was as anxious as I was to get that airplane together, so we could get it in the air by the weekend if that was possible, and it all depended on the parts coming in."

Indeed, Fred was all keyed up about getting his hands oily with plane parts—quite a different person, actually, from just three weeks prior, Byrd remembered later, when the two of them had gotten together to talk. On that day, Fred said he was worried about one of his co-defendants in an upcoming corruption scandal he had gotten himself deeply involved in. "He was very upset," Byrd later recalled. "Disturbed. Extremely depressed." Fred had been set to testify against one of the ringleaders of an extensive, three-year-long corruption probe. The guy Fred was going up against was an overweight, cigar-chewing, burly man by the name of William Paroli, someone who had "contacts," Fred told friends. A man who knew "people" and, Fred believed, could make him disappear without a hitch. "We were at Fred's house," Byrd later said, describing the conversation he had with Fred the previous month. That's when Fred said, "I've been having trouble sleeping. Nightmares about Paroli." Fred was certain Paroli was going to have him killed so he couldn't testify. Fred was facing serious time himself for getting kickbacks and giving out town contracts, shaking people down for money, among other illegal deals he had been running in town for many years. With his testimony against Paroli, he was looking at a much lighter sentence. He was prepared to testify that Paroli was the bag man. The person behind it all. Ever since the scandal broke and Fred had resigned from his high-paying job as the Town of Poughkeepsie water super-intendent back in May 1999, he had been looking over his shoulder, scared someone was going to, as he put it to several friends, "whack me. I've been working with the FBI," he said, adding how the decision to become a snitch was weighing heavily on him.

Still, others claimed Fred made it all up—that the last thing William Paroli was going to do was knock off such a small player in such a small-town scam. If Paroli kept clean, he wasn't going to get any more than a few years behind bars. Why would he jeopardize his case by getting back at Fred and receiving a possible life sentence? It made little sense.

Fred sounded upbeat, Byrd noticed, on the afternoon of October 28, 1999, as they discussed getting together that night. He was a different person. Maybe all that legal stuff was behind him now? He was going to admit his crimes, do his time, and come out of it all a different—better—man.

Byrd was worried about his friend, however. He had called Diana a few days after having that conversation with Fred and made a few suggestions, noting how "medication might help."

"After Fred contacted the FBI," Diana admitted to Byrd, "the agent in charge convinced him to get an appointment to go see a doctor for medication."

And so on that night, October 28, Richard Byrd waited for his wife to get home so they could take a ride over to his parents' house for dinner and then proceed to Fred and Diana's house in Hyde Park to work on that new plane.

CHAPTER 2

One of Richard Byrd's colleagues, twenty-four-year Poughkeepsie Police Department (PPD) veteran lieutenant Jef Fassett, had confronted his wife, Susan, on September 19, 1999, about an affair he knew for certain she had been having with Fred Andros—an affair that mostly everyone in Susan and Jef's small circle of friends had known about for a while now. Susan was well-known in town and certainly well-liked. She had been the personnel director at the Poughkeepsie Town Hall for years. She and Fred had met through their jobs, passing each other in the halls, and sneaking around for about the past forty-eight months. Some were shocked, while others shrugged their shoulders and knew it was part of life, no matter where you lived or who you were. Couples grew apart. Susan's then-twenty-year-old son, Jason Fassett, later told me that she was the type of person who "didn't want to say no to anyone. . . . She was a people-pleaser. She kept things to herself, didn't want to burden anyone with her problems." Thus, if she was having difficulties in her marriage, Susan didn't want to place that load on anyone. It was her cross to bear. She would work through it herself.

"Susan was kind, loving and attractive," her mother

later said. "She had a good husband and two fine sons. But, as happens in many marriages, she and Jef were having some problems. They were going through a difficult time—and then Fred came along. Susan was gullible and Fred took advantage of the situation."

"Sounds like Fred," said a former friend. "Fred took advantage of *any* situation he could. Real scumbag."

What baffled many was that Fred had such a magnetic attraction over women. Not being a ladies' man by appearance or definition, Fred's many affairs with different women became a strange dynamic some in town had scratched their heads over. How in the heck was this guy—by all means an ugly, short, cigarette-smoking, foulmouthed charlatan who wore cowboy boots and outdated Western shirts—able to manipulate women to such a large extent?

"It's incredible, really, when you look at it later," a friend of Fred's later said. "We couldn't believe Fred had that kind of power over these women."

"I see him as a selfish, egotistical, manipulative and immoral person," Susan's sister said later. "He always had to have control. The only person Fred loved was Fred Andros."

Jef was an odd way to spell his name. But it had always been one of John Fassett's pet peeves, people spelling his name the conventional way, with two *F*'s. It was wrong. Same as calling him John. He liked Jef, which was born out of his full name, John Edward Fassett.

Names were not on Jef Fassett's mind, however, on this night. Tonight Jef knew—like any man *knows*—that his wife had been stepping out on him. It comes with years of learning how a spouse acts, how she reacts to what you say, how she responds to your affections—good, bad or indifferent. A seasoned husband can notice subtle changes in demeanor, same as a wife can. On top of that, Jef had been a cop for a quarter of a century, with not a blemish to his record. He had an instinct for sniffing out this very type of situation. But, of course, Jef Fassett likely denied it in his heart for years, hoping it would all just go away and fix itself.

On the night of September 19, 1999, Jef had the evidence to prove his theory; he was finished playing games and acting as though nothing was wrong. It was time to expose the white elephant. Get it over with and deal with the consequences—however hurtful or repulsive they may be.

"You're busted," Jef told Susan that night. It was as simple as that. There was nothing more to say.

Susan dropped her head. Her cloud-white hair and bubbly demeanor suddenly cut short by Jef's accusatory words. She winced. She *was* caught. Red–handed. And this time she *knew* it. She could hear it in Jef's voice. It was the tone: *busted.* After all, Susan was dealing with a cop. Did she actually think she could hide her affair with Fred Andros from a seasoned police officer working in the same building?

"Jef . . . ?" Susan started to say.

Forty-eight-year-old Susan Taber Fassett grew up in Pawling, New York, on the sprawling Taber Farm her father had been given by his parents. Pawling is on the Connecticut border, north of Danbury, directly west of Sherman. It is as rural as rural gets in this part of upstate New York. On the outskirts of Dutchess County, it is a calming parcel of land with some history behind it, as George Washington had set his headquarters in Pawling for a spell as he contemplated moving his troops into New

York City and actually sent his troops to the Taber Farm
to buy milk and cheese.

The Tabers lived on the crest of a hill in a four-room
farmhouse when Susan and her only sibling, an older
sister, Mary Ann, were born. The family built a larger
home above the farmhouse on the edge of the property
line that Susan's son Jason lives in today.

"Being the youngest of my grandparents' two kids,"
Jason recalled, "my mom was definitely a farmer's daughter, daddy's little girl, if you will. My grandparents were
pretty exceptional people."

Susan's parents had given their children a Rockwellian
upbringing. Mrs. Taber worked as a schoolteacher in a
one-room schoolhouse that is a museum today. Her father
worked his fingers to the bone tilling and tending the land
and met his future wife in church. "Their whole world,"
Jason recalled, "was built around small-town living."

A legacy, in fact, they had passed on to Susan and
Mary Ann. There was a seven-year difference between
Susan and her sister. When it came time for Mary Ann to
think about life after school, she chose the big cities—
Poughkeepsie and Newburg—and nursing school. And
so when Mary Ann took off into adulthood, Susan was
left alone in a small town, living on a farm, with rolling
hills and miles of grass and cornfields separating her
from that "other" life beyond the country. She dreamed
of leaving the farm herself one day and being a career
woman.

"She loved this life on the farm," Jason later clarified.
"But growing up here all her life, Poughkeepsie seemed
like 'the city,' and she wanted to experience that different part of life."

Like her mother, Susan wanted to become a teacher.
Yet, as she grew into maturity, the timing was off. When
Susan graduated high school, the seventies had ushered

in a time when there were more teachers than schools. Every little girl wanted to be a teacher, and so the marketplace had become saturated, or at least that's how Susan perceived it. So she instead opted—some said "settled"—for what she saw as a professional job in a big city, working for the Town of Poughkeepsie.

"Get out," Jef said when Susan cracked under the pressure of being caught and admitted her affair with Fred Andros. She was crying. Hunched over. Sitting on the edge of her bed.

Jef was livid, of course. Who could blame him? He wasn't going to be treated like he didn't matter. He deserved more. He hadn't been Ozzie Nelson and had probably drifted away from Susan over the years and into his own shell, but his behavior certainly didn't warrant an affair. Therapy, perhaps, but Fred Andros, the troll of Poughkeepsie? *Come on, Susan, you're better than that! If you wanted attention, you should have come out and said something. I mean, for crying out loud, Fred Andros?*

There was a section of the Fassett home in Poughkeepsie that had been converted into an apartment for Jef's mother, who had at one time lived with the family. The house was a dark, cranberry red Colonial on Dutchess Turnpike (Route 44), which runs directly through Poughkeepsie into Pleasant Valley. From the outside, the house looked sort of run-down and in need of some maintenance. Pine trees wept downward and hung below the roofline blocking much of the view inside. One could easily determine with a quick look that the house and the yard were a metaphor for the marriage: neglected.

Jef told Susan it was best if she moved her stuff into the area of the house where his mother had lived, at least for the time being. Emotions were too raw at the moment.

Too volatile. They needed to sleep on things for the night and talk about it all in the morning. It wasn't a quick fix. But the separation would benefit the two of them so each could consider the next step—a thought neither really wanted to mention or confront right now.

For months—perhaps even years—Jef had suspected Susan was cheating. But having two sons and nearly two-and-a-half decades of marriage behind them, he didn't want to believe it, or deal with it. He wanted to be certain before he went ahead and said something. But then his law enforcement intuition took over. So he rigged a tape recorder to the telephone and recorded Susan having a conversation with Fred Andros, the cacophonous fraud of Dutchess County himself. Through that conversation, it was easy to tell that Susan and Fred were much more than town employees working in the same building.

Jason had even worked for Fred years ago. Imagine that, Jason thought later, the guy was bossing me around during the day and running around with my mom at the same time. Made him sick to his stomach to think about it. But then as he thought about things more and more, Jason understood now why his mother—and Fred, for that matter—acted the way she did the past few years.

For Jef, it was indeed a bitter pill to swallow, especially seeing that September 20, the day after he confronted Susan, he and Susan were supposed to celebrate their twenty-fourth wedding anniversary. That night, however, September 19, after things settled down, the anger and disappointment both felt had turned more restrained. Sadness had replaced most all other emotions, and both Susan and Jef realized their dream could only be quashed if they *allowed* it to be. They had control over their future. Not Fred. Or the kids. Or anyone else. It was up to the two of them where their lives went next.

Susan walked from her new bedroom into where Jef

was sleeping. It was near midnight, Jef said later. In a whisper, Susan asked, "Would you consider reconciling, Jef?" She wanted to save her marriage. She was a God-fearing woman. She believed the soul could be cleansed and forgiven of its sins, if only the sinner repented. She was willing to do that.

Jef looked confused and yet relieved. It wasn't over.

Susan handed Jef a pager and cell phone.

"What's this?" he asked.

"I used to use these to communicate with him. No more, Jef," she promised. "I won't talk to him anymore."

Susan pledged, right there and then, to participate wholly in rebuilding the marriage. Start over. Get rid of the deadweight holding down her spirit and focus once again on what had made her and Jef such an affectionate, devoted couple to begin with. It wasn't over. That love they had once shared could be reawakened. They could work and get it back. Love was a decision. They just needed to give it a try.

"Susan made a mistake," her mother later said. "She made a horrible mistake when she got involved with Fred Andros. She realized this and wanted reconciliation with her family."

Susan might have been a churchgoer and prude around the house, but she did have a "fun side to her," Jason later said of his mother. (Incidentally, Jason said he was his "mom's son," whereas his brother, Christopher, was his "dad's son." Jason admitted that he was closer to his mother. "I could share anything with her and she'd listen, not judge, and advise me as a parent and friend.")

Susan and Jef met at a bar in town one night when they were both starting out in their professional lives in Pough-keepsie after college. It was the mid-seventies. Both liked to go out and sit and drink beers together and fill the bar with cigarette smoke and have a good time, with limitations, of course. They were both responsible people. Focused on their careers. "She wasn't reckless," Jason Fassett said, "but she and my dad liked to have some fun." Still, when Jason looked back, he could see how his mother might have allowed her life to stray off course. "I've led myself to believe that at the time my mom never really did some of the things she wanted to do in life and she wasn't truly happy, she was trying to do something different and, unfortunately, being kind of naïve and innocent, not really being assertive enough with her own life . . . she kind of let situations develop around her and some of them were, again unfortunately, pretty bad situations. She was weak. We're all weak sometimes."

Jason recalled his dad being an introvert for much of their lives—the type of guy who really never caused any problems around the house, but was never there in an emotional sense. "He would get up for work before we were all up, so we wouldn't see him then. He'd come home after work and he'd take a nap because he worked so hard, such long hours. We'd have to wake him for dinner and then he'd be grumpy from just waking up. I love my dad, don't get me wrong. It just felt like we didn't get to see him very much."

There were days when Jason would sit at the dinner table next to his dad and yearn to know what his life was like. "What'd you do today, Dad, did you arrest anyone?"

As a young kid, Jason was fascinated with police work. He wanted to hear the stories some cops cannot help telling. Chasing bad guys. Wrestling bad guys to the ground. Drug busts that would make Pablo Escobar blush. The stuff Jason had seen on television. His dad was living it. He wanted to hear all about it.

On the other hand, working for a town like Poughkeepsie didn't leave Jef much to talk about. When it did, he still chose not to. He had his job, and that was it. He left it at the office.

"Being a cop creates a type of person," Jason astutely observed. "Because of that, it kind of made us like a family of three: my mom, me and my brother. And then—oh, yeah—my dad was there, too, sometimes."

So as the years progressed, if it was all that indirect and unemotional for him and his brother, Jason wondered, his mother must have went through the same. She likely wanted attention: *How do I look?* But never got it in the way she wanted.

Tell me I'm pretty.

"And my mom," Jason explained, "wasn't the type to come out and say, 'Hey, give me some attention.' She went out and found it where she could. Whereas my dad, on the other hand, wasn't doing anything malicious or intentional with his neglect. That's just the way he was."

On the following morning, September 20, after Jef confronted Susan, Jason and his girlfriend got up late and headed down the stairs. When they arrived in the kitchen, Susan and Jef were sitting at the table, "teary-eyed," Jason's girlfriend later remembered, "with a bottle of liquor between them."

Jef spoke first. "I'd like to talk to you and your brother." Seventeen-year-old Christopher was in the other room with his girlfriend.

Realizing how intense and private the moment was, the two girls waited outside. After a few moments, Jason emerged, saying, "My parents are splitting up."

A few days went by. The kids came and went and not much had changed around the house. It was just quiet.

Unresponsive and solemn. As if there had been a death in the family.

Eggshells.

And then, all of a sudden, one day Jason and his girlfriend walked into the house and saw the two of them, Susan and Jef, sitting on the couch, "cuddling," as Jason's girlfriend put it.

"We decided to work things out," Susan told Jason and his girlfriend, smiling, "and stay together."

Jef and Susan decided they'd take a week off from their jobs and begin to rebuild the love they had once shared. Rekindle that early romance. Start all over. An affair wasn't worth tossing away nearly twenty-five years of marriage. They owed it to themselves, if no one else, to at least give it a try.

As a token of their renewed relationship and rebirth of their marriage, they agreed to purchase new wedding rings as a dedication to each other. And as the next few weeks, leading up to October 28, went forward, things in their new life together seemed to be back on track. Susan and Jef were once again enjoying a transformed sense of love. Renewal. They had worked hard at bringing back that initial connection and it seemed to be working. Yet, Jason said later, "My mom was fooling us all—she was still talking to Fred Andros."

CHAPTER 3

The town of Pleasant Valley is quite literally what you'd think a town by that name might be like if a city planner, in theory, created it in a lab: acres of cornfields spreading out for as far as the eye can see; supple sugar maple and oak leaves, beside pine needles, drifting gently in the wind; the limbs of the trees, like tassels, hanging over streets as winding as spring coils; antique shops and traditional Colonial homes dotted about the countryside as if plucked from one of Laura Ingalls Wilder's Little House novels.

In town people mill about, primarily minding their own business, carefully watching out for one another, asking appropriately how so-and-so is, and how Johnny made out in Little League this year, and how Sally is coming along with piano and dance lessons. In the fall, roadside stands present an abundant pumpkin crop, caches of dried corn husks bundled together like gifts and bales of hay to decorate one's home. "See you in church on Sunday" is as common a gesture as the town's total disregard for big-city politics and bureaucracy. People in Pleasant Valley, perhaps like most suburban American towns, want to be, beyond anything else, left alone, if not to dwell in their own simple lives, to keep up the façade of wholesomeness and purity their lives are perpetually built around.

Situated at an area where Route 44 intersects with Route 82, heading out of town toward the hills of Connecticut, the Troop K Barracks of the New York State Police (NYSP) seem to act as some sort of tollbooth or gate out of town. Both roads cut a Y-shaped pattern and the barracks sit as if in the belly of a martini glass, there at the center of it all. In a moment's notice, troopers can peel out of the driveway and head to a crime scene, accident, domestic disturbance, homicide, burglary, or any number of other crimes in and around Dutchess County. A mile or so east of Troop K is the Taconic State Parkway, which is, essentially, a two-lane highway in each direction, north and south, taking commuters through the mountains of upstate New York as if on a roller-coaster ride to Albany and beyond, and, on the opposite end, down to Manhattan. Poughkeepsie, the largest metropolitan city near Pleasant Valley, is a short ride southeast on Route 44. Most who don't own their own businesses or commute to Albany or Manhattan work in Poughkeepsie or its nearby metropolitan counterpart, Newburg.

Up here, not too far from the birthplace of Franklin D. Roosevelt in Hyde Park, hitting a deer while out for a night's drive is more common than running into someone committing a felonious crime. In fact, in a town that is split down the middle—50/50, male to female, 93.7 percent of whom are white, mostly German, Irish and Italian descent—there are nearly three hundred people per square mile of space, which offers a wide open area of, well, absolute nothingness. This is the reason why some people move to Pleasant Valley to begin with: the quiet solemnity of thousands of acres of woods juxtaposed against fresh air and the soothing sounds of babbling brooks and soft streams sifting gently through the rocks. Plain old-fashioned country living: charming, graceful, not too all-encompassing or stressful, and—one might think—trouble-free.

Pleasant Valley boasts an income per household of about $64,000 in a state with an average of $50,000. Houses are expensive, though. Land is dense. And a majority of the town's residents are married. Moreover, if you wanted an American town where the least likely crime you'd ever expect to be victimized by is a sex offense, Pleasant Valley is the place, having a resident to sex offender ratio of 4,842 to 1. In fact, quite surprisingly, Pleasant Valley residents are more likely to be killed by a tornado—the town holds the record in the state, being 23 percent above the overall U.S. average for tornadoes, with two Category 4 tornadoes hitting the town within six years, killing three people and injuring nearly one hundred. Truth be told, when a common thunderstorm rolls into town, some residents look up, gaze slowly around and wonder if Mother Nature will whip up a whirlwind of misery and pain all over again—a memory that, for some, will likely never dissolve into the rigors of old age.

All this being said, however, while looking from afar, one might view Pleasant Valley as entirely safe, entirely innocuous and entirely off the radar of the world. And this was why on the cool morning of October 28, 1999, few residents in town, save for perhaps a nosey neighbor or two, *ever* considered the idea that not one but two murderers were waking up and preparing to put into action the best plan they could to kill one of Pleasant Valley's own. In a town with so little focus on the same immoral problems that contaminate much of the America landscape, in the breadth of twenty-four hours, things were going to change in a dramatic fashion for residents of Pleasant Valley. Those who would soon wake up fearless and comfortable living in Mayberry would go to bed, on the same night, wondering and questioning the lives of their next-door neighbors. A simple walk to the local market might yield stares and quiet whispers. Secrets would soon emerge that would have the little old ladies at the post office and regulars at the diner shaking their heads in disgust, wondering how in the world such things could take place in an area of the state so proportionately spectacular. The sanctity of small-town life and love would be rattled as residents began to ask, "How could this happen *here,* right under our noses?" The salacious acts of ill repute that were going on—rocking the foundation of principles that had, until this day, kept the town and people of Dutchess County bustling along on an uninterrupted ride—were soon going to shake up the core of this graceful small town.

CHAPTER 4

It was 4:00 P.M. on Thursday, October 28, 1999, as she—the shooter—drove toward Pleasant Valley from where she worked in upstate New York. It was mostly sunny. Cool, though, about fifty-four degrees most of the day, and the mercury was heading down now with the sun, and temperatures were expected to bottom out at about thirty-eight degrees Fahrenheit.

Beside her on the front seat of her station wagon was a loaded .45-caliber handgun. She had spoken to Fred Andros earlier that morning and he insisted that "it" be done today.

No more waiting. No more excuses. No more back talk.

"Friendship is friendship and business is business. Get it done!" he raged.

"It" was another one of his damn code words. Fred would never say "kill" over the telephone. She was tired of Fred and his code words, his threats and orders. But here she was—on her way to a murder.

On her way to take care of Fred's "business."

When she spoke to him a while later, he had calmed down some, and using his master manipulation tactics, he turned on the tears, speaking about something having to do with the Town of Poughkeepsie Republican Party chairman, William Paroli, who, he said, was still after him. Then he reiterated: She—Susan Fassett—was going to sink him when she testified. They were in this together, he implied: Paroli and Susan. They were going to turn him in and testify against him. Susan had to die.

Today.

"I know," she said. "You told me yesterday."

"I received a call," Fred added, "threatening me . . . if I didn't keep my mouth shut about Paroli, I would wind up . . . floating in the river. She needs to be eliminated."

Fred's shooter said she understood. "OK. I know. Tonight it will be done." She promised. "I'm on my way now."

"Put the pistol under her chin and blow her f***ing brains out," he said, breaking one of his golden rules of never talking about "it" over the telephone.

"I knew then how serious he was," she told me later. "I was scared for my family." She tensed up when she heard him say those words. "He wouldn't yell," she said, "scream or holler. He would just give you that quiet tone of voice." Which was much more intimidating, anyway.

After arriving in town, she stopped at the Kmart on Route 44, just down the street from Susan's house. She bought a pair of shoes, T-shirt, bottle of Excedrin over-the-counter headache medicine (maybe the stress was getting to her) and a ski mask (the kind burglars wear in the movies: the ones with the three holes for nose, eyes, mouth). She'd wear it so nobody saw her face. She was a big woman: five feet eleven inches (maybe taller), 271 pounds. Burly. Manly, even. Curly gray hair that was once brown, short and tight. She wore large-framed glasses (which she could take off and leave in the car). She walked lazily, skulkingly, like she had a bad hip or something. With a mask on, she could pass easily for a man. On any other day, it would be an insult. But tonight, well, she wouldn't mind if that's how she was perceived.

Walking out of Kmart, she looked at her watch. It wasn't even dark yet. Susan wasn't at church, either. *I need more time.*

So she drove to Dunkin' Donuts, which was just down the street from Susan's house, and purchased two dozen doughnuts. The counter girl, she remembered later, "had a bad cold."

In the parking lot of Dunkin' Donuts, she called Fred again. "I need to see you."

He was expecting company, he said. "You know that. Don't f***ing call me anymore. Just get it done."

"I need those plates."

It was still early. His guests—the Byrds—wouldn't be at the house for another couple hours. He had the time.

"OK. OK. I'll be right there."

He drove over to Dunkin' Donuts. He got into her car and they took off. She needed to fix the license plates he had given her over the existing plates on her car. The plates he had obtained were brand-new, she noticed. "Not a screw mark or blemish on them," she later recalled. "I have no idea where he got them, but they had never been used." He was supposed to do it himself, but, of course, he backed out. He needed an alibi. He needed to be home, in his basement with his friend Richard Byrd working on model airplanes. *How pathetic,* she thought as they drove. *He's like a little kid with those planes.*

"Pull over there to that hardware store," he told her.

He went in and purchased a roll of double-sided tape. "Here," he said, "use this to fasten the plates over yours."

She took it. "It'll work."

"I got company coming," he said, looking at his watch. "I need to get back home. Hurry up now."

She could tell he was upset with her. He had that

snappy way about him she didn't like, an irritated tone
to his voice. She knew he was impatient that it hadn't
been done already.

"What is it?" she asked as they drove.

"Nothing."

"What?"

"What the f***," he said angrily, "you better finish this
tonight."

She was in tears.

After he left, she took the double-sided tape and fas-
tened the plates to her car. This way, after it was all over,
as Fred had planned out days before, she could tear off
the plates and toss them into a garbage bag with the
mask and anything else she had used during the crime.

He would take care of the bag, she was told. "Just make
sure to drop it where I f***ing told you to. You got it?"

By the time she was finished at Dunkin' Donuts, it was
dark. She drove around for a while—and then decided
to drive over to Susan's house. Maybe she could get it
over with there and head home and be done with this
business of killing.

"You can do it there," Fred had told her a few weeks
back. "In the driveway."

It seemed like she should at least have a look. Maybe
he was right. Susan would walk out of her house, not sus-
pecting a thing. She could walk up from behind Susan
and put several slugs in the back of her head and tear
out of there before anyone realized what had happened.
She'd be on the interstate and long gone before the
cops were even dispatched. On paper it sounded perfect. With all the trees in the yard, it was dark and secluded. No one would see her.

Maybe Fred knew what he was talking about, after all?

Across the street from the house was a restaurant. She
parked on the side of the road to Susan's house, opposite

the restaurant. She then pulled the itchy wool ski mask over her face, grabbed the weapon, took a quick look both ways, got out of her car and stepped onto the street.

No one had seen her. If someone had, he or she would probably think it was some sort of Halloween prank, anyway. A person in a wool mask walking around Pleasant Valley?

No way. It *had* to be some sort of joke. People would drive right by.

She hustled from Route 44 (Dutchess Turnpike) and ducked over into the bushes in back of an abandoned garage. It was the perfect spot to sit and wait. Sooner or later, Susan would have to come out of her house. Maybe then she could get it over with. She never liked the idea of doing it in the church parking lot. It seemed all at once creepy and sacrilegious—even though God was the last thing on her mind as she stood in Susan Fassett's driveway, waiting to kill her.

CHAPTER 5

Poughkeepsie PD lieutenant Jef Fassett drove over to the jeweler during the afternoon of October 28, stopped in and picked up his new wedding ring, the one he and Susan decided to get in order to renew their love. After that, he made his way over to Susan's office at Town Hall so he could show her how it looked.

Susan beamed. What a great idea. A rebirth of their love. And now it was complete.

Jef kissed Susan on the cheek and told her he'd see her at home for dinner.

She liked the sound of that—it seemed so much like old times. No more secrets between them.

In actual fact, however, shortly before Jef arrived, Susan had just gotten off the telephone with Fred Andros. It had been one of five calls that day, telephone records would later indicate, Susan had made to Fred.

Near 6:30 P.M., Jef and Susan were at home eating a wonderful dinner Susan had cooked for the family. The worst was behind them. They could forgive and forget and move on.

One big happy family.

Susan was in a hurry, though. She had been running late

all day, it seemed. And that two minutes she had gotten behind earlier that morning seemed to follow and plague her throughout the entire day. Wherever she went, whatever she did, Susan had run just a tad late. Standing in the kitchen preparing dinner of green beans and breaded chicken, she hadn't even changed out of her work clothes. She was stirring the sauce, looking at the clock.

Some time later, "Jason . . . Sarah," Susan yelled up the stairs, "it's time to eat." It was something Susan did every night, Sarah later recalled. Call her and Jason down for dinner. One of those little things mothers do that most take for granted.

Jason and his girlfriend, Sarah, had blown off early from work that day to renew their driver's licenses. They'd gone to the Uno restaurant after the Motor Vehicle Department, stopped at Jason's house, napped and were now upstairs just hanging out.

A moment later, Jason, Sarah, Jef, Christopher and, of course, Susan were sitting around the dinner table together, chatting about everyday things. It was a pleasant family sit-down dinner. How nice it was going to be to sit and eat without secrets turning in one's stomach. Without silence acting as a wall between everyone. Without having to stay quiet for fear of saying the *wrong* thing.

This might just work out.

"Choir practice," Susan said more than once, eating fast. She never missed it. "I have to get ready for choir practice."

"Relax. Enjoy your dinner," one of them said.

At some point while they ate, Jef noticed what he described later as a "shadowy figure" lurking outside the home. He was staring across the table at Susan, and someone had walked directly by the large window in back of where she was sitting.

So he decided to get up from the dinner table and check it out.

It was Fred's hired gun, of course, dressed down in black, making her way up the driveway, peering into the windows, looking for Susan.

To the kids and Susan, it was probably nothing. But Jef was a cop. His intuition was that something was wrong. Something didn't seem right.

Just around the corner from the dinner table was a door leading to the deck that everyone used as an entrance to the house. Most country homes had a front door that no one used.

Jef walked out and stood on the deck, looking into the darkness of the yard shadowed by the trees and hazy moonlight. It was an ominous, foggy night, not in a warm way, but a way that made seeing ten feet beyond nearly impossible. Jason was right behind his dad. Sarah quickly got up and, with Susan, walked over to the window in the living room to see what was going on outside. When they didn't see anything, Sarah went outside to follow Jason and his dad, while Susan went back to her motherly chores of collecting the dishes and getting ready to leave.

"What's going on?" someone said.

Outside, Jef walked down the driveway, a long roadway, essentially, situated next to a private road that ran in back of the Fassett home. There were a few houses on the private road. It was routinely common for people to get lost looking for those secluded homes and think that the Fassett driveway was that so-called private road.

Maybe someone's lost?

As Jef walked onto the driveway from the wood deck, Jason behind him, a large figure—it was cast-iron black out by now—dressed in a sweatshirt with a hood pulled over, walked up the driveway. It seemed strange. Felt weird. Something wasn't right.

"Who is it?" Jason asked.

Jef didn't answer.

"What's going on?" Sarah yelled to Jason as he hurried to catch up to his father. Sarah stood back and waited on the porch deck.

"Stay there," Jason told her.

The person's car wasn't parked in the driveway, though, which was even more bizarre. The person had parked past the Fassett mailbox on Route 44, the main road. It wasn't every day someone pulled over on the side of the road and got out of his or her car to walk up the driveway.

Why not just pull into *the driveway?*

To Jason, it wasn't all that unusual. But, he said, "My father, being a cop, *right* away, no situation is 'normal.' Everything had to have a sort of 'what's going on here?' sense of urgency to it. It couldn't be that someone was just walking up the driveway and that person was, like, lost or something; it had to be 'Who's that? We better check this out.'"

And wouldn't you know, this time Jef's instincts were right on.

At that point, the person saw Jason and Jef walking through the yard. Startled, the figure (Jason and his dad still weren't sure if it was a man or woman) turned and began heading back down the driveway toward his or her car.

"In the distraught mental state I was in that night," the shooter later said, "there was something inside me that told me I couldn't do this now." "*Not where this woman lives,*" that inner voice told her as she stood there debating what to do next. "I could never give anyone an adequate answer to the question of why I decided to abandon the murder there, at that moment," she later said.

At that moment, Jason's girlfriend stood alone on the porch. Tall and skinny, with blond hair, from a distance—especially in the silhouetted darkness—she looked a lot like Susan, who was back inside the house getting ready to leave for choir practice, not paying much attention at all as to what was going on outside.

Jason Fassett recalled his grandmother, Helen, Susan's mother, as a humble little woman who worried more about others than herself. "Which was where my mom," Jason offered, "got it from. She was the light for people," he said. "Being the light is far different from having to tell people the light switch is over there. Instead of telling them, it's like giving someone the example to follow. Be the light and lead. That was my mom, whether she knew it or not."

Jason had no reservations about talking to his mother about drugs, sex or anything he would generally only talk to one of his peers about.

"She was pretty humble herself, but I could make her blush. From the time I was doing *anything*, I could talk to her about it. It wasn't even a question. I was lucky to have a mom I could be that real with."

Admittedly, Jason never had that type of relationship with his dad.

"I think they would have divorced if it wasn't for us." It sounded clichéd, Jason added, that his mother stayed in her marriage "for the kids"—but it was the truth. "There was no way she could have left us or thought about splitting up the family we had."

Susan was the one who took the kids to soccer practice and paced the sidelines cheering them on during games. School functions too. Every time one of them wanted to go over to a friend's house, it was Susan who dropped them off.

"Every one of my friends had their own relationship with my mother," Jason said. "They would all talk to her outside of me. The almost unbiased ear for me, as my mom sat and listened to my problems, was definitely that for all my friends. She had that one degree of separation with them where she wasn't 'their mom' and they could talk to her openly. She also had a sense of compassion and understanding with people I admired."

Leading up to October 28, 1999, Jason said he watched as his mother and father became happier than he had ever seen them. "They talked about divorce after he caught her with Fred," Jason said, "but that was behind them, we believed, during the last few weeks of October. They were really, *really* happy." One of the ways that Jason knew how happy they were was that they had started "doing stuff to the house again." Repairs. Home improvement projects. "They were things my mom and dad had wanted to do for the last ten years."

They had both contributed to the demise of the marriage, realized it and were both dedicated to working at making amends and "doing things right" the second time around, Jason explained.

There were anomalies inside this life that Susan led, however—some of which she could do little to stop from surfacing. She had made mistakes. She was ready to correct them and move on. But others had a different view of this—one being Fred Andros. He had videotapes of Susan with another woman, engaged in lesbian sex. Was Fred Andros holding these videotapes over Susan's head? *"I'll show your kids if you leave me!"* Moreover, had Susan actually left Fred Andros and broken off the relationship, as she had told her husband?

"We found out later," Jason said, "she hadn't."

CHAPTER 6

Besides the person outside in the driveway spooking everyone, the life Jef and Susan Fassett were celebrating on that night was better than it had been for years. As Jason Fassett recalled, it was actually "getting better every day." It seemed as though Susan and Jef had fallen back in love. "Genuine." Whether Susan was just going along with it, and still chasing Fred Andros, didn't really matter.

She was *happy* again.

When Jef, Jason and Sarah returned to the house after checking on the person in the driveway, Susan asked, "Who was it?"

"Dunno," Jef and Jason said, "couldn't see."

"We thought it was probably someone who was looking for directions but, for whatever reason, decided not to ask and just left," Jason said later.

Meanwhile, Christopher's girlfriend had arrived just as everyone finished eating. Rushing out the door a moment later, one arm inside her coat, throwing the other over her shoulder, Susan greeted the young girl and, at the same time, said, "I'll see all of you later. I'm late for choir practice. Gotta go."

"Bye, Mom," Jason said.

Sarah followed, "Bye, Mrs. Fassett."

"See ya, Mom," Christopher said.

"Bye, Susan," Jef added.

As Susan walked out the door, Jason watched her leave. A minute later, Susan was sitting in her car, waiting for it to warm up a bit before taking off.

Fred Andros's shooter, the big woman with the ski mask and .45-caliber weapon, had taken off by this point.

Susan was safe, at least for the moment.

As Susan drove away, Jef went upstairs and changed. A while later, he came back down the stairs with his coat on and addressed Sarah. "I have to go pick up my paycheck."

Jason was upstairs in his room.

"OK," Sarah said.

"I'll be back as soon as I can," Jef said.

The daughter of dairy farmer William F. Taber, Susan was the "tallest member" of her church choir. She told people she was five feet nine inches, but was at least an inch taller, perhaps even two. She stood out from the others with her shortly cropped white-blond hair and sparkling blue eyes. She was active at Pleasant Valley's United Methodist Church, organizing shut-ins and always busy as a member of the caregiver's group. Still, between piano lessons and going out with friends to dinners and concerts, Susan found time to help those in need. Although Susan's life hadn't been the picture-perfect union of godliness Jesus might have wanted it to be, she understood how important it was to make time for others, and especially to work toward repentance of her sins. It was part of who she was, not only as a Christian, but a mother, wife and caring human being. Even though she had problems of her own, Susan clearly knew that she could redeem herself and, hopefully, make things better by extending a helping hand.

United Methodist Church wasn't far from Jef and Susan's home on Route 44. It was a small church by big-city standards—what, with its bright red cross greeting parishioners as they came upon the building from the main road. The parking lot connected to the church was small, unable to sustain the growing number of parishioners on any given Sunday, or the various groups who met at the church during the week, including Fred Andros's model airplane club. So any overflow parking traffic was directed into a dirt and gravel area across Martin Road, a large field, several acres long, a few acres across. There was one streetlight in the middle of the yard. People who parked in the second lot had a short walk across Martin Road into the church lot and into the building. When a motorist turns onto Martin from Route 72, the church jumps out as soon as one begins to turn the short corner and head up a slight hill.

Choir practice was packed on this particular night. It was *that* time of the year. During the fall, all the local churches began to practice regularly for the upcoming winter holy Advent season. There was a certain bounce in everyone's step. Church attendance always rose in the fall and beginning of winter, toward Christmas, after school started and kids went back to holy classes. Choir practice was one of those moments in Susan's life where she could slow down and step into the world of Christ, ask for forgiveness in her own way, and forget about her problems outside church doors. A sanctuary from sin. The one place in the world where Susan Fassett didn't have to be *perfect.* A wife. Someone's lover. Sneaking around. Stealthily making telephone calls. Whispering. In church and in choir practice, Susan could just pray and meditate and sing until her heart was content.

The parking lot connected to the church must have been full, because Susan parked her brand-new 2000 Jeep Cherokee across the street in the second lot. The 2000 models had just come out the previous month, and Susan, ecstatic, had just gotten hers.

As she pulled into the lot and backed in slowly to a nice safe spot right underneath the overhead streetlight, the knobby tires on her vehicle crunched the stone underneath. She had made it on time. After all that hurrying all day long, being late here and there, she had finally been on time for *something*.

Thanks be to God.

Within a moment, Susan grabbed her bag, chirplocked her doors with her key ring and headed into the church to meet her fellow parishioners and choir members. It was time to sing and talk with friends. Undoubtedly, a calmness washed over Susan as she looked both ways before crossing the street, walking into the church.

CHAPTER 7

Living at the base of the Catskill Mountains for a little over the past decade had turned her into an "avid hunter." An outdoorswoman. Someone who, with her husband, test-fired handguns in the backyard, using an old oak tree as target practice. Thinking about it, perhaps murdering a human being wouldn't prove to be all that difficult, after all—maybe like killing a deer or a pheasant.

Both of which she had already done.

She had never been arrested or—for that matter—done anything even remotely as evil as murdering a fellow. And yet, from what she would say in the coming months, she had backed herself into a corner and felt she *needed* to do this for Fred Andros—or else.

"The only way he could ensure that Susan wouldn't blow up his deal was if she were to die," the shooter said later. "He wanted her dead."

The shooter wasn't some sort of innocent, docile housewife, as many of her friends and family later said they had seen her evolve into over the years. This was part of her social mask. Sure, she was married. Had a kid. And lived a somewhat solemn life, working for a company that assisted disabled, mentally challenged adults. On the outside she might have appeared to have integrity and honor. But there was another side to her personality: a person she couldn't later explain, nor could those who thought they knew her quite fathom. Several of her former friends later said, when it came down to it, she was someone who could, at the drop of a hat, do *anything*. And tonight would prove that point most assuredly.

A family friend later said he had known her since she was seven years old, and she was "always well-behaved and never exhibited any tendencies toward violence to people or animals." She often helped people, he added, "anyone who needed assistance of any kind."

Another friend said she seemed to have a "great deal" of "respect" for her fellow human beings, as well as "genuine concern."

Certainly not the characteristics of a killer.

For Fred Andros, the one who had arguably convinced her to commit this murder, she had performed sexual acts—deviant, sadistic acts at that. It had started years ago. He'd call her up at work and summon her like some sort of slave. He had friends waiting. Friends who wanted sex for money. He had paid her; she hadn't done it for nothing. She'd even bedded Susan Fassett for money. She'd had five lesbian encounters with Susan, all while he watched, some of which he participated in and videotaped. At times he'd stand behind the video camera, which was situated on a tripod, directing them, telling them what to do and how to do it. He'd pull out his "toys" and explain to them what to do with them. They'd be in his garage behind his house or out at one of the waterpumping stations he managed. He'd be wearing a robe, like some sort of porn star, saying things like, *"OK, you do this. . . . OK, do that now. . . . Yes, yes, like that. . . ."*

She and Susan would be going at it, and he would

"disrobe and participate." He said it was Susan's idea from the start: that she had always wanted a threesome and had always dreamed of making love to a woman, and so he obliged her desire because he loved her, he said, and wanted to give her whatever she wanted.

Others said he was full of it. The only reason why Susan did it was to please him. Even the shooter agreed that Susan wanted nothing to do with the lesbian side and was only doing it to satisfy Fred's sexual desires and fantasies. He was semi-impotent. He needed diverse sexual experiences to keep him going. To keep things interesting.

Love didn't seem to play a part in his life anymore, however. *"Blow her f***ing head off. . . ."* That's what he thought of Susan Fassett now. Was there any love—save for himself—in wanting her dead?

The day after Fred Andros had showed her those photographs, they met and talked about how he wanted Susan murdered. Fred had it all planned out, he said.

"Listen to me. Drive into town and park in the Big Kmart parking lot." She sat and listened at first, without asking questions. They were standing outside her job in upstate New York along the interstate in the parking lot of the rest stop where she worked. "Make it around eight o'clock," he continued. "Leave your gun in the car. Go shopping for a while. If you come out of the store and your car is gone, go back into the store and wait awhile more."

She nodded her head, which indicated she understood. He knew she had kept a spare key inside the driver's-side wheel well. Apparently he was going to take her car and change the license plates. This way, she could zip in, do the deed, and zip out without anyone fingering her. If someone saw her plates, it wouldn't matter.

"I want her dead," he said on that afternoon, quite matter-of-factly. There was a hint of revenge in his tone. Hatred too. It was definitely *personal*. He had been slighted in some way by Susan and he wanted her dead.

There was no other way around it.

He explained where Susan could be found. There were two locations, he clarified, both of which she would be guaranteed to be at during certain times of the week.

"Do you understand me?"

The shooter nodded.

"Follow me," he said. They took off and drove to the Jewish Community Center in Pleasant Valley, not far from where Susan lived.

"She has Jazzercise classes every Monday night," he said.

She took a look around the parking lot. All the cars. All those windows in the building. All the people. Thinking about it, she said, "This is too public a place. . . . I cannot do it here."

He looked impatient. "Follow me, then."

They drove to the second location: the United Methodist Church on Martin Road in Pleasant Valley.

After they pulled over, she looked around. Nodded her head in agreement, picturing herself doing it here. *This might work. . . .*

"Definitely more suitable," she told him. "I can do it here."

The church was located in a secluded section of land, at the bottom of what is a steep incline, an average-sized rural neighborhood in back, and yet totally out of sight from the main road. There were trees lining Martin Road like a fence. Woods across the street.

At the right time of night, this could be the ideal location.

As they studied the area around the church, not for one moment did either of them consider that—if one is subject to believe in such things—although killing a woman is one thing, and there would be a time and place to answer to that immoral act, killing a woman in the parking lot of a holy house, a temple of the Lord, was another matter entirely. There was likely, some might say, a separate furnace in hell set aside for people who did things like that.

It didn't matter, of course, because unlike Susan Fassett, neither had much grace or even considered the church part of their lives. The shooter had been baptized Catholic, but hadn't practiced the faith in decades. They were here to discuss a murder and make sure it went off without a hitch. God played no part in that diagram—other than providing a stage.

He pointed to the road, asking her to notice how it went up a hill and around a sharp corner. "OK, you do it here"—pointing to an area near the church door where Susan would be exiting—"and take off that way, up the hill."

She looked.

"You understand me?" he asked.

She nodded. It seemed practical. Even *doable*. There was a tree blocking the view. Once she got up the road and around the corner, she could follow the street for about two hundred yards, take a sharp left and disappear back onto the main road into the population of everyday traffic.

Sitting in her car as he continued talking about something, she stared at the road: *This will work.*

On October 25, 1999, she drove to the Jewish Community Center by herself, sat in her car in the parking lot and waited.

This could work, too, she considered. After knocking the idea around some, she figured that if she did it at dusk,

there was a chance no one would see her. She had her
.45-caliber Ruger beside her. A good shot, she had grown
up around weapons. She took target practice out in back
of her Catskill home. She'd have little trouble with the act
itself, but people concerned her. She didn't want to clip
an innocent bystander and make this more than it was.

Maybe there are *too many people.* . . .

She scanned the parking lot again, but she didn't see
Susan's vehicle. It would be quick, she considered. One
quick pop. Maybe a few follow-up shots to "make sure."

Looking around, watching people coming and going,
she realized her first instincts were right: there was no way
it could happen at the Jewish Community Center. As she
had suggested already, there were far too many people
coming and going.

So she left.

The next morning, she called him and told him what
happened. In fact, he had just gotten off the telephone
with Susan, who still didn't suspect a thing, he said.

"I know," he said after she told him she couldn't do it
at the Jewish center. "It *has* to be done fast."

"I know . . . I know," she said.

"It has to be done by Thursday," he fumed. "Her testimony was postponed. You've got *one* more chance."

He didn't say it then, but in days past, he had piled on
the pressure by telling his hired killer that she would go
down with him if the murder wasn't completed soon. She
thought about what he had said. She remembered running envelopes for him, delivering cash money to certain
people. That made her a part of it all. A conspirator. A
pawn in his chessboard of corruption. In that respect, he
had once told her a story about Susan getting ready to go
in and testify against him for bilking the Town of Poughkeepsie out of tens of thousands of dollars, threatening
people, harassing and extorting contractors until they

paid him off. She knew things about him. She was sure the target was going to sit in front of a grand jury and hang him—any day. And then he would, in turn, hang *her*, the hired killer. If she didn't complete the job now, it was over for the both of them. Susan was going to provide evidence to put them both away.

And she knew what that meant.

"You're involved," he had told her more than once. "She's going to hang us if you do not get this done."

She said, "OK. I understand. I *get* it."

Things hadn't worked as planned back at Susan's house. She had snuck around the yard for a few moments, walked up the driveway, took a quick look, saw Jason and Jef coming toward her, then decided to leave. There were other people around that she could see. Someone else might get hurt. She didn't know, of course, that it was Sarah, Jason's girlfriend, standing on the porch. From a distance, Sarah looked a lot like Susan.

It's a good thing she didn't just shoot blindly.

Besides those five sexual encounters with Susan, she didn't know her. Not one bit. She had no feelings for her, one way or the other, which maybe made killing her that much easier, or at least *easier* to justify. She had participated in the lesbian affairs because, she later claimed, she owed Fred money. He'd knock $350 off her bill every time she met him and Susan, or even hand her cash. More than that, she was doing it so he could get off. He had some sort of Svengali power over her: she found herself over the years doing whatever he asked—and she had no idea why.

For that matter, neither did Susan.

In any event, he threatened her family again on the previous night, October 27. That's why, at that moment, she later said, she was on her way to Susan's church, determined to kill her there—this, as Susan sang hymns with her fellow parishioners and smiled and filled her heart with God's word and grace.

"I'll have them killed," he had told her, referring to her family once again. "You have to do this. She *must* die."

She had left the Fassett home and pulled off to the side of the road and cried.

I cannot do this. Banging on the steering wheel. *No, no, no. . . .*

So she called Fred to let him know. "I can't do it. . . ."

"Look," he said, "go through with this or I am going to see to it this time that I damn well carry through on my threats!"

She was terrified. She knew that her family was at home and he could possibly send "his people," as he put it, up there right now and have them killed.

"OK," she told him, then hung up the telephone and headed over to the church.

It never occurred to her why, if Fred Andros actually had "people" waiting in the wings to harm her family, he didn't use those same henchmen to kill Susan and not involve her at all?

CHAPTER 8

It was somewhere near 7:00 P.M. when she pulled off Route 72, near the center of Pleasant Valley, onto Martin Road, took a sharp left-hand turn, and there in front of her stood the United Methodist Church, where Susan was, at that moment, inside practicing with the choir.

After pulling around the corner, driving up the slight hill, in between the two church parking lots, she noticed a large group of children playing outside.

They must be waiting for their parents, she realized, and then drove by them as if she had just been passing through the area.

As she started up the hill, she took a quick look to the right and saw Susan's Jeep Cherokee parked across the street from the church in the overflow parking lot. She knew now that the woman she had made love to several times—the same woman that Fred needed dead—was definitely inside.

But what was she going to do about the children?

She drove into the center of town. It was about fifteen minutes after she had first driven by the church. She parked at a local A&P supermarket. Then she sat for a moment in her car, wondering what to do.

Those kids. I cannot do this with the children outside.

She had a doughnut.

Call him.

She approached the pay phone, looking in all directions, as if someone might be watching, and dialed his pager. She was a bit conflicted. There was a number on the pay phone, but she wasn't sure if the phone accepted incoming calls.

When his pager beeped, she keyed in the number, hoping he would call back.

As she stood, smoking a cigarette, bouncing her foot a mile a minute, she heard a "little chirp" from the pay phone and suspected it might be Fred.

"Hello?" she said hastily. "Hello, Fred?"

"What!?"

"There are children out front at the church," she said.

He sounded hurried. She could tell he had people over to the house. His wife, too, was in the background, talking jovially to another female. "What's the problem?" he asked in a whisper.

"There's *children* out there . . . I won't do it," she said.

"I don't give a damn about the children"—she could barely hear him, he was speaking so low—"they'll be gone soon. Get your ass back there and take care of business."

She thought about driving home and running into her house and telling her husband what was going on. But he made it clear that he had people in waiting, closer to her house than she was, who would act on a moment's notice for him.

"OK," she said.

Still, Susan Fassett, a woman he had proclaimed his undying love for, had been condensed into a piece of *business*, a job that needed to be done. A love affair that was now nothing more than a plan.

"Take care of business," she heard him say in her head.

* * *

Hanging up, she began to think about those photographs of her son once again. How her son was by himself, smoking a cigarette outside the building where he worked. Whoever took the photograph had been watching him. Stalking him. Much like the rest of her family. Fred had warned her. And then she asked her son one day if he had ever noticed anything peculiar. He said he was in a bar one time, somewhere far away from Hyde Park. Hours away, in fact. He was just sitting at the bar watching TV and having a beer. This man had come in and sat beside him. "He was about five foot six, brown hair, slicked-back, wore jeans and plaid shirt and cowboy boots."

"I was stuck on stupid," she said later, describing that moment, "because my son had described Fred Andros without ever having seen him."

Fred had apparently gone from bar to bar in towns where she lived in the mountains, specifically looking for her son. As her son explained it further, she knew Fred was trying to send a message. Her son had introduced himself to Fred and given him his first name, but not his last. As the guy in the bar was preparing to leave, he said, "I guess I better shove off now. It was nice to meet you, Mr. [her son's last name]."

And so the hired gun left the A&P parking lot and drove back to the United Methodist Church.

When she came around the corner of Martin Road, she decided to park next to Susan's Jeep Cherokee. The streetlight hanging over the Jeep, like a drooping sunflower, cast a clarity over the immediate area around the vehicle. Although she would be out in the open and under a spotlight, at least she'd be able to see what she was doing. She didn't want anyone else to get hurt.

Looking over toward the other parking lot, she noticed that the children were gone.

Thank goodness.

One could argue that it was at this moment where she had truly showed the genuine person she had become. Or, if you believe her, the person Fred had turned her into with his threats and intimidation and manipulation. The truth of the matter was, however, she could leave right now. Take off. Tell her kid to watch his back. He was old enough to protect himself. She could explain to her family that Fred was out to get them. Threatening her. Everyone. She could admit to her husband she had been sleeping with him—and Susan and the others and some of it had been videotaped—and take responsibility for her behavior, for her life. She could take out a loan and repay Fred every penny she owed him.

She could call the police.

She could call Fred and tell him no.

She could wait for Susan and tell her.

She could drive away and keep driving.

The fact was, there were plenty of options available, besides murdering a woman in cold blood as she left, of all places, church choir practice.

"A million things went through my head as I sat there waiting for Susan," she later explained to me.

How am I going to do this?

Reach for the key, start the car . . . leave.

The other part of this was that she knew Susan. Had slept with her.

"I made love to this woman. I thought about seriously waiting for Susan to come out, explain to her what was going on, tell her I wanted to follow her home and tell her husband. He would know what to do."

But murder was the decision she had made. Her only way out. She felt backed into a corner and pressured and vulnerable and unable to do anything else. Or that's what she would soon tell people. This was a weak argument, of course. Terribly selfish and narcissistic. But it was sustaining her at that moment, allowing her to face off against any trepidation or spinelessness that might lead her away. It was enough, surely, to take her from hunter to murderer.

From mother and wife to killer.

Her brother-in-law once said all this business of killing was "totally out of character for the person" he "knew," as it was not "what he would expect of her." He also said that this one murder (she was about to commit) was an isolated incident . . . that he was hard-pressed to think that "there would be any future acts of violence on her part."

It is easy to fool certain family members, if we rarely see them. And when we do, we are generally on our best behavior, admitting to only those deeds in our lives we want to share. The true self—the mishaps and broken parts of our character—is something many of us keep tucked deep down inside. Away. Hidden. Certainly, the shooter could relate to this. In reality, it was, one source later told me, "stimulating. . . . I think she enjoyed it . . . that she actually liked the idea of killing someone. She might have even done it for the thrill! I'm not sure she was threatened by [him] and I'm not sure she needed a reason." Killing a human being, in other words, was something she *wanted* to try.

The other point of the matter was, why not kill *him?* Why not turn the tables and put a cap in the back of *Fred's* head someday when he wasn't looking? That would certainly end all her problems. If she was going to cross that line and murder a fellow human being, why *not* kill him? She had no reason, essentially, to kill Susan.

"She was an Amazon woman," noted a former friend.

She chopped wood. She did physical work at home. Fred was nothing but a pip-squeak. She had about a foot on him and over one hundred pounds.

"She could have crushed him with her bare hands."

She said the thought had crossed her mind once or twice to kill him. "But you know, I—I . . . actually," she said, thinking about it further, "it was later suggested to me that that was the route I *should* have taken."

But she didn't. Instead, she parked her car next to Susan Fassett's Jeep on the night of October 28, 1999, and she waited for Susan to walk out of choir practice so she could, as he had been suggesting, "blow her . . . head off."

CHAPTER 9

And so she sat and waited in the parking lot near Susan's Jeep, having backed in patiently and deliberately, so the passenger-side door of her beat-up Ford Taurus station wagon was directly opposite the driver's-side door of Susan's Jeep. She planned to scoot over and sit in the passenger-side seat of her vehicle and wait for Susan to emerge.

It was 8:30 P.M. now. Her Ruger was under the back-seat. She could reach into the back easily and grab it as soon as she got herself situated.

"She'll come out somewhere near eight-thirty," Fred had told her, explaining his plan specifically. "The Jeep is gold. Brand-new. Get it done."

She slid over to her passenger seat after backing into the parking spot and reclined the seat all the way back. "As far as it would go," she said, "and . . . I then placed a magazine in the gun," locking it into place, making that snapping sound as it seated, "and chambered a round."

Then she rolled the window down.

And positioned herself perfectly.

She had said that saving her son's life had primarily driven her to murder. Still!, she didn't consider that

Susan Fassett had a family: two boys and a husband. People who loved her. None of that bothered her now as she focused her mind on murder.

It had been two months since she'd started taking medication for an anxiety disorder, she later explained. "Fred kept pushing the buttons," she added, "that kept exacerbating that situation." In other words, Fred knew that he could get her to do anything he wanted if he ratcheted up her fear and worry enough to the point where she didn't know what to believe anymore. "He manipulated my own weaknesses to his advantage."

One of her nieces would later say that she "has always tried to live by the law." The niece explained further that she "is not perfect, but none of us are," adding that her aunt had always taught her and her sister "right from wrong," that she had never "hurt anyone before all this. . . ." On top of that, she "was under extreme duress from him when she pulled the trigger that night." If it were under "normal circumstances," her niece continued, "she never would or could have pulled the trigger." She just wasn't that type "of person to take the life of another human being."

For some, killing becomes almost a reflex: to anger, love, greed, whatever. The act itself becomes a sort of malfunction of the brain in a sense that some people can convince themselves that death is the only answer to a *problem.*

Waiting, she had the gun in her hand, her arm stretched out by her side. Every once in a while, she'd peek her head up over the dashboard to see if anyone was coming. At this moment, she *was* that type person. She was that monster who could penetrate a knife into the abdomen of his or her victim. That rapist who could choose a victim at random, pluck her off the street and have his way with her, then strangle her as if her life didn't matter. Sitting in that car waiting for Susan Fassett to walk out of choir practice, she was just like all of them. What perhaps made her worse, however, was that she *knew* it. She was aware of what she was doing and the responsibilities of taking a life.

Fifteen minutes seemed like forever, she said.

Where is she?

She waited and stared at her watch: 8:30 turned into 8:45.

Susan was nowhere in sight.

Inside the church, Susan finished choir practice at 8:30, right on schedule, and began packing up her things by about 8:35 P.M. as several choir members came by and said, "Good-bye, see you on Sunday."

That casual, social gesture we all expound upon one another without actually thinking about what we're saying—more out of comportment and sensibility than sincerity. Of course, members of the choir loved Susan, and she them. But no one ever suspects that a simple departure from a social event—much less at church—will be the last time he or she actually sees that someone so dear to one's heart. You don't expect that you'll never be able to say good-bye again.

One of Susan's fellow choir members, Richard O'Hearn, was still rehearsing with some of the other men, who were staying a bit later, when Susan and another woman, one of her close church friends, walked out the door. *Madeline Kerns* walked with Susan into the parking lot. According to a police report, another one of Susan's friends followed behind shortly after and caught up with them. They all stopped for a moment and talked about the same mundane, domestic issues plaguing every American housewife. *"It was a beautiful night, wasn't it? So perfectly autumnesque, chilly and wonderful."*

"What a time of the year it was, indeed."

At some point, Susan mentioned to Madeline and the other woman about parking across the street, and Madeline said something about seeing her on Sunday morning, bright and early, when they'd be putting to the test what they had been practicing for so long now. The women then nodded to one another and smiled, and that was it.

They parted ways.

Just then, Susan walked across the street, making sure to look both ways before she crossed, as Madeline stood outside for a few moments more, digging in her purse for her car keys. Susan's other friend walked toward her vehicle and began getting in.

CHAPTER 10

She was raised Catholic. It bothered her that she was about to kill a human being in the parking lot of a church, but she later said, "I had two choices—the Jewish Community Center, which had a neighborhood watch sign directly in front of the building, which would have been suicide on top of murder. The other choice was the church."

Still lying on her back, she waited in the parking spot near Susan's Jeep. She had her ski mask on by now, plus a pair of rubber gloves. (She had used a second pair of gloves earlier that day to wash each bullet before placing it in the clip, and both sets of gloves were going to be tossed after the crime.) She had been waiting for about twenty minutes now, but as she poked her head up over the dashboard, for what seemed like the tenth time, there she was: Susan Fassett. She recognized Susan immediately, because she had made love to her on several occasions.

Finally.

Get this over with.

No one else was around—at least not in the second parking lot.

A moment later, Susan walked over to her Jeep and fidgeted inside her pocketbook for a moment, looking for her keys. She never saw the white of the hunter's eyes in the car next to her Jeep, the oversized woman she had performed sex with over the summer, who was reclined, staring at her through the tiny diamond-shaped cutouts of the woolen ski mask.

Breathing a bit more heavily, the shooter could feel the warm air through her nose bouncing back at her face off the wool mask. She was scared, she later said, but also quite confident she could get the job done. However, "If she would have made eye contact with me," the shooter later told police, "I would not have shot her." She was ambivalent.

But Susan never looked in back of where she was standing, and certainly hadn't expected a killer to be hiding out, waiting for her.

"She's a tough person to figure out," a friend of the shooter's later said. "She would never engage you in any type of personal conversation … . you know." Indeed, she was monotone and flat when she spoke. Sort of matter-of-fact. You couldn't tell, friends and others said, if she cared or not about what she said, because she said it with so much emotional secrecy.

Susan Fassett stepped into her Jeep after opening the door, never looking at the car parked next to her. Did she think there was someone out there, in the parking lot of her church, no less, waiting for her to come out of choir practice so she could unload the contents of a .45-caliber Ruger into her head? Susan might have stressed over the affair her husband had recently exposed and felt bad about the way her life had progressed. But she wasn't looking over her back, thinking someone was about to kill her. It made no sense, really.

In the course of a moment, a breath, three seconds, perhaps, Susan opened her Jeep door and sat down. She took a minute for herself, and then started her Jeep, turned the headlights on and reached over and grabbed her seat belt so she could latch it.

Madeline Kerns and the other woman who had walked out of the church with Susan were still in the parking lot across the street, standing outside their vehicles. By all accounts, it was just like any other Thursday night in late October at Pleasant Valley United Methodist Church. The common muffled noise of the church organ and the choir rehearsing inside replaced the mild buzzing of cars passing by Route 72 nearby, behind the parking lot. It was just a calm and peaceful end to a month that had been chaotic for Susan Fassett. This year's holiday season was going to be quite special, indeed. New. Festive. For once, Susan wouldn't have to sneak around and wonder if she was going to get caught buying a gift for him or having lunch or taking a ride.

No more. It *was* over.

Or was it?

Meanwhile, the shooter sat reclined back in her 1997 Taurus, poised and ready to end Susan's life. She was thinking about everything all at once. There was something about what Fred had said regarding Susan's new Jeep that she had thought about earlier. It had state-of-the-art features. "The Jeep automatically locks at fifteen miles per hour . . . once the door is closed," Fred explained. "You won't be able to get into her vehicle." He had even asked a friend of his who owned the same type of vehicle about this function. He understood it wrong, however. Because the vehicle remained *un*locked until the vehicle reached fifteen miles per hour. Then again, maybe it was what he wanted her to think. He had told her, point by point, how to carry out every aspect of the murder. He planned every detail—or so she later said. What did the Jeep locking really have to do with anything? She knew what she was going to do and how she was going to do it. The fact that

Susan had started her Jeep and revved the engine a bit, though, was the spark that got things moving.

"I thought she was going to leave right away," she said, "and so I sat up and I pointed the gun in her direction. . . ."

As the shooter sat reclined, thinking about when she would actually do it, she could hear the buzz of Susan's Jeep as its engine idled just next to her.

And so when she sat up—without looking anywhere else besides into the eyes of her target—and faced Susan, she leveled her weapon, and as she later described it, "I started pulling the trigger." When someone later asked her, "Do you know if you struck Susan?" She answered, quite arrogantly, "I think I did—but I'm not sure."

The first shot broke through the driver's-side glass window on Susan's Jeep and hit her squarely in the neck, piercing two major arteries. These two common carotid arteries deliver most of the blood to the brain. Sever one or both and the brain will cease functioning within five to ten seconds, thus rendering the victim unconscious.

But not dead . . . not yet.

The first shot could not have been more accurate. It actually went through the window, entered Susan's neck at her common carotid artery, traveled on a flat plain of what would be her throat on an east-to-west trajectory and exited her body through her common carotid, on the opposite side of her neck. It subsequently passed through the passenger-side window and jetted off toward a wooded area near the north side of the parking lot.

When Susan realized what had happened—or maybe she didn't—she went for the door. Maybe it was instinct? Maybe she knew she had been shot?

Either way, Susan opened her door and fell out of her Jeep onto the ground.

That was when the shooter unloaded her weapon: *Pop. Pop. Pop. Pop. Pop.*

Five more. In rapid succession. The empty hot shells flung out of the gun and landed inside her car on the seat and floor.

"I fired the gun until it wouldn't fire anymore," she said later. "My mind was racing."

CHAPTER 11

Susan's friend Madeline Kerns was still standing outside the church in that second parking lot—it all happened so quickly—when she and another choir member heard what Madeline later described as a "firecracker" sound coming from across the street. Six loud "pops," Madeline recalled in court later.

Realizing that the sounds were more than fireworks, Madeline first looked toward the noise and saw a "vehicle," she later told police, "leaving the west exit of [the parking lot] at a high rate of speed, traveling west on Martin Road *away* from the church" (which she described to the police fifteen minutes after the shooting as a "light-colored, possibly tan sedan or station wagon"). After she heard the shots and looked toward them, Madeline ran into the church and shouted to the male choir members, who were still practicing, "Shots . . . call nine-one-one. . . ."

In opening her door, Susan had smashed the passenger-side mirror of the shooter's vehicle. The glass didn't break, but it left a pretty solid mark.

Susan ended up unconscious, on the ground, with half of her body propped up against the Jeep. Forensics would later find a bullet actually lodged in the door frame of her Jeep, so we can decipher from this piece of evidence that those shots the shooter described were fired very quickly as Susan fell *out* of her vehicle.

In all, Susan sustained four gunshot wounds to her body.

Richard O'Hearn, who had stayed late with some choir members to continue practicing, heard what Madeline had said and ran outside toward Susan. As he darted across the street, the shooter took off, kicking up dirt and gravel in the process, chirping her tires ever so quietly on the tar as she left the parking lot and then drove speedily up Martin Road toward Barbara Lane and Gateway Drive, two rural neighborhoods in back of the church.

It was dark. That light hanging over Susan's car and several lights in the second lot were the only sources of light on the street.

O'Hearn reached Susan and immediately knelt down beside her, picked up her head and torso, placing her upper body in his lap. All he could do, he knew, was offer her comfort. As he looked at Susan, the way in which she was breathing laboriously, it was rather obvious that she was not in good shape. Those shots had hit vital areas of her body.

"She was having a hard time breathing," O'Hearn said later, "it was an awful sound. She was lying there, moaning. She wasn't coherent."

Indeed, in this situation, wheezing would be common right before death. Susan's lungs were filling with blood. Her heart was beginning to slow down.

O'Hearn looked closer and, he said later, saw "the hole in her neck." The only thing he could do for Susan, he realized, "was pray."

And so, as EMTs, the NYSP and the Dutchess County Sheriff's Office (DCSO) rushed toward the scene after church members and a local man who had heard the shots had called 911, that's exactly what O'Hearn did: he prayed for Susan Fassett's soul as she lay in his arms and, possibly, breathed her last.

CHAPTER 12

The shooter peeled the ski mask off after she tore up the hill and was far enough away from the scene so that no one would see her, tossed it on the seat next to her, took off the gloves and pitched them onto the floorboard.

Oh, my God, she kept telling herself. *I just killed Susan.*

Every car she passed or saw was, of course, a threat. She was terrified of getting caught. All she wanted to do was get home and see her husband, who she knew would be waiting up for her. He always did. For him, it was a routine Thursday night. He would be sitting in front of the television, waiting for his wife.

She later said that from the time Susan Fassett got into her car and "I shot her and took off out of the parking lot, it was probably the longest six seconds of my life. I won't *ever*... get that image out of my head," she told me, choking up, crying, "It is now something I dream about every night."

Fred had given her specific instructions to follow Martin Road toward Route 71, then back onto Route 44, where, she was told, to drive four miles back to Poughkeepsie and stop at Van Wagner Road to dump everything she had used to commit the murder in the woods there, on the side of the road.

As she came to an intersection, looking both ways, a state trooper, lights flashing, sirens blaring, whizzed by, heading in the opposite direction.

She knew where he was going.

"Put the gun in a plastic garbage bag behind the tree," Fred Andros had explained. There, on Van Wagner, was a short dirt pull-over off to the side with several acres of woods off to one side. There was an old oak tree on its side, which had fallen over near the beginning of a trail. He told her to put everything behind that dead tree, promising, "I'll pick it up later that night."

As she drove, she was crying and shaking and hysterical. "My heart was in my throat."

Leaving the bag where he had told her to, she drove to her sister's house, just around the corner. She gave no reason for this move later on—only that her sister lived close by and she might have thought it to be a good alibi.

She loved to help people, her sister wrote later. It didn't matter, she added, who it was, either, *a family member, a friend or stranger. . . . She is not a threat to anyone or anything. . . .*

Her sister wasn't home. So she took off from Poughkeepsie and drove to Hyde Park and stopped at a Stewart's convenience store/gas station out on Route 9G to use the pay phone.

"Don't call me with your damn cell phone. Page me when it's done and the bag is in back of the tree," he had said before explaining the code she was to use once the murder was complete.

She looked around the parking lot to make sure no one was watching. She then pulled up to the pay phone, ran out of her car and dialed his pager number, nervously waiting for the beep.

When she heard it, she punched in the number he had told her to use: *666.*

They had committed murder. Together. He the puppeteer, she the puppet. And now it was a scramble to clean it up and make sure the cops didn't figure it out.

"You're leaving the gun in the bag," he had explained, "so that if you are stopped by the police, you won't have the gun on you."

She agreed. It sounded like the best thing to do at the time.

Fred Andros was at home, downstairs in the basement, working on his model planes with his friend, a cop, Richard Byrd, when his pager buzzed its way across the table making a noise like a piece of paper caught in a fan.

He picked it up. Fred's friend was saying something about the model planes.

Looking down, Fred saw the page: *999*.

It was upside down.

666.

It's done. Susan Fassett, the problem, was dead.

"He loved using codes," the shooter said later. "He had the same setup with Susan. He didn't have to call you back or speak to you. That code—six, six, six—was to tell him that I had completed as he had instructed. It was a done deal."

Jason's girlfriend, Sarah, was sitting in the living room of Jef and Susan's Pleasant Valley home when she was startled by the piercing sound of an ambulance siren tearing down the road outside the house. So she got up and looked.

A while later, she recalled, Jef Fassett walked through the door after driving over to the PPD to pick up his paycheck.

"I remember an ambulance," she said, "screaming down the street . . . and Mr. Fassett was back at the house . . . but, of course, had no reason to think twice about it."

CHAPTER 13

New York State Police lieutenant Art Boyko, who worked out of Troop K in Pleasant Valley with the Bureau of Criminal Investigation (BCI), was at home on Thursday night, watching television, when his pager went off somewhere near nine o'clock.

Shots fired . . . victim hit . . . Martin Road, United Methodist Church.

Boyko knew the place. Exactly where the church is located. He had grown up in the area. Worked for Troop K most of his career. An experienced investigator, having been on the job for ten years by that point, Art Boyko embodied the character of an investigator, right down to his sharp, superhero good looks, lean and muscular athletic figure, perfectly trimmed suits and steely gaze. His demeanor, like his haircut (blond buzz cut), screamed *cop*. On the job, Boyko spoke directly to the point, rarely mincing words. He often didn't say much at all, as a matter of fact. Boyko, who had just turned thirty-four, was one of those cops who listened more than he talked. He liked to get a handle on a situation first and think about it some before making judgments or even commenting.

If he didn't know something, well, so be it, he wasn't afraid to say so.

A trooper had paged Boyko and, through a sign of his own, let him know that they had a possible DB, dead body—quite a rare occurrence for the town of Pleasant Valley. Even odder, the crime scene was inside a church parking lot.

Boyko took a look at his pager, realized the address, and couldn't believe it.

No one knew for certain if Susan was alive or dead. She had been removed from the scene and was, at that moment, on her way to the hospital. It didn't look good, of course, but she was still breathing when she left the scene, Boyko was told.

Boyko needed to get down to United Methodist Church as soon as he could. Witnesses were scurrying around. Standing. Talking. Wondering about Susan and what had happened.

So Boyko left his house hurriedly and raced to Martin Road in his jet-black state-issued Chevy Impala, where a stretch of yellow police tape and gaggle of churchgoers and rubberneckers and detectives were gathering, filling up the short road, roaming about and bumping into one another. Within moments, it seemed, after the first call had come in, EMTs had rushed Susan to St. Francis Hospital in Poughkeepsie to see if her life could be saved.

As Boyko got out of his car, he was briefed on the situation. Forensics was on its way, he was told. The scene had been secured. Several choir members were reporting having seen a "light-colored station wagon, possibly a Ford" leaving the scene speedily after shots had been fired. According to one witness, several of Susan's choir members were outside at the time of the shooting. They were stunned, naturally. Shocked and remarkably upset that Susan had been unconscious when she left the scene. There was still blood on the gravel by her car.

"Is she going to be OK?" someone asked.

No one could answer that question.

Boyko began to survey the scene and hand out assignments. Walking toward Susan's Jeep, it occurred to the seasoned investigator that it was going to be a long night. This was an odd occurrence—a murder in Pleasant Valley inside the parking lot of a church. The media was going to have a ball with this one.

According to the National Institute of Crime Prevention statistics focusing on family violence, 95 percent of victims are female, while *thirty-eight percent of women who are murdered are killed by their husbands, ex-husbands, or boyfriends. More than 4 million women in the United States are victims of domestic violence during an average 12-month period.*

Staggering numbers by any means.

Susan Fassett's murder, investigators knew immediately, could very well fall in line with those statistics. Nobody wanted to jump the gun and start tunnel-visioning, or profiling. But cops working the beat in cities all across the country know that nine out of ten times when a woman is murdered or abused, her husband or boy-friend is the likely culprit and the situation involves either love or money.

The "problem" that BCI would soon face as the information became available was that Susan Fassett's husband was a cop himself. This would certainly throw a kink into the early stages of the investigation. Anytime the spouse of a cop is involved in a crime, either by osmosis or a deliberate plan, it puts a different spin on how the investigation will unfold over the course of the first twenty-four hours.

It had taken Art Boyko five minutes to drive to the

United Methodist Church from his house, but no more than five seconds to realize that he had a touchy state of affairs on his hands, seeing that Jef Fassett was a Poughkeepsie police officer and his wife had been brutally shot several times at point-blank range. In fact, as Boyko soon found out, there was no shortage of choir members who had heard the shots.

"Her killer used a .45," Boyko said later, that much was pretty clear immediately, because "it sounds like a cannon going off, and several people from the church reported how loud it was."

From the BCI's perspective, it was fairly obvious that no one from choir practice had killed Susan. And, quite sensibly speaking, the crime was almost certainly not a random act of violence—some sort of thug in town who just happened to be passing by the church and decided to rob (and kill) Susan.

What became clear was that Susan Fassett was the target of the crime, which made a big difference in how the investigation would proceed.

Gathering details from those witnesses at the scene right away was a vital part of solving the crime. Information was fresh in their minds. If someone got a plate number or a make and model of a vehicle, an APB could be put out over the radio and wire. There was a chance the shooter was still in town or somewhere in the close proximity of Pleasant Valley. Having a description of the vehicle or maybe even a plate number in the hands of troopers all over the immediate area might produce a suspect, and save a trooper, perhaps, from walking up on an armed suspect running from a crime scene.

Finding out that Susan had a husband and family was a part of the sequence of events that confused things early on. Someone had to notify the Fassett family. But then, after Boyko ran the registration on Susan's car and it came back with Jef Fassett's name, things became complicated.

How to tell a cop his wife was just shot and might possibly die from those wounds? Not only that, but it would have to be done in a way that allowed troopers to begin asking Jef Fassett some tough questions about where he was and if he knew anything about the shooting.

It had to be done. There was no way around it.

Inside the church, someone reported that Jef Fassett had called. "But nobody said anything to him about Susan," Boyko was told.

"Good."

"What should we tell him if he calls back?" someone asked.

"Nothing."

Play dumb.

Sure enough, Jef called back moments later. Being a cop, he was beginning to ask pointed questions. He knew something was wrong. He could hear everyone in the background. Sirens. People yelling.

The one thing Art Boyko and his investigators knew from interviewing witnesses and finding some things out about Susan was that "this was no robbery," he later explained. "It wasn't a carjacking gone bad. There was motive behind it. That was clear from the little bit of evidence we had at the scene."

Moreover, a professional hit was quickly ruled out as soon as investigators learned that Susan had been shot multiple times, and none of those shots had been to the back of her head.

Boyko sent a car over to the Fassett residence to sit conspicuously and watch the house. Jef Fassett, Boyko said later, noticed the car outside his house immediately and called the church, this time *demanding* to know what was going on.

But no one would tell him—which only heightened his anxiety.

Then he called Troop K and asked the same series of penetrating questions.

As well, no one at Troop K would offer any relevant information.

Every law enforcement agency in the surrounding region—including the Poughkeepsie Police Department, where Jef worked—was in the loop, but no one wanted to tell Jef that his wife had just been gunned down, and he was a potential suspect.

After a time, several troopers, along with BCI investigators, drove over to the Fassett residence. "At some point— I don't know who actually told him—Jef Fassett learns what has happened to his wife," Art Boyko said later. "Rightly so, he's now got concerns about the welfare of his wife. He wants to go over to the hospital and be with her."

By this point, however, Susan Fassett was dead. Renowned forensic pathologist Dr. Michael Baden, working for the state of New York at the time, had already been called in to conduct an autopsy and determine a cause of death, aside from collecting any evidence Susan's body might yield. Jef Fassett, it was thought, might begin to complicate matters. Plus, he needed to be questioned. His weapon, issued by the Poughkeepsie Police Department, needed to be test-fired and checked. Many things had to be done, the least of which included Jef Fassett visiting his wife at the hospital or morgue.

CHAPTER 14

The shooter left Stewart's and proceeded north on 9G until she came to the Rip Van Winkle Bridge, which connects Hudson and Greenport on the east side, with Catskill on the west, and continued on her way home. She had to compose herself and walk into the house as if it were just another night working with the disabled.

"I had the car on cruise control most of the way home because I didn't trust myself to drive without speeding," she later told me.

There was one point during the trip where she drove by a state police barrack and one of the cruisers pulled out as she made her way by and followed. She was petrified. She thought for sure they had figured it out.

Up at a light as she was making a turn, the cop pulled up alongside her car, turned, looked over, smiled, and then sped off.

When she walked into the house, her husband was up, as usual, watching the news. It was somewhere near eleven.

"You're up?" she said.

"Yeah . . ." He seemed surprised that she was getting home so late.

"I had a little problem with the car. There was some problem somewhere. Cops were all over. So I went slow."

She sat down after putting her coat away and getting a glass of water. The news was still on.

"There's your problem," he said. He was referring to the story on the news about a shooting in Pleasant Valley. "Cops are looking for a killer."

She got up quickly and walked toward the bedroom. Standing in back of him, so he couldn't see her heart in her throat, her pale skin, she said, "Oh, my God. That's down near where your sister lives," referring to the shooting scene.

He was more interested in the news than perhaps thinking his wife was the murderer. He paid no mind to her anxiousness.

She got herself ready for bed and slid under the covers to try to sleep, saying later, "A lot of things went through my mind. A lot of guilt. A lot of remorse."

A report soon came in that a car had been seen leaving the scene of the crime. That car, the witness had said, was identical to Jef Fassett's car.

As the NYSP investigator sat outside Jef's house, while investigators figured out how to best handle the situation with Jef having kids in the house and possibly being responsible for Susan's death, Jef walked out of the house and approached the investigator sitting in his car.

"Why are you here?" Jef asked the cop. He banged on the glass. "What's going on?"

The investigator wouldn't answer.

"What's happening?" Jef wanted to know.

"Please go back into your home, Mr. Fassett," the investigator finally said.

At this time, the same men and women Jef had known

and worked with for over twenty years, the Poughkeepsie Police Department, went into action. It was a complicated issue: the NYSP and PPD couldn't sit idly. They
had a witness claiming Jef had speedily left the scene of
a murder.

Jason Fassett, who was inside the house watching the
entire incident unfold before him, didn't quite see it the
same way. "It was as if they (the Poughkeepsie PD) had
been waiting for something like this," he later said, "to
test all their new equipment out."

The Poughkeepsie PD SWAT team dressed and read-
ied themselves for a rendezvous on the Fassett residence.
They put on their vests, grabbed assault rifles and goggles
and helmets, and went into combat mode, racing over to
the Fassett home. All because they believed, Jason suggested later, Jef Fassett was a *suspect* in his wife's murder.

BCI knew that Jef Fassett was inside his home and, most
important, he had weapons in the house. Many felt that if
Jef had murdered his wife, he was preparing to make a
stand against the police and was a suitable candidate for
suicide by cop, or maybe even a hostage situation.

"One thing led to another," Art Boyko said later, a bit
docile and reflective with his choice of wording, "and we
start doing, with the Town of Poughkeepsie, what's
called a 'negotiation' to get him out of his house."

It was a tandem effort—each department working together to try and get Jef out of the house without anyone
getting hurt. Jef's frame of mind had to be taken into
consideration. His wife was dead; she had been gunned
down while coming out of choir practice. If Jef didn't do
it, he was likely distraught and upset over the murder,
nonetheless. Either way you looked at it, the situation
wasn't easy to deal with.

"We didn't know what he was thinking inside his

house," Boyko added. Moreover, BCI didn't know if Jef even knew if Susan was dead.

Jason and his girlfriend, Sarah, had made plans to go over to his friend *Kevin's* house after dinner and "hang out," as Jason later put it. "We were going to . . . chill out."

So Jason and his girlfriend got into his car and proceeded to work their way down the driveway. When he got to the end of the driveway, where it crossed like a T with the main road (Route 44) out in front of the house. He looked across the street and saw two cars in the parking lot of the pizza restaurant directly across from the house. Each car was facing him.

When their headlights met, Jason recalled, "I saw all these faces pop up."

What the hell? he thought.

In fact, there were cops scattered all over the place: in the yard, across the street, in back of the house. They were dressed in black and had rifles. Jason knew the cars across the street were cops, because he recognized some of the men as his dad's colleagues. Jason had met them over the years at cookouts and at the department. In fact, one of Jason's best friends' father was sitting in one of the cars, staring back into Jason's car.

Come on, Jason told himself, *all this for a little bit of weed?* He had grabbed some pot on his way out of the house and believed he was being busted.

When the cops saw Jason, they were all very surprised, he said, and had no idea what to do next.

"They're looking at each other, looking at me, looking at each other, then looking at me."

It was like a movie, Jason said.

"What the f***?" Jason said aloud.

Sarah asked him what was going on.

OK, Jason thought, *I'm busted. I'm in trouble again.*

So Jason backed up his driveway, got out of the car and went back inside the house.

"Dad," he said to his father, who greeted him at the door, "I don't know what's going on, but there's a bunch of cops in the parking lot across the street."

Jason ran upstairs, put the weed into a boot in his closet. It made no sense to him that that many cops would be staking out the house for such a small amount of pot.

Jason, his dad, his brother and his girlfriend had no idea that Susan had been shot dead, or the true reason why the Poughkeepsie PD was encircling the house at that moment.

"No one told us a *damn* thing," Jason recalled. "No one said, like, 'Hey, you guys got like fifteen minutes to see your mom . . . she's dying. . . .' Instead, they immediately started investigating this SWAT team effort, blocking off Route 44 to traffic, initiating a mobile command unit at the local firehouse, and here they are with all this fancy equipment they probably had to dust off before they used it, and no one had any proof that my dad had done *anything*. All his years with that police department and they believed he was this vicious killer."

Unbeknown to Jason or anyone else in the house, although Jef had probably guessed, seeing that he knew how his colleagues would react, the house was entirely surrounded. Jef called the Poughkeepsie PD. "What's going on? Why are there two unmarked cars sitting across the street?"

According to Jason, who later spoke with his father about that night, the Poughkeepsie PD played the telephone game with him: "Hold on, let me transfer you. . . . You need to speak with . . . so-and-so . . . ," and kept giving him the runaround.

Jef hung up and turned to Jason. "Something's not

right here. I need to know your mom is OK. Call the church, Jason."

Jason picked up the phone.

"Is Susan Fassett there?" In the background, Jason could hear whispers: *"Oh, my goodness, Jason's on the phone, what do we tell him?"* Jason knew everybody at the church. He had attended holy classes as a child growing up in the church, had been confirmed and, as a youngster, went to church with his brother and mother. He could tell something was wrong. No one wanted to speak about Susan.

His heart sank. His stomach went into knots. "I realized at that moment that this is not about me smoking a little weed."

Finally a guy from the church choir Jason knew got on the telephone and said, "Jason . . . um . . . your mother's been shot."

Jason went silent. "That was," Jason later said through tears, "probably the craziest thing I have ever heard in my life."

Jason turned and told his father, "Mom was shot."

"What?"

For Jason, life at that moment, he said later, "had just become permanently skewed. It was never what I thought it would be again—and hasn't been since that moment. Life had grinded to a halt and become this long, dark *waiting* period."

Things seemed to move in slow motion from that moment forward.

What Jason was waiting for, he didn't know. Maybe for Susan to return from choir practice. One long period of expecting her to walk through the door any day, any moment, but knowing she would never again enter the house or smile or be there for him to turn to in a time of need.

And yet, at that moment, all Jason and his family knew was that Susan Fassett had been shot. Nothing more.

Later, Jason had a tough time with what happened that night. He was upset that the Poughkeepsie PD didn't treat his father—and his family—with a bit more dignity. "If the cops were so interested in helping us or 'saving us,' why didn't they come out and say so? Why not talk to me or my brother to see if we were OK? It seems like there were a lot of possibilities they completely overlooked and instead went right for the macho, guns-blazin' approach. . . . Despite what anyone says, I believe they wanted to make this a 'huge ordeal.' What's an army without a war? What's a SWAT team in a town that doesn't ever get to use one? . . . Part of me will never get over how horrible we were treated that night by my father's supposed friends, coworkers and peers."

The Poughkeepsie PD refused to respond to Jason's obvious anger.

CHAPTER 15

Inside the house, Jason called his friend, *Kevin*, whom he and Sarah had been on their way to visit when everything went wrong. Kevin and Jason were close. Jason was at a loss. He didn't know what to do. His mother had been shot, or so he was told, but by whom? For what reason? Was she alive or dead?

"A little communication would have gone a long way at this point," Jason later said.

When Kevin answered, the words, Jason said, fell from his mouth without effort: "My mom's been shot!"

"What?" Kevin responded.

"Somebody shot my mom."

Jason and Kevin had always joked around, but Kevin could tell immediately that his friend was serious.

Nothing else was said. Kevin hung up.

"And I knew he was on his way over to the house."

There wasn't any pandemonium in the house after the news about Susan being shot settled on everyone. They all knew then and there that Susan was never coming home again. Their lives had just changed forever.

A weird, scary silence took over the house after Jason hung up with the church and spoke with Kevin, Jason remembered. Nothing happened in a rapid fashion. The entire night came to a screeching halt.

The cops outside the house didn't make matters any better. In fact, for Jason and his family, their guarded omnipresence only added to the growing confusion, fear and anxiety that seemed to be building.

"OK," Jason later reflected, "we learned my mom had gotten shot, but then why were there cops in our yard? Why weren't they coming into the house to console and talk to my dad about it? This was all wrong to me."

Jason was sitting in a blue chair in the living room, bouncing his foot a mile a minute, thinking about what was happening and why no one was explaining anything, especially a group of guys whom his dad had known so well and worked with for decades.

"Turn off all the lights in the house," Jef Fassett said. He gave no reason. Then Jef went around the house—as law enforcement outside watched—and closed all the blinds.

For cops roaming around the property, when they saw this, many considered it to be a "defensive posture." At best, Jef's actions were extremely peculiar.

There Jason sat in that blue chair, his brother and Sarah by his side, wondering and waiting for something to happen. "Terrified," he said later, "curious and scared."

Inside the home, there was the idea that Jef Fassett was being stalked by someone he had put in prison. Maybe Jef had arrested some dude years ago and that guy had gotten out of prison, shot Susan and was now on his way over to the house to kill the rest of Jef's family? That's why, they all thought at one point, the cops were outside: they were protecting the house from some lunatic out to get Jef Fassett and his family.

But why wasn't anyone explaining this to the Fassett family?

On the other hand, the NYSP and the Poughkeepsie PD were in a tough position. As things progressed and Jef's behavior continued to seem peculiar, any person of average intelligence could have certainly made an argument that Jef was involved in his wife's murder. What Jason and the others didn't know was that a witness—that person who said he spotted Jef's car—had actually placed Jef at the scene of the murder. What could have solved the entire situation would have been to allow Jef to approach an investigator and speak with him, one on one, but then no one could tell Jef his wife was dead or give him any other details. And so Jef was left in the dark and a standoff ensued.

"It was turning into this sickening picture," Jason said, "that I didn't want to see completed. My stomach was beginning to twist and turn."

Nerves.

"The tension was getting to us all."

Not knowing.

"My head's racing a mile a minute. . . ."

The anxiety of *What's next?*

"My brother's upset." Christopher, Jason explained, was never one to talk about his feelings. But as he sat there that night, not knowing the outcome, he opened up to Jason and told him how much he needed and appreciated him.

Jef was making calls. Trying to find out what the hell was going on. But whoever Jef called wouldn't answer his questions.

At some point, Jason looked outside toward the backyard, where there was a hill by the pool, and saw something: more cops in SWAT gear moving down the hill as if they were preparing for something.

Then Kevin pulled into the driveway, a cop car closely following behind him. As Kevin parked, Jason said, near the top of the yard by the back door, "he was immediately 'ambushed' by the SWAT team."

What is going on here? Jason thought, staring out the window. His friend was being pulled out of his Jeep like some sort of criminal. They threw him to the ground, with guns drawn, handcuffed and seemingly arrested him.

Some of the cops out in the yard had worked with Jef for twenty years. But there they were, stealthily working their way toward Jef's house, preparing to converge, surround and take Jef and his family into custody.

No one in the house, however, understood why, or truly knew what was happening.

Jef Fassett called the Poughkeepsie PD again after Jason reported seeing the cops on the hill making a move toward the house and Kevin being taken down.

"What's going on?" Jason heard his father say into the telephone.

They wouldn't tell him.

Next a hostage negotiator called the house. Jef was alarmed. Shocked. All those strange feelings that go along with being accused of something you haven't done. Jason saw his father's face go from worry to dread.

"They told my dad that they wanted us all—including my girlfriend—to come out of the house with our hands up."

"What's going on?" Jason asked his father. ("I just wanted to go to my friend's house [party], and now there's this SWAT team outside my house, my mom's been shot, and one of my dad's colleagues on the phone telling us all to come out of the house with our hands in the air.")

Surreal.

Jason watched as his father walked out onto the porch first, his hands behind his head, turning on command, dropping to his knees, bowing his head.

This is crazy. He couldn't believe what he was seeing.

"My father was being arrested in every sense of the word—the only difference was that no one ever came out and said, 'You're under arrest.'"

One by one, Jason, Christopher and Sarah were ordered to exit the house, hands on back of their heads, while walking backward toward cops pointing assault rifles at them.

After they were all on the porch, kneeling, several cops came up, handcuffed all of them like common criminals and walked them to the middle of the dirt driveway.

When they got to the driveway, the cops made them get down on the ground, on their stomachs, spaced apart.

Sarah was crying. When she went to kneel down, she dropped from her knees onto her face into the dirt driveway very quickly. "And the cop standing there beside her," Jason said, "just let her go. She just fell on her face!"

Jason looked up at the cop. "Could you *please* pick my girlfriend up off the ground?"

He stood over Jason, assault rifle by his side. "Nope" was all he said.

From there, they were placed in separate police cruisers and driven away to Troop K, where the reality of the situation for Jason, Sarah, Christopher and Jef would begin to sink in.

According to the NYSP, it took BCI and several state police troopers hours, but they watched from afar as everyone was "systematically" removed from the Fassett house and brought down to Troop K to be interviewed.

Jef Fassett was a potential suspect, he couldn't deny BCI the benefit of *that* doubt. It went with being the husband of a murder victim and a report that his car had been at the scene. But more important to the investigation, one source later cleared up, was that Jef Fassett "could shed light on a motive for this crime—he possibly had information that could have been extremely helpful to the early stages of the investigation as far as tracking down potential suspects."

The PPD didn't see it that way, obviously from their behavior, but the NYSP had a murder investigation wide open that they needed answers to. Jef could be helpful in that respect.

By about midnight, heading into the early-morning hours of October 29, Art Boyko and his team of BCI investigators learned through several interviews with PD officers who knew Jef and Susan that Susan had been having an affair with Fred Andros, the former Poughkeepsie water superintendent, who, they had learned also, had signed a deal with the FBI that May to plead guilty in a corruption scheme involving other town officials. Fred was the government's key witness.

Realizing this new fact, one had to wonder, was Susan Fassett a witness for the government as well? Was she also involved in the corruption probe?

"It began to get messy," one investigator later told me.

Someone is going to have go over there and talk to Fred Andros, Boyko realized.

With the revelation of Susan's affair on the table, it opened up all sorts of possibilities, not to mention potential suspects. Her lover. Husband. The wife of her lover. Maybe it was a hit, after all? Perhaps Susan Fassett knew *too* much?

Art Boyko decided to make a call to Fred Andros and head over to his house to conduct an interview.

Meanwhile, Jef, Christopher and Jason Fassett, along with Jason's girlfriend, Sarah, were at Troop K, in separate rooms, being periodically interviewed by members of BCI.

"When I was seventeen," Jason explained later, "I was arrested for selling acid in school. They brought me in and, understandably so, handcuffed me to a desk. Here I was, now twenty years old, my mother had been murdered (they knew this!), and I was once again handcuffed to the same desk inside the same police station."

Jason had no idea what time it was or why he was being detained. No one explained to him what had happened to Susan, or why, for that matter, they were all there, being kept apart, being questioned, not to mention why they had been handcuffed and taken out of their home like terrorists.

"What did your father say in the house?" was one question Jason remembered being asked repeatedly. "Did he mention anything about your mom, or what happened to her?"

"What? Could you *please* just tell me what happened to my mom? I need to know."

No one was telling Jason what was going on. He was livid. Someone would pass by the desk and he'd say, "Can you help me out here?"

But, according to him, "They ignored me like I was a common criminal."

Part of it was that BCI needed to figure out what Jason knew about a potential role his dad *might* have had in Susan's murder. Although handcuffing the kid to a desk might have been taking things a little too far, keeping information from Jason was an investigative tactic, nothing more.

At times a cop would show up in the room and ask Jason a few questions.

"I realized my mother was dead, when, after being handcuffed in a police station all night long, no one had told me anything *good*. After such a long period of time, my mind just concluded that my mom must be dead—that this is what this is all about."

Jason felt humiliated. Why would the police not tell him about his mother?

"There's something not right about those cops not telling me right away that she was gone. It was eight hours at the police station before they told me *anything*."

CHAPTER 16

Some husbands and wives grow apart. It's an ingredient inside the evolution of some marriages. For a great marriage to work, there has to be a complement: the yin to the yang. Sacrifice and unconditional love. Anger and forgiveness. Withdrawal and care. Resentment and compassion. Hurting and healing. "Very normal things happen," Jason Fassett said of his mother and father's marriage. "After twenty years, they stopped loving each other. They don't tell each other they love each other anymore. They don't compliment each other. Lack of communication. Sometimes parents can be just like grown-up kids, acting the same, doing the same things, but on a deeper level."

Susan loved to travel. Jef didn't. As they grew older and the kids were at an age where they could truly enjoy traveling and spending time with their mother, the three of them began going places together. You sit and you look through the photo albums of the Fassetts' life together and, as Jason so observantly pointed out, "it's like every third or fourth picture is the three of us: my mom, my brother and me." They went to Mets games. The Statue of Liberty. Church picnics. There they were, the Three

Musketeers. After a while, Jason recalled, "We came to realize that my dad was there, but he also *wasn't* there."

On paper, "my dad was everything a father is supposed to be," Jason added. "He went to work. Came home. But it seemed like he just wasn't really in our life."

Susan loved nothing more than to tape her favorite soap opera, *Days of Our Lives,* then sit in the living room at night and watch hour after hour of the show. Perhaps it was because a part of her life began to mimick those events in the show.

"She was probably," said Jason, "as loyal to *Days of Our Lives* as she was to the Methodist Church." He laughed lovingly at the memory.

Susan believed. She felt the presence of God and Jesus Christ and knew there was a place in heaven for her and her kids and husband, regardless of the mess she'd created out of her life with Fred Andros.

"I really think she was trying to do something positive," Jason said, reflecting back on his mother's affair, "but she was probably at this point in her life feeling very much alone. She had a lot of friends, a husband, two kids, and we were all close and everything, but I think where she was personally in her head, she didn't see that she had anybody to help her out with life."

The Town of Poughkeepsie was another sore spot with Susan. She was underpaid, according to her son. But, at the same time, she would never speak up for herself. She'd just accept what was given to her and never complain.

"She wasn't assertive. She would never stand up and say, 'Hey, I'm important. You're mistreating me. You need me.' She let them decide when she'd get a raise."

Susan wanted people to like her. She didn't want people to think negative things about her and would hardly ever tell someone what she truly thought of them or anyone else. Everyone around her was first in Susan's life. The unselfishness she displayed, Jason explained, came from her mother, who, he believed, was the sweetest old woman Dutchess County had ever produced. The type of person who fed the neighborhood before ever thinking about eating herself.

"My grandmother," Jason recalled, "would do *anything* for *anybody* else and never think of herself first."

On the one hand, Susan's mother had a much more simpler life than her daughter. Susan was a child of the 1950s and celebrated the peace and love movements of the 1960s and '70s. She had many more choices than her mother, and certainly more temptation.

Humility and honor drove the Taber parents in raising Susan and her sister. Jason remembered friends of his stopping over and always warming up to his grandmother. There she was, apron on, smile across her face, always with something positive to say.

The Tabers were the light, Jason said. "My mom and my grandparents didn't have to sit us down and tell us to be good people—they led by example. After my mom's death, my grandmother became the light I learned to follow."

Somewhere within all that goodness Susan had grown up around, however, entered the abominable Fred Andros.

CHAPTER 17

Back up in the Catskills, the shooter was in bed toss-ing and turning. She couldn't sleep. So she got dressed, took a walk, returned home and played solitaire on the computer most of the night, chain-smoking cigarettes and reliving over and over the bloody scene at United Methodist.

Her husband didn't move a muscle all night.

She considered going back into town to see Fred. But was afraid of, she said, "what I might do. I was really upset. He had put me in a terrible situation and caused me to do something that was totally against my nature."

Not a good idea . . . , she had told herself every time the thought came up.

By 5:00 A.M., she was getting dressed for work. She had not slept a wink all night.

Driving toward her first pickup—she was in charge of picking up all of the mentally challenged workers she worked with and supervised all day—she began to go through the night. It was odd, she suddenly thought, to leave the gun in a garbage bag on the side of the road for Fred to pick up. But that's what she had done. It was her gun. She had bought it and registered it. Now it was in *Fred's* hands. And he controlled its whereabouts.

She'd put her entire life in Fred's hands.

Fred Andros was an awkward-looking son of a gun. He kept his salt-and-pepper hair greased back and fluffed up in a pompadour in the front, like he had perhaps just come from an audition for *Grease.* His rough, sandpapery, pockmarked face made for a strange canvas. Fred was short, too. Some called Fred "repulsive," "ugly," "filthy," "nasty." Others viewed him simply as a huckster. A charlatan. A man who thought he could take what he wanted without repercussions—including someone else's wife.

In his own twisted psyche, Fred had fashioned himself a sort of big shot within the towns of Hyde Park and Poughkeepsie. He lived in Hyde Park with his wife, Diana, and a son from a previous marriage. Hyde Park, located on the east bank of the Hudson River, like Pleasant Valley, is about halfway between New York City and the state capital, Albany, and was the home of Franklin Delano Roosevelt, the thirty-second president of the United States. *The Roosevelt Estate is the only place,* reads the Hyde Park Chamber of Commerce literature, *in the nation where a President was born, grew to manhood and lies buried in the Rose Garden, which is located on the grounds of the estate.* So Fred Andros, who grew up in Poughkeepsie and had always been known around town as a thug, a wannabe bully and a two-bit criminal, had lived near royalty all his life. He could taste it. And certainly wanted his share of it without putting in any of the effort and hard work.

Much to his own chagrin, Fred Andros was quite efficacious when it came to getting what he wanted. Despite the fact that he was myopic and even obvious about it, Fred was a "master manipulator," one former friend later recalled. Others claimed, he could, with enough time and opportunity, talk a nun into converting to Judaism.

NYSP investigator Art Boyko knew nothing about Fred Andros, beside the fact that he was facing some serious time for his involvement in a scam he had been running for years out of his Town Hall office as Poughkeepsie's water superintendent. The scandal involved some fairly heavyweight political people from the area Republican Party that Fred had been dropping a dime on since getting caught and turning government witness. Thus, Boyko knew as he walked into the interview with Fred Andros, he was dealing with a liar and thief.

It was 3:48 A.M., according to Boyko's personal notes, when he and another BCI investigator skated by Fred Andros's house on Violet Avenue in Hyde Park to, as Boyko later said, "take a quick look and survey the house."

Seeing that everyone in the Andros house was sleeping, Boyko decided he might fare better by phoning Fred first before banging on the door. So he pulled off to the side of the road a little ways past Fred's three-story gold home on the generally busy street and made the telephone call.

Diana Andros, Fred's fourth wife, answered the telephone with a groggy, sleep-deprived, raspy whisper, "Hello?"

"Mrs. Andros, this is Art Boyko, from the New York State Police. . . . I need to speak to your husband."

Silence. Then, "Hold on."

Boyko could hear Diana say, "Fred . . . Fred," getting louder each time. "Fred! It's for you."

"Yeah?" Fred said after a moment.

"Mr. Andros," Boyko said, introducing himself. "Can I stop by and speak to you?" Boyko explained who he was, but didn't say what he wanted or what had happened to Susan.

Fred thought about it.

"Sure," he said, reaching for his glasses on the night table beside the bed. "I'll get up."

Fred Andros had no shortage of people who would have loved nothing more than to see him behind bars, looking out into the world from a safe distance. Jef Fassett, of course, was likely the first in line. Jef and Fred had a run-in a while back. Jef had a feeling that Fred had been sleeping with Susan. So he called Fred. "Meet me at the Poughkeepsie Police Department," Jef said.

From his office at town hall, Fred made the drive over.

"Are you f***ing my wife?" Jef came right out with, according to what Fred later told police.

"No, no, no," Fred said, pleading with Jef to believe him. The truth was, like any bully, when Fred was confronted or someone stood up to him, he backed down and walked away with his tail between his legs.

He was scared. He could tell from the tone of voice Jef used that he meant business. He wasn't so much bigger, but Jef was definitely stronger, and certainly could have pummeled Fred if he wanted.

Susan had explained to Fred it was over. And yet, just a few days before her death, Susan had met with Fred. The day of her death, in fact, she had telephoned Fred several times.

One of Fred's biggest adversaries at the present moment, however, wasn't Jef Fassett, who was still at Troop K being questioned by BCI investigators. Fred's big rival at present was none other than William Paroli, the former chairman of the local Dutchess County Republican Party, who had himself been under investigation since 1997 for pilfering monies from local developers—some of whom were found to be paying Paroli and the Republican Party over $100,000 in exchange for permits and tax breaks. It was a typical small-town scam by politicians who thought they could pull one over on the little guy and slip their corrupt ways under the radar of what was going on in the larger cities. Authorities claimed Paroli had enlisted Andros and another man, Basil Raucci, who was, at the time, the Town of Poughkeepsie's tax assessor, in an elaborate scheme of taking kickbacks for favors and contracts reminiscent of Gilded Age heyday sleaze.

When the *New York Times* later caught up to Paroli after his arrest, and asked him to describe Fred Andros, Paroli, a roly-poly barrel of a man heading into his golden years, told reporter David Chen, "He's a small man with a Napoleonic complex who wants to be bigger than he is."

This quote summed up Fred's life pretty convincingly. He was an aspiring wiseguy type—someone who liked to play dirty politics as though he was a big shot himself around town, when federal prosecutors would soon prove that Fred Andros was merely a player.

But Fred was certainly not one of those so-called "strongmen" the *Times* had mentioned. Once Fred got with the real bad guys, he was just another divorced man, pushing sixty, who was looking for a free ride at the expense of much bigger fish—and thought his position as a water superintendent could bring him wealth in a corrupt world of rural community politics.

Fred was watching his back these days more than he had let on to friends and family. Paroli's second man, Basil Raucci, had been found in the Hudson River, his death ruled a suicide. But those in the know felt they knew better. Raucci certainly could have been shut up, the old-fashioned way.

"You think a guy," one source told me, "who was afraid of water," referring to Basil, "would drown himself in the Hudson River as a means of committing suicide? It makes no sense. Fred Andros knew this—and he was watching his own back every step of the way."

CHAPTER 18

BCI investigator Art Boyko knocked on Fred's door near four o'clock on the morning of October 29, 1999.

It took a few moments before Fred answered. "Come in, come in," he said. Still quite muzzy from waking up so suddenly, Fred was wearing a full-length bathrobe. His wife, Diana, was behind him, asking, "What's going on?"

Boyko and his partner, Investigator Eric Underhill, walked into the kitchen and stopped there. As they moved into the dining room to sit down and begin talking, Diana Andros said she was going back to bed.

"We'll want to speak with you, too, Mrs. Andros," Boyko pointed out.

She nodded.

Fred took one look at Boyko and said, "I know why you're here."

Boyko would later say he didn't recall Fred coming out and saying this until later on in the interview. In any event, according to a judge's order, Fred continued, saying, "Special Agent James O'Connor (from the FBI) called me around eleven last night and told me Susan was dead."

It made sense. Fred was the FBI's key witness in a

three-year corruption investigation. Agents working with him knew that Fred had been having an affair with Susan Fassett. So when she turned up dead, they likely thought it most appropriate to call Fred and let him know, or see what he had to say about it.

"I know you had a relationship with Susan, Fred," Boyko said as he sat down at the dining table. Fred sat next to him. Listening, Underhill stood nearby.

"I've known her twenty years," Fred answered. He looked distraught, Boyko later said. He was seemingly broken up by Susan's death. Anytime cops are in your kitchen in the middle of the night, it's not going to be a pleasant moment.

"How long have you guys been intimate?" Boyko wondered.

"Four years," Fred said, shaking his head.

Boyko had no reason to suspect that Fred had had anything to do with Susan's death. He and Underhill were simply following the evidence, seeing where it led. Getting to know Susan Fassett, they understood, would yield new leads and new information. There was, after all, a reason behind her murder, which meant that Susan, in somebody's view, needed to die.

"We went there because we wanted to learn about her," Boyko mused later, looking back on that first interview with Fred. "We wanted to see what he knew. It was basically to learn some information about *him*. See what type of person he was. He knew our victim. Background on him. His family. His employment. It was all going to help us figure out who committed this brutal crime."

Boyko steered Fred into a discussion about his relationship with Susan and when it was they had last seen each other, either intimately, personally or in town.

Fred didn't hesitate: "Last time we had sexual intercourse," he admitted, "was a year and a half ago. I'm impotent," Fred added casually, unabashedly, not ashamed in the least. "Since that happened, our relationship consisted of hugging and kissing and no intercourse."

Boyko took copious notes. He studied Fred. Checked his mannerisms, his movements, how he used (and chose) language. It was all part of the mystique of investigating a murder. Everyone was a suspect until he or she could be crossed off what was a growing list.

"Have you seen her lately, or spoken to her?"

"I spoke to Susan, um, let's see, at about four o'clock yesterday. She paged me and I returned her call. She was at work. Just getting ready to go home." It was nothing more than casual speak, Fred insisted. Susan liked to talk to him several times a day. Just to say hi, or maybe ask about his night.

"And when did you see her last?"

"September twenty-seventh," Fred said without a second thought. He was firm with the date, as if he had written it down. "But we spoke on the phone many, many times after that."

Boyko paused. Then, "Can you go through and tell us where you were earlier tonight?"

"I was at home here at the time of the shooting. We had company between seven and nine, a friend of mine, Richard Byrd, and his wife were here."

Byrd was a Poughkeepsie police officer, which was, in the scope of things, "a pretty decent alibi," Boyko said later.

As Boyko sat and listened, he kept going back to one thing in his mind: _Why did the FBI call and tell Fred Andros about Susan? What was the motivation behind the call?_

Fred continued talking as Boyko, he later explained, tried to gage his reaction to Fred's responses.

"I have no idea what happened or why?" Fred said at

one point. Boyko wrote it down. "Susan was a lovely woman." Fred hesitated, then lowered his voice some, adding, "I have no idea who would want to hurt her. Look . . . I'm *still* in love with her."

Boyko didn't want to make it a long, drawn-out interview. They were already an hour into it. It seemed that Fred was hurting, totally taken by the death of his lover.

Mr. Andros appeared to be emotionally upset, Boyko later wrote in his report, *crying, visibly shaken about the death of the victim.*

From that moment in Fred's dining room and on, Boyko became the liaison between Fred Andros and the NYSP. "I was the point of contact," Boyko said, "between him and us, and anytime he needed something, Fred would call me and ask."

Boyko stood. Closed his notebook. "Here, Fred," he said, reaching across the table, "here's my pager and cell phone number. . . . If you ever need anything, Fred, you call me. You understand?"

"Thanks a lot, Boyko," Fred said.

Leaving, Boyko said, "Fred, you mind if I come back and talk to you some more on another day?"

"Hey, my door's always open for you," Fred answered.

As Boyko was leaving, the sun was just about coming up. He told himself the interview went well. "I never walked out of the house," Boyko added later, "saying that he did or didn't have anything to do with Susan Fassett's death. I couldn't say. We had a rapport building. Fred was good. He manipulated me. He was good at it."

CHAPTER 19

While the shooter was at work that same morning BCI was beginning to unravel Susan Fassett's life, she was spooked every time a trooper pulled into the thruway plaza for a cup of coffee or a restroom stop. "Every time a police car pulled into that lot, I thought in my mind they were after me."

She had suffered from anxiety, to begin with; she was on medication. And now, here she was, standing in the middle of a rest stop plaza, sweeping and emptying garbage and polishing floors and water fountains, and New York State Police troopers were walking by, brushing elbows with her. Some even stopping to chat for a moment or two. It was all she could do not to drop her broom, throw up her hands and give herself up.

"I knew then that it was all over for me. It was just a matter of time."

Troop K brought in over forty officers, including more than a dozen crime-scene technicians, to investigate Susan Fassett's murder as Friday morning sunshine broke over the Catskill Mountains and illuminated Pleasant Valley.

"At this point, we have not identified any suspect," Major James Schepperly, the Troop K's spokesman, told the media that morning, "and we have not focused in on any one particular individual."

Because Susan's husband was a cop himself, it was important to keep the rumor mill from gathering steam. Schepperly insisted that the gun provided to Jef Fassett by the Town of Poughkeepsie PD was being tested by ballistics. But the results wouldn't be available for several days. "Everything is a possible lead and everything gets investigated," Troop K lieutenant Michael Regan told the press. "It would be foolish not to test Jef Fassett's weapon."

Regan warned everyone, however, that the testing of Jef's weapon was not indicative to guilt on his part, and should not be viewed as such. It was standard police practice. No one should be looking into it any other way.

Senior Investigator Tom Martin grew up outside Manhattan, in Westchester County, but was born in the Bronx. No one in Martin's family had entered into law enforcement, yet Martin wanted to become a cop ever since he could remember. Moving from Westchester County to upstate New York into Dutchess County, Martin lived directly behind one of the NYSP barracks. "So maybe that's what made me want to become a state cop, I don't know," he said.

Solidly built and rather husky, Martin speaks with an obvious Bronx accent, and has a sort of street toughness, like a boxer. Martin's shaved head is a metaphor for his well-mannered, clean-cut comportment. Yet even the toughest, most disciplined cop can be brought to his knees by what he sees. Martin recalled being straight out of the academy as a highway patrolman and driving up on an accident that truly showed him how the decisions he was going to be making throughout his career as a NYSP trooper would effectively decide life and death.

* * *

It was a quiet night. A slight drizzle was falling, Martin recalled. "The kind of night where you couldn't really see too well out on the road."

As he was driving down a state road in the backcountry, he came up on an accident: two cars had hit head-on. It appeared that the driver of one car had fallen asleep and drifted into the oncoming lane.

Martin got out of his squad car and ran up to the first vehicle. A young girl, maybe eighteen, was in shock, quite banged up, but appeared to be alert and responding to his questions. "I think I'm all right," she said, "but my knee's a little bit numb." It was dark. Foggy. Hard to see. Martin had his flashlight out. He shone it on her leg.

"Her femur sticking right out of the skin."

She was bleeding profusely.

Martin gave her first aid as quick as he could and then ran over to the second car, a minivan with two kids, a mother and a father. One of the kids was in his car seat in the back, screaming. The other child had gotten out of the car and was running alongside the road. The father was in shock. "He was lost," Martin remembered. Frozen by the fear of what had happened.

The mother was in her seat—but there was blood, Martin recalled, "spurting out of her face." Her face had been completely torn off: no upper lip, no nose, no skin whatsoever. Like the other woman, she was bleeding copiously.

Assessing the situation in his head, Martin faced a dilemma: one woman was in the other car and her ephemeral artery, he knew, had been severed, which meant that she had about two minutes before she bled to death. The other woman, in front of him, was bleeding so badly she would likely die within a matter of minutes if the bleeding wasn't contained.

And for a passing moment, Martin said, the thought occurred to him: *Who do I save?* He couldn't stop the bleeding for both. He had to make a choice: Who lived? Who died?

Before he could make up his mind, however, Martin turned and, to his amazement, the fire department had rolled up to the scene.

Both women ultimately lived.

Martin's career eventually led him into forensics, which meant his daily life at work now centered around all types of death. "People ask me," he said, "how do you deal with so much death? I've been to the autopsies of children and countless murder victims, young and old. I tell them, death is *easy* to deal with. It's the living that are tough: that person screaming for help from inside a car that's upside down on the road and you cannot pull that person out. It's the ones that die in your arms. Death is easy. It's final. It's what leads up to death that's hard."

Martin worked on the Kendall Francois case. Dubbed the "stinky killer," serial murderer Francois, a Poughkeepsie native, was responsible for murdering eight prostitutes and storing the victims' decomposing bodies inside his Poughkeepsie home for up to two years.

"Even with that case," Martin said, "you get to a point where nothing shocks you anymore."

There was a young boy who had been tortured by his mother and her boyfriend. Martin had to rush to the intensive care unit (ICU) of the hospital and gather evidence off the boy as he fought for his life.

"I ended up holding his hand as he died."

The Susan Fassett case didn't pose many problems for Martin from a forensics standpoint. It had its interesting, even confusing aspects, but it seemed to be, at least in the beginning, a pretty straightforward murder scene—if there could ever be such a thing. What stood out to Martin and his forensic colleagues immediately was that there were no shell casings anywhere at the crime scene. They searched the area two times over and came up with nothing. Moreover, the bullet wounds in Susan's body didn't tell them much. "Whether a shooter is two feet away or two hundred feet away, the entrance wounds will be the same," Martin said. "So with the Fassett case, we really didn't know how far away the shooter was standing."

Martin said that forensic investigators are prone to use *deductive* reasoning: *Let me see what I have, let me see where the pieces fit, and I'll try to draw a conclusion from it all later on.* Criminal investigators, Martin added, generally look at crime scenes and murders from an *inductive* reasoning point of view, or the opposite way: They gather information and allow it to lead them down a path. They bank on theories and formulas, and see if things fit or don't fit.

Both working together is what solves homicides.

For Martin, murder is pretty clear-cut: *This is the evidence, this is what I have so far.* "What 'could have been' is not part of what we do in forensics," he said. "Here is the evidence. This is what it is—and nothing more."

So what did Martin and his team have at the Fassett crime scene? Multiple gunshot wounds to the body; glass fragments on the ground by Susan's Jeep; a vehicle with its lights on, engine running; several witnesses claiming different styles of vehicles sped away from the scene; and a bullet lodged in the door frame of Susan's Jeep, which would become the most important piece of a not-so-perfect puzzle.

The most popular theory developing among BCI investigators was that a "station wagon" type of car had left the scene speedily from the parking lot where Susan's Jeep was parked. In that sense, Jef Fassett still needed to answer some questions. This much was fairly clear as the second day of clues came in. And so as Tom Martin and Troop K's team of forensic investigators began to look closer at the case, that bullet he extracted from Susan's door frame would have to give them some answers.

CHAPTER 20

The investigation took an unusual turn on October 30, 1999, when Dr. Michael Baden released a portion of his autopsy results to members of the BCI. It was a piece of evidence that would soon cause BCI a number of investigatory problems. Four bullets had entered Susan's body, two of them fatal, which wasn't so shocking. What became an issue for BCI was that Dr. Baden found a specimen of semen in Susan's vagina that was, as far as the doctor could tell, no more than twenty-four to forty-eight hours old. It now appeared that whoever had sexual intercourse with Susan last could very well answer some key questions.

Baden sent the semen out to be analyzed—and yet, without a few DNA donors on the other end, what good were those results going to be?

Jim Karic had been an investigator for two decades, but one of BCI's polygraph experts now for a number of years. Karic had an incredibly calming manner about him. He spoke soothingly and quite comfortingly. Talking to Karic was like talking to your grandfather. You wanted to tell him your secrets because you felt safe.

One of the things a polygraphist needs is a subject who is well-rested. Karic was called in to the Fassett case to do a number of things right away, one of which included giving Jef Fassett a polygraph test. Jef had been questioned by BCI for a good fifteen hours, depending on whose count you want to go by. He was not, necessarily, the best specimen for a polygraph test.

"The circumstances for a polygraph test," Karin later said, "were less than ideal."

The problem the BCI had with Jef was that, circumstantially speaking, all the evidence pointed to him. Jef knew Susan was having an affair with Fred Andros; he also knew that there was a good possibility that although she had said it was over, the affair was still going on at the time of Susan's death. What if . . . yes, what if Jef found out he had been duped and snapped? Could be this situation played out all the time.

Another important piece of information that came out was that one of the men involved with Fred Andros in the corruption probe, a guy who had some pull in Town Hall, had been responsible for getting Jef Fassett his lieutenant's job on second shift. Not the position itself; Jef had earned that job with his decades of stellar service to the department. But one of Andros's friends had made sure Jef was put in second shift so Fred could have access to Jef's wife at night.

Karic sat down with Jef and for five or six hours and asked him pointed questions about everything. "I sat down with him and we did the test, and for the purpose of the charts, he didn't give me anything glaring. His posture, additionally, was very good."

Jef was mainly "fired up," Karic recalled, about the way in which his kids had been treated by the Poughkeepsie PD's SWAT team during what they had termed to be a standoff. He was shaken by the fact that they had made the kids out to be criminals and bullied them while their mother lay dead in the morgue.

As the interview progressed, it seemed Jef answered every question easily, without one bit of animosity or resentment. At one point, Jef looked at Karic and said, "Look, I don't care what you do. You can ask me anything you want. You can turn on the hot lights, beat me with rubber hoses. But when you're all done with me and you get me out of the way . . ."

Karic was startled, and yet not surprised. He knew Jef was telling the truth.

"What's that, Jef?"

"We can stay here as long as you like." Jef was wearing a paper suit, prison orange jumpers. Forensics had taken all of his clothes. He had been questioned over and over again. He was exhausted. But yet he kept saying the same thing: "I'll answer all your questions . . ."

"OK, Jef."

". . . but when you're done with me, you go see Fred Andros," Jef said rather pointedly, quite sure of himself. "He did this! He was involved in this."

After the interview, Karic sat down with his BCI colleagues to discuss what he found out during the polygraph.

They all looked at him. "Look, I don't think so," Karic said. "I don't feel he did it. I believe what he said. I don't think he's involved in this thing. Let's stay friendly with him and keep him on our side. Let him go."

They all agreed.

"Jef was very cooperative," Karic recalled. "He could not have been better or helped us any more than he did."

When BCI got the results of Susan's autopsy from Dr. Baden, Jim Karic was chosen to go over to Jef's house and see what he could find out. Karic had a rapport with Jef going already.

"Hey, Jef, how's it going?"

Jef shrugged. It wasn't going so well.

"Listen," Karic said, "I need to know a few things."

"What's up?" Jef asked.

"When was the last time you and Susan had sexual relations?"

Jef thought about it. "At least four or five days before her death," he said.

Karic was a bit apprehensive about the next question. But he had to do what he had to do. "We need to get some blood work from you, Jef. Will that be a problem?"

Since he was a cop, the lightbulb went off for Jef. Karic could see it on his face. The dread and gloom. He believed Jef was saying to himself, *Oh, man . . . I thought this woman was in love with me again. . . . What was she doing?*

It broke his heart, Karic knew. But he wanted to help solve his wife's murder. After thinking it over for a moment, Jef said, "Let's go. I'll do it."

What was significant for Karic was that Jef never asked for a lawyer or balked. He did all these things he was asked—without once complaining about it.

CHAPTER 21

On Halloween night, a peacefully cold Sunday evening, Art Boyko put in a call to Fred Andros. It had been a few days. Boyko wanted to stop by and talk to Fred once again. Maybe pin down another portion of his story and begin what was going to be the long dance into learning about the relationship he had with Susan. So far, locating a viable suspect wasn't turning out to be so easy. Theories abounded, but not one piece of evidence pointed to anyone in particular.

"I need to talk to you, Fred," Boyko explained over the telephone.

"Sure," Fred replied. He was gracious, as always. More than willing to comply with Boyko's requests.

They spoke in the dining room again, which seemed to become a staging area for Boyko and Fred to meet and discuss the case. Along with Boyko, investigator John Ryan, one of Boyko's BCI colleagues, was there. From what Boyko and Ryan could tell, Fred's wife, Diana, wasn't home.

Fred confirmed everything he had said the previous time Boyko had interviewed him, which told Boyko that Fred was either a good liar, had a great memory or was telling the truth. Either way didn't matter to Boyko. Any investigator worth his or her salt will tell you that a lie is just as good as a truth in the grand scheme of an investigation.

"Let's be clear," Boyko asked again, knowing what he knew about Baden's findings, "the last time you had sex with the victim was one and a half years ago. Is that correct, Fred?"

"Yeah, I told you that," Fred answered.

"How would Susan get hold of you?" Boyko wondered. Investigator Ryan glanced around the room, taking in Fred's home, watching Fred's mannerisms, while Boyko did most of the questioning.

"She'd page me," Fred explained, "every day when she got in to work." Fred wrote the pager number down on a piece of paper. "Sometimes she'd page me six times a day." Then he slid the paper across the table.

For the most part, Fred and Susan met for lunch. On some days, they'd take a drive out into the country or hang out at a park and relax together, hugging and kissing, like two teenage lovers sneaking around town, staying out of view of their parents. Fred seemed to condense the affair down to more of a friendship than an actual romance. It was as if they were just two friends enjoying each other's company.

Boyko was reserving judgment until all the details and facts were in. He didn't want to make any leaps just yet. What Fred was saying seemed buyable. Perhaps Fred Andros had very little to hide.

"That's a lot," Boyko said, responding to how many times Susan called Fred. It was strange how Fred had wrested the levers of power over Susan and controlled the relationship. That much became clear as they talked about the relationship more and more.

"I know," Fred said. "I know it was. We decided in September to a mutual breakup. It was a week or so before our last face-to-face meeting, oh . . . maybe the seventeenth or eighteenth of September." He explained further that after he and Jef Fassett had that altercation inside the Pough-keepsie Town Hall, he and Susan broke off their relation-ship. It was clear Jef was going to find out, or begin putting pressure on the two of them, Fred suggested, and it wasn't worth the trouble anymore, he said. Up until that point, Fred insisted, no one knew about them. They had "dated" for four years and Fred's son was really the only person who knew. They were careful, Fred explained, about how they communicated. "We never used e-mail or wrote things down. My son would e-mail Susan for me, but not me."

He said Susan stopped paging him as often as she had in the past after they decided to split up. "It went from six times a day," Fred explained to Boyko, "down to about two or three. We were still friends."

"OK, but the last time you saw her—"

"I have *not* seen her," Fred reiterated, "since September twenty-seventh." He was adamant about the date. It was important to him that Boyko understood that he was sure of himself and this particular date.

Boyko made a mental note that this date was *after* Fred and Susan had broken up.

Among other tasks, BCI investigator Jim Karic was as-signed Town Hall detail, meaning that he had been chosen to interview a list of Susan Fassett's coworkers and friends. On that same afternoon when Boyko met with Fred Andros for a second time, Karic began speak-ing with some of Susan's coworkers, many of whom also happened to be good friends with her.

What was significantly obvious almost right away, Karic later said, was that every one of Susan's friends and coworkers knew about the affair she was having with Fred

Andros. As Fred sat in his dining room, telling Boyko that no one knew about the affair beyond his son, Karic was having trouble finding someone who *hadn't* heard about it.

"Everybody that knew Susan knew about the affair," Karic kept hearing. "Everybody who had had contact with Susan knew."

What was even more surprising was how open Susan and Fred seemed to be with the affair. The fact that Jef slept all day and worked all night helped, of course; but it seemed that all of Poughkeepsie knew that Susan Fassett, "the cop's wife," was running around town with Fred Andros.

Art Boyko and his colleague were still at Fred Andros's house, interviewing the embattled ex–water superintendent, as Karic began putting together a clearer picture of the affair. Soon the two would meet up and swap stories. For now, however, Boyko wondered about the federal case Fred was involved in. Before heading over to Fred's, Boyko had spoken to Special Agent James O'Connor, of the FBI, and gotten a fairly decent rundown of the federal case against Fred from him. But he wanted Fred's take on it all. He wanted to see how Fred would explain things.

"Was Susan involved in any of that?" Boyko asked, referring to the federal probe.

"No," Fred said. "She had only gone to White Plains once," where the FBI investigating the case worked out of the U.S. Attorney's Office, "to, I believe, verify some records." Fred was adamant: Susan played no role whatsoever in the corruption investigation, either for or against Fred. Nor had she been involved on a co-conspiratorial level.

Boyko and Fred Andros talked some more about the

relationship, and Fred seemed to be going around in circles, saying the same things over and over. Boyko guessed it was out of sheer shock and surprise—here was Fred, according to him, having put the affair behind him, sitting in his house and talking about it to the police. He was uncomfortable, to say the least.

"Do you have any guns in the house, Fred?" Boyko asked rather casually. It was a back-and-forth chat, nothing more, as Boyko pointed out later (and which his reports confirmed). It was not an accusatory sort of interrogation. Boyko was collecting information about a murder victim, and Fred understood that he would be helping them out if he answered some questions.

"No, no," Fred said. Having guns in the house would be in violation of his federal plea deal. It was strictly forbidden under the indictment he had agreed to and signed with the U.S. Attorney's Office. Although they didn't discuss it, both he and Boyko knew the law.

"Does Mrs. Andros know about the affair?"

"Sure," Fred answered. "We talked about it after the breakup last month. She knows. Yes. Yes."

"And you were here all night on October twenty-eighth? Is that right?"

"I was."

Boyko had spoken to Richard Byrd already, the Poughkeepsie police officer who was with Fred on the night Susan was murdered. Byrd and his wife established that they had dinner over at the Andros house that night with Fred and his wife. Byrd said he and Fred went downstairs after dinner and worked on Byrd's remote-controlled model airplane. They were down there for about an hour, hour and a half, he said.

Fred went on to explain that besides his son, who lived in the house, he had three other children, who didn't live with him and Diana.

Boyko had Fred go through and explain what he and Byrd did downstairs in the basement, particularly asking if Fred had received "any phone calls" while he and Byrd were downstairs.

Fred said, "No." After which he explained the entire night, adding, "The Byrds left around nine." Then he paused a moment, looked at Boyko and said, "I hope no one else has to die before you catch who did it."

What an extraordinary statement, Boyko thought, sitting, staring at Fred. He didn't know what prompted Fred to just come out with it. It was as though he was thinking out loud and didn't realize it.

"What do you mean, Fred?" Boyko queried.

Fred thought about it. "I don't know," he said. "I don't know why I said that."

Boyko later explained: "During the early stages of the investigation, our attention began to focus on one individual as he slowly developed into a viable suspect. Basically, my role was to obtain any and all information on the conduct and character of Fred Andros." Still, the problem for Boyko and the BCI was that Fred had an alibi. His story checked out, no matter how they added it up. He had three witnesses claiming he was at home. There was no way Fred Andros could have been at that murder scene.

Boyko wasn't quite ready to end the interview just yet. He had come to Fred's house on a specific mission and wasn't leaving until he at least let Fred know why he was actually there.

CHAPTER 22

From what Jim Karic found out from Boyko and other members of the BCI team investigating Susan Fassett's murder, Fred Andros kept rising to the surface of what was turning out to be a very small pool of suspects. It was rather obvious that Fred was, in most instances, talking in circles. And although he could not have been at the scene of the murder, his alibi certainly didn't toss out the idea that he could have hired someone to do his dirty work. Fred was good at that, Karic began to learn: making other people do things he didn't want to do, or didn't have the guts to go through with himself.

What fueled the matter was actually an "urban legend" around town regarding Fred Andros and one of his co-conspirators in the corruption probe. The rumor was that Fred and this other guy had had a witness in the corruption probe murdered some time ago. Because of it, people feared Fred Andros in some respects and believed he could get things done if he wanted.

"This was absolutely untrue," Karic later told me. "I think this rumor could have possibly been started by Andros himself. It would be the kind of thing Fred would do to make himself out to be some sort of big shot."

Fred loved to boost his reputation, no matter what type of person it made him out to be—as long as he appeared to be a tough guy.

"The death of this man empowered this little guy [Fred] to the point of, I found out, people in town being terrified of him."

Karic knew, however, there would come a point when the BCI could throw that death in Fred's face and use it against him—but first, Boyko knew, he had to work Fred a little bit more.

BCI needed to acquire any pager and telephone numbers Fred could offer, so forensics could begin to put together a timeline, using Fred and Susan's telephone numbers as a means to track communication between them. In doing so, it would open up a vein into whomever else Fred had been calling during the weeks leading up to Susan's murder and the days after. If the BCI knew Susan's number—which they did—and had Fred's numbers, a crude timeline of Susan's last few hours of using the telephone could be established. Not that it would tell the BCI anything more than they knew already, but telephone records have a way of opening up new avenues and presenting new leads.

As they continued talking on the evening of October 31, Fred told Boyko that he and Susan would use a code number to communicate. "Eight, nine, five," Fred explained. "If I saw that number, *895*, it meant 'call Susan.'" Sometimes, he added, she would use *895XXXXX895*. "It was a code."

"You said you have no handguns here, Fred. Is that right?"

"My daughter has them," Fred answered.

Boyko didn't know it, but Diana Andros had been

home the entire time they were at the house talking with Fred. She had been upstairs during the interview. Realizing she was in the house, Boyko asked Fred to go get her. He wanted her to answer some questions, if she would agree to it.

"But it's up to her, Fred."

"Yeah, no problem."

Diana looked scared. She had a true sense of purity about her that Boyko picked up on immediately. She definitely wanted to help, but she didn't know how much help she could be, or if she was going to hurt her husband in the process. She was caught in the middle.

Boyko went through and asked the same set of questions he had posed to Fred. In the interim, Fred left the room and went upstairs.

"Yeah, he told me about the affair. . . . It ended on September nineteenth," Diana confirmed.

After several more questions: "What about guns in the house?" Boyko asked out of curiosity. It wasn't that he didn't trust Fred, he wanted to hear what Diana had to say about it.

"Sure," Diana said, "we got guns in the house. They're here. You want to see them?"

They walked into another room and there they were: six handguns. All different makes and models. According to Boyko's notes of the conversation, Diana spoke up and identified all of them. "Three .38 revolvers," she said as if she had handled guns her entire life, "a .22, a .40-caliber . . . and a [six-shot pistol]."

"Interesting," Boyko said. *But no .45-caliber.*

Then again, chances that a murderer would be stupid enough to use a handgun to kill someone—or lend it to someone he had hired—that was registered to him were slim to none, anyway.

Boyko didn't want to confront Fred on the lie immediately. He needed to get out of there and allow it to settle on Fred, who, Boyko knew, had been listening in on the conversation and he now understood that Diana had showed them the guns. He was caught in a lie, and he would have to somehow explain himself at an appropriate time.

As Boyko and his partner were walking out the door, Fred came down the stairs and told them he had diabetes and other health issues. "Depression too," he added. "I take medication for both."

"Thanks, Fred."

"Anytime you guys need to come back," Fred said pleasantly, "you just call and come over, OK?"

"Sure thing," Boyko said.

Having weapons in the house and lying about it was interesting, Boyko thought, but it still didn't mean Fred had hired someone to kill his lover. For all anyone knew at this point, Jef Fassett could have hired a hit man to take out his wife, Susan.

CHAPTER 23

The story had become major news in Dutchess and Albany Counties, which sent a further shock down the back of the shooter's spine. Local newspapers and regional television stations weren't letting go of it. POLICE HUNT CLUES IN KILLING, read page one of the *Poughkeepsie Journal,* accompanied by a large photograph of troopers roaming around near the church. The first line in the article said it all, describing how, in a town like Pleasant Valley—where its name alone conjures images of white picket fences, mailmen waving to town residents and people walking around in some sort of blissful, suburban fog—it seemed remotely impossible that this sort of crime might have taken place: *Susan Fassett, a 48-year-old mother, was fatally shot Thursday night as she left choir practice at the Pleasant Valley United Methodist Church.*

Looking at the newspaper that morning after the crime, the shooter was plagued as she went about her normal routine of work and home. As much as she had wanted to say something and call Fred, she had done what he had demanded and waited.

But then, out of the blue, Fred called her. She was sitting at home, in her living room, going over the crime in her head. Her husband had asked what the problem was, why she was so quiet. But she blew him off, saying, "I don't feel well."

But now, Fred was on the telephone. "Meet me at the information booth near the [New York State] Thruway entrance," he said quite demandingly. "I have something to give you."

"I'll be there." She couldn't stand the silence. She needed to see him.

Hours later, she was sitting in her car, smoking a cigarette, when she looked in her rearview mirror and spied his plates heading toward her: *FREDDEE*. How appropriate: a vanity plate for a guy who was entirely full of himself.

It was shocking to many in town when they finally found out that Fred was this man behind the curtain who "wielded such power" over these women. At best, Fred was a coward who convinced others to do his dirty work because he was too afraid to do it himself.

Indeed, Fred Andros, the wannabe of wannabes.

As the shooter sat and watched, not moving from her seat, just as he had instructed, little Fred Andros got out of his car and waddled toward his trunk. Checking in all directions first, Fred then leaned in and pulled a dark garbage bag out of the trunk and then sauntered over to the driver's-side window of her vehicle. She noticed there was someone else in the car with Fred—his elderly father—but she didn't care. The old man could hardly see two feet in front of himself, better yet figure out what Fred was up to, or whom he was meeting.

Watching Fred come toward her, she thought, *I need to clean this mess up, get this guy out of my life and try to move on best I can.*

"He had already ruined my life," she said later. "I knew I was done. I was just going through the motions with him. I wasn't sleeping, not eating. I couldn't work. It wasn't going to get better."

Fred handed her the bag. "I went fishing," he said casually. "I caught some really nice ones, too. Here are the fish you wanted."

She didn't say anything.

"You OK?" Fred asked.

"Not really, Fred. What do you expect?"

"It's over now."

"I hope so."

After she took the bag, before he walked away, Fred gave her a sharp ("you better not blow this") look of discontent, which was quite sobering. Then he turned without saying anything more, got back into his car and sped up to the side of her, saying, "I'll be in touch soon." Then he took off.

She drove nervously up the New York State Thruway, looking in her rearview mirror, side to side, hoping no one had seen them, and made it home sometime later. When she took the gun out of the bag that Fred had given her, it wasn't hard to tell that the barrel had been honed and/or drilled out in some fashion. Holding it, she noticed immediately how scratched up it was. Apparently, Fred had drilled out the barrel to protect them both from ballistics matching the gun with any of the bullets taken from Susan's body.

Susan. My God, she thought, *I killed that woman.*

Not thinking too much about it, she put the gun back underneath her water bed in the drawer where she had stored it originally. But then she took the rest of the stuff—the mask and the gloves and the shell casings—and walked out in back of her yard. She and her husband had a "burning barrel," in which they'd torch old wood, brush and leaves, and sit around sometimes with a few beers and enjoy the fire. And so, with no one around, she tossed the bag inside the barrel, doused it with fuel and lit a match. A puff of black smoke whooshed toward the sky in one quick breath and the remainder of the tools of the murder were gone, just like that.

CHAPTER 24

Art Boyko called Fred Andros on November 3, but no one was home. The next day, November 4, somewhere near 3:00 P.M., Boyko got in touch with Fred and set up another interview. Fred seemed once again eager to jump in and help the NYSP out with anything it needed to catch Susan's killer. He thought he had been playing things smoothly, telling Boyko exactly what he wanted to hear. A few interviews, Fred knew, were going to be part of the crime he'd have to deal with successfully.

Boyko was slowly beginning to figure Fred out, however. Little by little, bits of information here and there weren't adding up to the seasoned investigator. Boyko was sure Fred wasn't being entirely straight with him, and yet Boyko was still holding back, staying in the information-gathering mode, allowing Fred to talk himself into a corner and dig himself a bigger hole.

Boyko entered the house and immediately explained to Fred that he needed him to do something important. "We want to compare your blood to semen we found in Susan's body," Boyko said.

"I don't know," Fred said. He was clearly a bit frazzled. A friendly rapport between them had suddenly turned into a DNA blood test. "I'd like to talk to my lawyer first, you know, Boyko," Fred said. He was looking down toward the floor.

"We understand, Fred."

"Look, I have no problem talking to you guys, you know that. But I need advice from my lawyer on this."

"Hey, I can understand, Fred," Boyko said comfortingly.

Fred Andros wanted people to think he was more important than he was; and it drove everything he did. When Boyko mentioned a blood test, Fred knew he was going to have to come up with an excuse to get him out of it. He knew that the blood test would lead to more questions.

"OK, Fred," Boyko said as he got up to leave.

"I'll call you, Boyko, as soon as I speak to my lawyer." Waving as Boyko walked out of the house, Fred added for no apparent reason, "You guys are great. I'll talk to you tomorrow morning. How's that?"

"No problem, Fred," Boyko answered.

Art Boyko was in his office first thing the next morning, wondering if Fred was going to call him. By now, he knew that it was a given he had likely heard the last from Fred Andros. Things were getting a bit sticky for the guy. A few routine conversations had turned into potential DNA evidence. As Boyko waited, he couldn't help but think that Fred definitely had something to hide—otherwise, he would have, like Jef Fassett, dropped everything and agreed to the test.

At 11:00 A.M., Boyko called Fred after not hearing anything from him all morning, asking, "How's it going?"

"Good. Very good, Boyko. How are you this morning?"

"You speak to your lawyer yet, Fred? Just wondering

about that. I'd like to get the blood test out of the way and move on from here."

Fred went quiet. Boyko knew his mind was racing.

"On the advice of counsel," Fred said rather slowly, a bit broken up, "I would be unwilling to take a blood test. I hope you understand. But listen, Boyko, I've got no problem speaking with you guys. I'll talk to you guys *anytime* in the future."

"That's a shame, Fred."

"My attorney said I could talk to you guys all I wanted to, though."

"Who's your attorney, Fred?"

Silence.

"Fred?"

"Yeah . . . I . . ." He refused to give Boyko his attorney's name.

The little things Fred was beginning to do, Boyko told me later, "started to hurt him. We knew otherwise when it came to Fred saying that he hadn't seen Susan for weeks before her murder."

Both Jef Fassett and Fred Andros had denied any sexual contact with Susan at any time near her death. Yet BCI had a seminal sample from a male donor. Tom Martin had done a complete sexual assault evidence collection kit on Susan. He'd taken several oral swabs from her cheeks, which were negative for sperm and positive for blood. Both anal swabs Martin collected turned out negative. And yet all of the vaginal smears came back positive for sperm. *Forensic DNA is a possibility in this case,* the Forensic Investigation Center out of Albany wrote in its report, but for the *examination to proceed,* the lab wrote, it required contrary blood samples to be collected and tested.

Fred had refused. Because of the rejection, Boyko had a sense that Fred had something to hide. Over the course of the week, Boyko had stood back and wrote down whatever Fred had to offer. Boyko made no judgments and refrained from listening to gut theories and instinct. "I just documented everything he had said because you never know what information you're going to learn that will later refute what he says. When I figure that out, it's ammunition to go back to him and get him caught up in what became a web of lies." Still, the seasoned investigator added, "You never want to rule anyone out." Jef Fassett didn't have such a great alibi, Boyko suggested. "He was home at the time of the murder." He had even left his house, one witness later reported. "But even so, you never want to draw any conclusions early on. You always want to keep an open mind. Unless you can positively, one hundred percent, rule somebody out, then you move on. But you never want to close that chapter."

The other problem Boyko faced: when Fred refused to give a blood sample and announced that he wanted to speak to his lawyer, had he invoked his "right to counsel"? If so, Boyko couldn't question Fred any longer without Fred's attorney present, or he'd have to read him his Miranda rights, which BCI had no grounds to do.

Boyko soon clarified things with Fred.

"I asked him, 'Are you sure you only want to talk to your attorney in regards to getting advice on whether or not you should consent to a blood test?'

"Fred said, 'Yup, absolutely.'"

The other part of it was that Fred had never asked Boyko to leave his house. All of the interviews Boyko had conducted were done inside Fred's house, on his turf, so to speak. Fred could have ended any interview at any time and thrown Boyko out of the house.

But he never did.

"In fact," Boyko said later, "he invited us in."

The point of staying in Fred's face, Boyko knew, was to keep asking questions, but also to allow some time to pass.

He had caught Fred in a lie once already—regarding the guns—but had not yet confronted him with it as of yet.

"Once you start lying and it goes over a week, you're going to start forgetting what you're telling me," Boyko said later. No one can keep track of lies over a period of time.

CHAPTER 25

BCI had routine brainstorming meetings, sometimes every morning, which allowed investigators to get together and swap ideas and leads about open cases. Detectives working different shifts would turn in what were called lead reports, and during the meetings, everyone would knock ideas around about a particular case to see what, if anything, new had turned up the previous day or night. Many times a case against a suspect would present itself to investigators as they went through, interviewed people, collected evidence and put it all together.

As for Fred Andros, if he had played any role whatsoever in Susan's murder, BCI knew it wasn't hard to tell that he was perhaps hoping to project a diminishment of culpability, in a sense saying that because he was so far removed from the actual act of murder, he had no blood on his hands. Being the mastermind behind the curtain would actually help Fred be able to conceal the crime and lie with a straight face, in other words.

BCI investigators had met scores of these types of murderers: the ones who think they can get away with a crime because they weren't involved with the act itself. In doing so, Fred Andros might have believed he could keep BCI at arm's length and even play its game. But Fred had no idea that Art Boyko and other BCI investigators were beginning to catch on to him—that his lies were catching up with the facts of the case—and there was little he could do to deflect it, besides, of course, staying out of the investigation entirely, which was something Fred's ego just wouldn't allow him to do.

If a couple days went by and Boyko hadn't heard from Fred, he was on the telephone calling him to see what was going on. At this stage, it was about keeping Fred talking. Boyko needed to maintain that comfortable relationship he had spent the past few weeks building with Fred.

"Everything OK, Fred? You need anything?" Boyko would call and ask when he didn't hear from Fred for a time.

"I'm good, Boyko. Thanks for calling."

Boyko knew that Fred was feeling the heat from the federal investigation, fundamentally being squeezed on both sides of the justice vise: state and federal. He wanted Fred to know that he was there for him, in any way he needed.

"Give me a call if you need something, Fred."

"Will do."

On the other hand, Boyko later explained, Fred wanted to make it appear as though he was helping out, providing BCI with information that, Boyko said, "generally amounted to nothing."

Nonetheless, it made Fred feel confident and also kept the line of communication between the two of them open.

On November 11, Boyko called Fred and asked him if he would be home. He wanted to stop by for a few moments and talk. "Alone," Boyko suggested.

"OK," Fred said.

It was around 3:30 P.M. Boyko was heading home for the night. Hyde Park was on his way.

Sitting in Fred's dining room sometime later, Boyko said, "Look, Fred, have you ever been to the United Methodist Church in Pleasant Valley?"

Fred looked surprised. "Huh . . . no. No." It was the first time Boyko had come out and made an accusation of sorts against Fred. Up until that point, they had exchanged "thoughts" and theories, but Boyko had never brought up any notion that Fred might be involved in the crime.

"Susan was murdered there in the parking lot after she attended choir practice," Boyko said next.

Fred had a look on his face: *Why are you telling me this? I know this.*

"I've never been there," Fred reiterated. (In truth, Fred had attended meetings with his airplane club at the church. He could have easily explained it.)

"Can you tell me about Susan's schedule? We're looking to pin it down."

Fred and Susan had been sneaking around town for years. Fred couldn't deny that he knew Susan's schedule, most likely better than anyone else.

After Boyko posed the question, Fred stared down at the dining-room table. Then went into it. "On Mondays she went to exercise class at the Jewish Community Center. And . . . um, choir practice on Thursday nights at the Methodist Church there in town."

Boyko was quick to write down in his notebook whatever Fred said. This served two purposes: one, Boyko didn't have to appear as though he was pressuring Fred, or interrogating him, but was instead still just collecting information and unsuspectingly taking notes; two, it allowed Boyko to sit and match up things Fred had said over the course of the past two weeks.

Compare notes, if you will.

"Did you two talk a lot during these times?" Boyko wondered.

Fred thought for a moment about it. He said, "Yeah, she would call me before both."

As the interview progressed, Fred told Boyko that he had recently given Susan a necklace "worth about ninety dollars." Fred seemed a bit more down-to-earth during this interview; he wasn't, Boyko reported, as broken up as he had appeared to be in the past. The way Boyko pitched it back to Fred was that as time passed, Fred was beginning to "get over" losing Susan, both in death and as a lover.

"Thanks, Fred, that's all I have. I'll be in touch."

A few days later, Boyko called. There was something he forgot to ask, he said.

"Shoot, Boyko, what is it?" Fred wondered.

By sheer planning, Boyko said, "About your guns, Fred. I had observed six weapons in the house on Halloween night." Boyko made it sound as though he was more confused than accusing Fred of lying.

"All of my guns," Fred said quickly, almost interrupting, "are at my daughter's house."

"Thanks, Fred. We'll be in touch soon."

"Anytime, Boyko. Anytime."

Fred was at home during the week before Thanksgiving. A friend of his he had known from his days as water superintendent, a woman who owned a water-testing business, called one morning. She sounded frightened, Fred later told police. Scared that something was going to happen to her.

According to what Fred later alleged, the woman had taken a call the previous night, in which the caller said, "Fred got a message. If you don't stay away, you might be the next *message*."

"I'm concerned for her safety," Fred told Boyko. "She's a longtime friend. I've known her for years." Fred sounded panicked and genuinely scared that his friend was going to be next.

"We'll check it out, Fred," Boyko promised.

BCI needed a DNA sample from Fred Andros. It was as simple as that. In the back of Boyko's mind as he and Fred played their little game of cat and mouse throughout the second week of November, and throughout the Thanksgiving holiday, was the pounding metronome: who had slept with Susan Fassett hours before her murder? BCI investigators were certain that it wasn't her husband, Jef Fassett—DNA had recently proven that. Fred said it wasn't him. Who, then, could it be? Without a DNA sample from Fred, Andros couldn't be completely ruled out. But how to get that sample?

Now it was December. For the past month, the investigation into Susan Fassett's murder had run its course; BCI was in a tough spot, not having many new leads to follow. If they could only scratch Fred off their list of potential semen donors, or put him on the top, it would change the focus of the investigation, at least for the time being. Some wondered if BCI was spending *too* much time worrying about Fred Andros. Besides Art Boyko, there were no fewer than six additional investigators working on the case, following it in several other directions. And yet there was a certain feeling about Fred amongst everyone; he seemed like a good candidate for murderer. Still, without that sample, there was no way to tell if there was another male involved in Susan's life—someone no one had yet named. If she had cheated on her husband with Fred, the possibility was another lover existed.

During a BCI meeting one morning, the focus became how was Boyko going to get that sample? Suffice it to say, if Fred wasn't interested in giving it up, how could BCI legally obtain a DNA sample from him? There were legal issues surrounding how Boyko could go about obtaining it secretly.

"I was in his house a lot," Boyko explained to me. "But I couldn't just grab a hair sample from a brush in the bathroom. Outside his home, however, if he abandoned something"—a cigarette butt, a glass, anything with saliva or skin tissue on it—"I could certainly take it."

On top of that, there was no way they had enough evidence against Fred to get a court order. So the problem Boyko faced was getting Fred out of his comfort zone. Fred had agreed to see Boyko anytime, but only inside *his* house, where he knew it was safe, a sort of neutral zone where he could, at any moment, ask Boyko to leave. Fred had felt so good about talking in his house that he hadn't once brought his lawyer in to sit in on the conversations.

"Lunch," someone in the morning meeting suggested. "Get Fred out of the house and buy him lunch."

That was it: Invite Fred to lunch. Play into Fred's ego. Make him feel important.

Another idea then surfaced—something that would placate Fred's ego. He would never see it coming.

On December 6, Boyko found himself once again in Fred's dining room, going over several discrepancies BCI had found in Fred's story. According to a report filed by the district attorney's office, one major conflict involved the number of times Fred had claimed to be married. In the report, Boyko reported that he and Fred had been going back and forth for weeks regarding how many times Fred had admitted he was married and how many children he had. Boyko knew Fred had been lying to him. BCI had tracked down Fred's first wife.

"Three times," Fred told Boyko again, on December 6. "Four children."

But Fred had been married *four* times and had *five* children.

In any event, Boyko got off the subject and asked Fred to give him a tour of the house.

"Sure," Fred said.

They eventually made it downstairs into the basement. Boyko noticed immediately that Fred had a drill press, and there were metal shavings all over the place. There were various model airplanes on a bench with tools and other items associated with Fred's hobby scattered around. Boyko guessed that Fred was an avid model airplane builder, like he had said, and spent a lot of time in his basement workshop.

There was a door in the workshop leading to the outside, into the driveway.

Fred mentioned he was home all night—but that he had been downstairs for an hour with his friend, Boyko thought, staring at the door.

Boyko then noticed two telephone lines. He pointed and asked Fred about them.

"Those," Fred said, "oh, yeah. They're for a fax machine and my computer."

"OK," said Boyko. "Can I get those numbers?"

"Sure," Fred said, reciting them.

Boyko headed out the door, turning and shaking Fred's hand. "Talk to you soon, Fred, huh."

"Take it easy, Boyko."

A day later, Boyko called Fred. Boyko was sitting in his car down the street from Fred's house. "Hey, I bought you lunch. Let's meet up. I need to talk to you about the federal side of things. It's getting a little sticky."

"I don't know—"

"Come on," Boyko said. "I have an autopsy report here that I bet you'd like to see." Boyko had former Town of Poughkeepsie tax assessor Basil Raucci's autopsy report with him. He explained to Fred that no one had seen it. With all the rumors floating around of Basil being murdered for his role in the corruption probe, Boyko knew Fred would jump at the opportunity to have a look at the report, so he could then turn around and go tell everyone how important he was that he had gotten his hands on the report.

Fred perked up. "OK, sure," he said.

Boyko had stopped at Wendy's. He purchased Fred a hamburger, fries and water. He told Fred he didn't want to meet inside the house today. "I'll meet you across the street," Boyko said, "at the Hoe Bowl. I'm eating my lunch."

There was a large parking lot directly across the street from Fred's three-story house. The Hoe Bowl was the only bowling alley in town. Boyko was parked there. Eating. Waiting for Fred to join him. If Boyko walked into Fred's house and gave him the bag of food and the drink, it would become Fred's property. Outside, in his car, it was public property. All Boyko needed Fred to do was sip the water through the straw and he'd have the DNA sample that had eluded BCI for the past few weeks.

"I don't know," Fred said, rethinking the situation. He seemed a bit more nervous now, most likely regarding leaving the house and meeting with Boyko at a neutral location.

"Come on, Fred, a free lunch. Who turns down a free lunch?"

"OK."

They hung up.

About five minutes later, Boyko sat in his car and watched Fred cross the street and walk into the Hoe Bowl parking lot.

"Come on, get in, Fred," Boyko said when Fred arrived at the car. Boyko had the autopsy report in his hand. "Sit down. Let's talk this through."

Fred sat down.

Boyko handed him his meal.

"No, no," Fred said. "I ate already. I'm not hungry."

Some time went by. They discussed the federal probe. Boyko showed Fred the autopsy report. Fred seemed on edge. Jumpy. He had reason to be. The federal case was heating up.

At one point, Boyko said, "Come on, Fred. I bought this meal and you're going to *refuse* it?" It came out in a joking manner. Boyko was acting as if Fred was hurting his feelings for not eating his food.

"OK," Fred finally said. "Give me that bag!" Fred grabbed the bag of food and the drink. Then he placed it down by his legs. "I'll eat it later. You happy?"

As Fred looked out into the parking lot, perhaps surveying the landscape to see if anyone was watching them, Boyko turned the heat up in the car. "I'm like cranking up the heat in the car," Boyko told me later, "hoping that he's going to take a sip of that drink. I'm hot as hell. The sun was shining into the car on me and with the heat blasting . . . I'm on fire."

After a while, Fred reached down, grabbed his drink and took a sip from the straw.

Boyko thought, *I met my objective, now I just need to take possession of the drink.*

Fred opened the door. "Thanks for lunch, Boyko," he said. "I appreciate it." He had the drink in his hand. "I'll drink this on the way back to the house."

Great.

Boyko had to be careful. He didn't want to break the trust between them he had spent so much time cultivating. If he showed his cards now, Fred would probably shut him down and stop talking. Boyko couldn't risk it—especially since he felt he had Fred on the ropes.

As Fred was getting up to exit the car, Boyko thought

fast and "accidentally" spilled his own drink all over himself. He grabbed some napkins and began dabbing at his blue suit.

"Fred, give me that water," Boyko said, "so I can get this soda out."

Fred handed Boyko the water.

"Thanks," Boyko said as Fred stood outside his vehicle. "I'll be in touch."

CHAPTER 26

According to some who knew him, Fred Andros had a certain primordial cry for power, wealth and status in him that was unmistakably evident in the way he carried himself. None of these things, of course, Fred could attain by his own means. This was one of the reasons why he was always leaning on others to do whatever "dirty work" he needed done. In the scope of his life, Fred had failed as a professional, destroying the only respectable job he'd ever had, taking kickbacks for permits and having town employees work on projects for his house, among other financially beneficial acts of corruption. There was one man in town who swore that Fred, who lived in Hyde Park right over the Poughkeepsie border, had rigged the water line from Poughkeepsie to feed his house, just so he could receive free water. Moreover, Fred had gotten "mixed up," according to one source, with a "burglary ring" when he was sixteen years old. He was an aspirant thug who, even as a child, wanted the other kids to fight his battles.

By the middle of December, about four days after Boyko secured the DNA sample from Fred (now out for testing), the focus of the investigation into Susan Fassett's murder zeroed in on Fred Andros.

"We're starting to catch him in a lot of these lies," Boyko explained. "There were discrepancies that needed to be addressed."

If someone didn't have a reason to lie, why would he? It made no sense to BCI why Fred Andros would lie about seemingly menial issues if he wasn't involved on *some* level. Fred had admitted to having an affair with Susan. He had admitted sneaking around with her and even getting into an altercation with her husband. Why, then, would he choose to lie about other issues surrounding that affair? Things, Boyko began to realize, that were inconsequential to the scope of the case.

Part of Fred's federal indictment, which included him testifying as a federal witness, also included a cooperation agreement with the FBI, in which he was required by federal law to cooperate with any *other* investigations, as well as the federal probe—i.e., the Susan Fassett murder. If Fred was obstructing justice in any way—lying, not revealing evidence, holding back valid information that could help BCI solve a crime—he would be in violation of his federal agreement, held in contempt and put into an awfully awkward position with the U.S. attorneys offering him what was a sweet plea-bargain deal.

BCI decided to confront Fred on his lies. Force his hand. Make him explain the slight differences in his stories that weren't adding up.

Accompanying Boyko this time out was Jim Karic. When he wanted, Karic could turn on an "in your face" attitude that spoke to the authority of his position, and yet showed how much poise Karic had as an interrogator. Karic had conducted polygraphs on suspects for years. He knew the ins and outs of squeezing a suspect. Not that Boyko didn't, but Karic knew how to handle guys like Fred Andros and get them to reveal things they didn't want to. He knew when to get in someone's face and when to lay back and catch a person in a lie.

"Art had caught Fred in these little lies, chickenshit, really, when you come down to it," Karic said later. "Fred keeps professing his love for Susan, she's been murdered, and even though they are little lies, he's lying to the police."

On the surface, Fred's conduct contradicted itself.

Boyko asked Fred about his and Susan's relationship and when the last time they had seen each other had been, and Fred gave the same answers he'd had several times already.

"Come on, Fred," Boyko said this time. The tone of the interview was a bit different from all those other times Boyko and Fred had met to swap stories. "Was it hostile?" Boyko later recalled, talking about this particular day. "No. He had explanations for everything. He continued his desire to speak with me without legal representation. But there certainly was a different tone to the interview."

Fred heard the difference in Boyko's inflection and it unnerved him. "What? What?" Fred asked impatiently. Boyko wasn't agreeing with him on everything he said, and he was suddenly calling him on it.

Karic watched Fred. Studied his reactions. Karic had been told by Fred sometime prior that he was impotent—same as Fred had explained to Boyko—and was taking medications that contributed to it. Karic had gone back and asked Fred's wife, Diana, about it. "Sure," she had told him, "we haven't had relations for at least five years. I love him. He's a good provider. He's kind to me. And it's OK."

Fred had floated the notion that Susan might have had "other" affairs, that he wasn't her only lover. But as BCI looked into it, Karic said, "We found that highly unlikely."

Fred was being boxed in now. "What is this?" Fred asked.

"When were you last with Susan intimately, Fred?" Boyko wondered.

"I'm telling you, a year and a half *before* her death," Fred said. He was adamant. He couldn't understand why they would question him about it.

The DNA had proven otherwise, Boyko and Karic knew. That semen in Susan's vagina was Fred's—the results had come in shortly before Karic and Boyko headed over to talk to Fred. Not only had Fred seen Susan a day before she was murdered—and lied about it—but he'd had sex with her, then lied about that, too, on top of the fact that he wasn't impotent.

"Fred, Fred, Fred," Boyko said in his deep, militarylike baritone. He meant business. It was easy for Fred to tell they weren't friends anymore. They had now entered into a new part of their relationship, to say the least.

"I'm telling you guys," Fred said, quite animatedly, looking quickly back and forth at both Karic and Boyko, "I'm impotent and suffer from sexual dysfunction."

"Fred, are you suicidal?" Boyko asked. They'd gotten a report from someone close to Fred that with all the pressure surrounding him from both cases, he was talking about killing himself.

"No," he said, rubbing his chin. "I would never blow my head off for anyone. But I am depressed. I won't deny that."

"Now, getting back to the last time you saw Susan," Boyko said, flipping through his notebook, stopping at a certain page, "you said that that particular meeting lasted from two to three minutes to no more than ten minutes?"

Fred shook his head up and down. "Uh-huh."

"We have witnesses to that meeting that claim you were with Susan for at least thirty or forty-five minutes, Fred, in the parking lot of Town Hall."

"Those damn people are sadly mistaken, Boyko. Come on."

"You told me," Boyko said, "over and over, that you didn't have a cell phone."

"OK, I have two. So what? I never told you I didn't have *a* cell phone."

Boyko ignored him.

"You say you last saw Susan on the afternoon of September twenty-seven—"

"Yes!"

"How 'bout our witnesses saying that you were with her on October twenty-fifth in the parking lot of Town Hall?"

"Damn it! I made no attempt to contact Susan on the twenty-fifth. What is this?"

In between the time Boyko had last spoken to Fred, BCI had uncovered Fred's pager records. Fred's pager, BCI knew, had gone off at 8:43 P.M. on the night Susan was murdered. (It was the shooter paging Fred, letting him know that Susan had been murdered.)

"Your pager, Fred, did you receive a page on October twenty-eighth at eight forty-three that night?"

"I don't recall. I generally turn off my pager at five or six, when my wife gets home."

Boyko made a note: Fred had always claimed that Susan had paged him on Monday and Thursday nights, so he left his pager on during those times and those nights.

"Do you know what Susan had planned for that night, Fred?"

He was a bit uncomfortable now, twisting and turning in his chair. It was clear the questions were bringing up things for Fred that he did not want to confront. "Look," he said sharply, "Susan had a board meeting that afternoon at around four. . . . I knew she was going to choir practice, she always did on Thursdays."

Boyko decided to come out with it: "You ever talk to anyone about hiring a hit man, Fred, to kill Susan?"

BCI had spoken to a source that claimed Fred had

asked him to find a hit man. This suggestion riled Fred. "No, no, no!" Fred seethed.

Leaving, Boyko and Karic were convinced Fred knew a lot more than he was admitting. Maybe it was time for a search warrant? BCI needed to search Fred's house to see what it could come up with. At this point in the investigation, what else did they have?

"By then," Boyko acknowledged later, "we had a good feeling that Fred was involved with Mrs. Fassett's homicide."

Now it was a matter of simply putting the pieces together—if, in fact, those pieces were out there somewhere.

CHAPTER 27

Two of BCI's narco unit investigators were sitting in downtown Poughkeepsie one night, inside their vehicle, several car lengths in back of Fred Andros, who was inside his car, parked off to the side of the street. Fred did not see the tail. He was too involved with what he was doing. It was one of those cold, rainy winter nights, when the roads become glazed over with a thin sheet of ice. Ever since Boyko had developed a "feeling" about Fred, BCI had been following him, especially at night. They wanted to find out exactly what Fred Andros was doing during his spare time.

What they learned was rather astonishing, this for a guy who claimed to be impotent. Fred was driving into Poughkeepsie, day and night, picking up hookers, sometimes two a day. BCI would interview the prostitutes after Fred dropped them back off and they reported how he was paying them in crisp brand-new $100 bills. All he requested was oral sex. The girls said he would pay them, but he would never produce, as they put it, "starburst" (no ejaculation). "He would get erect," one girl said, "but no starburst. . . ."

On this night, the undercover unit watched as a

known transvestite walked over to Fred's car. After a
short discussion, Fred summoned the guy to get in.

The unit laughed. Fred had no idea.

The transvestite got in and Fred began to talk to him.
A little while went by and Fred then threw the guy out,
likely figuring out the hard way that he wasn't a woman.

Over the radio, the guys had a laugh. "Ah," one of
them said as Fred became obviously heated and tossed
the dude out of the car, "he just found out that one had
a stem."

It was strange that Fred wasn't able to ejaculate for the
ladies of the night, but he had been able to inside of
Susan. BCI knew Fred was popping Viagra like Tic Tacs,
because they'd subpoenaed some of his personal papers
and found out. But no one could ever figure out the
reason behind his bizarre sexual appetite and how he
managed it, or where, in fact, those $100 bills were
coming from.

"Fred was into more than just skimming off the town,"
a former female friend later told me. "He had plenty of
deals going on all over the place, and even up in the
Catskills. He owned land and other property. As for his
impotence—Fred had a tough time getting it up and
keeping it up. As the years passed, he couldn't function
sexually much anymore and it really ripped into his ego."

Jim Karic stopped by Fred's one day to follow up on a
few things. He wanted to give him the opportunity to explain himself one more time. At this time, Fred wasn't interested in answering questions much anymore. Karic
said Fred would answer a question with a question.
Dance around the issue. Almost in frustration, Karic said
to him, "Listen, Fred, I'm going to ask you some direct
questions and please, just please, answer me directly."

Fred looked at Karic with a defeated air about him.

"Did you, Fred, have anything whatsoever to do with the death of Susan Fassett?"

Fred stared into the investigator's eyes. "I loved that woman!" he responded. "If I'd had anything to do with the murder of Susan Fassett, would I be here talking to you, Mr. Karic, right now without a lawyer?"

"Come on, Fred, that's not what I'm asking. Answer my question."

Fred wouldn't deny it. He kept talking about how much he had been helping BCI.

"Just . . . will you please answer me, Fred?"

After about five minutes of going back and forth, Fred finally said, "No."

Each time Karic spoke to Fred, he felt more strongly that Fred was their man. "Each time I talk to Fred, he locks himself into the crime more," Karic recalled.

BCI was finished playing games with Fred Andros. It was time to get with the feds and figure out what to do with Fred Andros.

Fred Andros realized he was in a vise, being squeezed at both ends by two different law enforcement agencies: he was lying to the feds about his role in the Susan Fassett murder and lying to the state police about his role in the corruption probe *and* the Fassett murder. Sooner or later, it was all going to come crashing down. And yet what could he do?

After some discussion between the FBI and state police, the FBI decided it wanted answers from Fred Andros. No more was he going to be able to dodge questions and play the fool. It was either answer the questions posed by BCI, or the deal Fred had cut with the feds was going to be taken off the table.

"We wanted answers from Fred," Boyko said. "We could not participate in that interview between Fred and the FBI. We were all here [at Troop K] waiting to hear what the FBI came up with."

It was decided that the FBI would call Fred in and put the chops to him. Until this point, the feds had left Fred alone and stayed out of things. The entire interview was designed around what Boyko and his colleagues had been finding out about Fred. The only difference was that the FBI would be asking the questions now, not BCI.

It all boiled down to the cooperation agreement Fred had with the feds, Boyko said. "He was required to answer our questions. If he reneged on the cooperation agreement, all bets were off."

They had him, in other words. Fred was suddenly facing some time behind bars, if his deal was stripped. Fred knew he could never survive prison. He might have talked it up around town that he was some sort of made man, but he was no more prepared for prison life than a child.

"We shared with the FBI everything we knew about the Fassett case," Boyko said. "We needed to, obviously, arm them with everything we could, to go after Fred. *They* had the hammer over him, *not* us."

To assuage the FBI, however, Fred was going to have to admit to something. He very well couldn't admit to being involved in the murder, or the time he was facing for the corruption probe would be nothing compared to conspiracy to commit first-degree murder. So after Fred heard about the request to come in and speak with the FBI, he began to think things through and come up with some sort of plan to get out of it.

Fred had been dealing with Special Agent James O'Connor. He felt comfortable with O'Connor. It was about 10:30 A.M. on December 21, 1999, when Fred and his attorney walked into the U.S. Attorney's Office in White Plains, New York, to discuss what Fred knew about the Susan Fassett murder, if anything. O'Connor mentioned to Fred immediately that his stories were beginning to break down. Was Fred trying to play both sides against the middle?

"No, no, no," Fred pleaded.

Besides Fred's attorney, Anthony Servino, Agent O'Connor, an investigator from the State Commission of Investigation and two U.S. attorneys were present for the interview. Fred looked awfully depressed and stressed. He had walked in with his head down, a look of total defeat on his face. He knew he couldn't lie—and get away with it—much longer.

Fred and Servino spoke privately for a brief period after O'Connor explained to Servino why Fred had been summoned.

"You're here, Fred," O'Connor said, "to clarify discrepancies and inconsistent statements between the information you've been providing to us in the course of the corruption investigation and that [was] related by you to the state police regarding the Susan Fassett homicide."

Fred looked on. Shook his head. His credibility with the feds had been severed. William Paroli's corruption trial was slated to begin in early 2000. How could the feds depend on Fred turning government witness if he couldn't be straight with everyone else about what seemed to be simple things? Did they need Paroli's attorneys dropping a bombshell during cross-examination? How would that look? Suppose they had information that Fred had been involved in Susan Fassett's death, or even that he had been involved with Susan on a deeper level than Fred wanted to admit. It would be a disaster in court.

"You need to provide truthful answers, Fred, based on

your cooperation agreement with us," O'Connor said as they sat inside conference room B of the U.S. Attorney's Office.

Fred said he understood. The last time O'Connor had spoken to Fred, Fred was rather hostile and bitter. In a spontaneous manner, O'Connor later wrote in his report, Fred had blurted out, *"I did not kill that woman,"* referring to Susan. *This statement was not made in response to any inquiry made to him by anyone else at the meeting,* O'Connor noted. It was a strange explosion on Fred's part.

"You want to tell us about Susan Fassett?" O'Connor said placidly after a moment. Everyone in the room looked at Fred. "And your relationship with her?"

Fred hesitated. His lawyer nodded, as if to say, *Go ahead. It's OK.*

"I had sex with her one and a half years ago in a motor home. That was the only time we had intercourse."

O'Connor dropped his head. It seemed Fred Andros still wanted to play games. Neither Fred nor his lawyer knew by that point, of course, that the DNA had proven otherwise.

"Wait a minute," O'Connor said. He was tired of the runaround. He knew the facts. They had other witnesses giving statements that didn't gel with Fred's stories. "Back on October twenty-eighth," the night of the murder, O'Connor said, referring to the telephone call O'Connor placed to Fred at home, "you said your sexual relationship had lasted for four years."

"I'm impotent," Fred said. "We got physical, yeah, by hugging, kissing and fondling."

"Come on, Fred?"

"We had sex on more than one occasion," Fred finally admitted. As Fred now explained it, he claimed he and Susan stopped seeing each other in late September. They had dated for "years," Fred added. "It was a mutual thing," he said of the breakup. "Jef Fassett had confronted Susan. I notified my wife with a telephone call to her at work. She told me not to do it again and forgave me. . . . I told the state police that I only had sex with her one time because I did not want them to tell my wife about the affair. They had told her other things."

O'Connor was still confused. He wanted Fred to be more specific.

"I had sex with her," Fred added, shaking his head, looking totally crushed, "on Monday the twenty-fifth, or Tuesday the twenty-sixth." He wasn't sure which day, exactly. "It was just prior to her death, though."

Before continuing, Fred said he wanted some water. After a quick swallow, he explained how the end of the relationship went down. He said he picked Susan up at noon on that day—the twenty-fifth or twenty-sixth—by her car in the parking lot of Town Hall. Then they drove to Fred's house in Hyde Park.

As soon as she got into the car, Fred told Susan, "Lie down on the seat so no one can see you."

"OK," Susan agreed.

They had already decided that the relationship was over. But Susan, Fred insisted, wanted to be with him once more. "She begged me to have sex with her one last time," Fred explained, adding, "I loved her as much as I loved my wife."

O'Connor looked at his colleagues. He didn't need to say it, but did Fred expect all of them to believe that Susan begged him for sex? Did they look like fools?

O'Connor wanted more. They had established that Fred lied about having sex with Susan shortly before her murder. What else had he lied about? And why would he lie about such a thing, anyway?

"You ever discuss with anyone the idea of hiring a hit man?" O'Connor wanted to know. BCI had explained

Fred had mentioned to a friend that he wanted to hire someone to "whack" Susan.

"No, no, no," Fred said defiantly. "I never discussed that or asked anybody about hiring a hit man." He seemed appalled that the feds would suggest such a thing.

"Why'd you tell the state police that you didn't have any handguns in the house, when you knew you did?"

"I was trying to protect myself and my wife," Fred explained, refusing to go into any detail.

"OK, fine," O'Connor said. "Tell us about October twenty-eighth, the night of the homicide."

Fred had been through this before. It was an easy memory to recall, simply because he *was* telling the truth. "I was home," he said. "My wife and I had friends over . . ." and he continued with the same story he had told Boyko several times already: dinner, then working on the model airplanes in the basement with his buddy Richard Byrd. "I never left the house. My dinner guests will back me up."

O'Connor asked if Fred thought his wife could have left the house on that night, without him knowing. After all, he was down in the basement with Byrd for more than an hour, which was plenty enough time to zip over to the United Methodist Church in Pleasant Valley, do the deed, and hightail it back home. Had he heard his wife leave? Maybe she became overcome by jealousy suddenly and decided to end the affair he was having with Susan once and for all.

"I don't think my wife had anything to do with killing Susan. . . . However," Fred said, stopping for a moment, "now that you mention it, you're making me think about it."

"Who do you think killed Susan, Fred?" O'Connor finally asked.

Fred didn't hesitate. "Jef, her husband! He's responsible."

"Fred, we're a bit confused. Explain to us why you didn't tell the state police any of this? Why were you so evasive with them?"

Fred ignored the question, and instead changed his mind. He now believed it was William Paroli who had Susan killed.

"What makes you say *that*, Fred?"

"I have no information to corroborate it, just a thought."

Fred became quiet at this point. He whispered something to his lawyer, who whispered back.

"Fred," O'Connor said, "why didn't you tell this"—the Paroli theory—"to the state police?"

It was odd that Fred was just now beginning to come up with all these wild ideas that he had never shared with Boyko or Karic. It was a fair question. Arguably, Fred and Boyko had a pretty good relationship until the end. Why wouldn't Fred tell Boyko he thought William Paroli had killed Susan?

"It was a woman," Fred came out with next, without warning, "by the name of Doreen or Darlene." He said he wasn't sure. "She killed Susan. She met Susan in early 1999 and had gotten together with her on a number of occasions."

O'Connor was surprised. Still, *"gotten together"*? What was Fred implying now? "What? Her name is Darlene, Doreen? Which is it?" O'Connor wanted to know.

"I asked Susan about her relationship with this woman," Fred explained. "She told me that it was a lesbian relationship. I was upset about it at first, but then accepted it."

From Jef Fassett to William Paroli, to possibly his own wife, now to a woman named Darleen or Doreen over a lesbian relationship gone bad. What was Agent O'Connor supposed to believe? With each question he asked, Fred's story became more unbelievable.

As O'Connor began to ask another question, Fred interrupted and added yet another story. This new tale Fred told was about the three of them—he and Susan and this *other* woman—and how he became part of the relationship between the two women. The question O'Connor and the FBI now faced, however, was if Fred was actually telling the truth. He had lied so much, who could believe him? Further, was he just trying to get himself out of the moment, as he had a history of doing in the past?

CHAPTER 28

Her name wasn't Doreen or Darlene. It was Dawn Marie Silvernail. She was a fifty-year-old, big-boned, heavyset woman with a wiry mop of gray hair. Married, Dawn Silvernail was born in Catskill, New York. She had lived a pretty much carefree life with her second husband, "Big Ed," and son by her first marriage, for the past twenty years that she and Fred Andros had known each other. With two older sisters from Poughkeepsie, one of whom worked for the town with Susan and knew Susan's husband and kids quite well, and a normal life of no legal trouble whatsoever, Dawn Silvernail was perhaps the most unlikely murderer one would ever expect to meet. She wore big, round-rimmed glasses that accentuated her rough features. She spoke with a raspy, nicotine-laced, leathery voice, but she had not an enemy among her small group of friends and family.

Everyone, it seemed, loved Dawn Silvernail.

There was another side to Dawn, however, that spoke to her naughty nature. According to one source, she liked to hang out in the dive bars and toss 'em back with the hard-core barflies. "She hung around disreputable people," one source noted. "Her husband, Ed, he had no idea what was going on. It wasn't even that she was a lesbian—I don't think she really was. With Dawn it was, 'Whatever.' Whatever came down the road that she felt like doing. The moment—whatever it is, it is."

BCI investigator Jim Karic grew up in Columbia County, near Hudson, where Dawn Silvernail was a fixture during the mid-1980s. The old cliché rang true, Karic explained of his days in the Hudson region: "Everybody back then pretty much knew everybody." In fact, Karic's mother had always purchased the family's appliances from a store in town called Silvernail Appliances, owned and operated by Dawn's in-laws.

As a teenager banging around town, Karic used to run into Big Ed Silvernail and his father, Tom. Ed was always known around those parts as being "strong like a bull." Moving those appliances around all his life as if they were toy pieces of furniture, Ed developed into a massive adult. Ed never said much. He did his work and kept to himself. "A great guy," Karic said of Ed. "Just an all-around nice man who always worked hard for what he had."

After school Karic joined the marines, enlisting from 1968 to 1971, missing out on going to Vietnam. When he returned to Hudson, Karic took the trooper test and made it on to the force. As the years passed, the blue-eyed, now white-haired, trooper worked his way up to an investigator's position with BCI. Before that job came along in 1988, however, Karic was stationed not too far from his home in Hudson, out of the Claverack barracks. Karic not only patrolled and worked the region, but it was his hometown turf. He knew people. He hung out at the local diners and bars. After his shift, with some of the guys, Karic would sometimes stop for a bite to eat and a few beers at a certain local watering hole. They'd sit and eat and share some laughs, maybe play a few games of pool. The bar would be packed, generally, with locals, hanging out and blowing off steam. Karic knew many of them. "Decent people," Karic said. "Hardworking common folks."

One night Karic went into the bar and noticed a "large-framed woman I hadn't seen around before." She was sitting at the bar with three of the locals knocking a few back and laughing and having a good old time. With Karic and his colleagues, there wasn't a lot of interaction between the two social groups. Each knew their place. The cops sat in the back at a table, and the locals stayed at the bar and did their own thing.

On this particular night, this woman, the big one—whom Karic later learned to be Dawn Silvernail—was at the bar with these guys engaged in, of all things, a farting contest. She'd let one go, the others would follow. To Karic, years later, when he thought about it, that one episode showed him the type of female Dawn Silvernail was: rough-and-tumble. A tomboy, really.

Karic stood stunned that night. "Does anybody know who this woman is?" he asked around.

"That's Dawn Pelton," someone said. "She works at the garage up the road." The same garage, in fact, that serviced some of the troopers' vehicles.

Six months after the farting contest, Karic stopped back in the bar and spied the same woman sitting with Big Ed Silvernail, whom he had known fairly well.

By now, Dawn and Ed were inseparable. Both big, lanky people, with the same sort of demeanor. Karic would hear them referring to each other as "dolly," "sweetie," "honey." Not occasionally, he said, but *every* sentence they spoke to each other would include some sort of term of endearment.

The night that Karic bumped into Dawn and Ed sitting

together, slobbering over each other with saccharine gestures and vows of love, was the last time Karic saw either one of them—that is, until nine years later, when Karic knocked on Dawn's door after Fred Andros had finally come clean and given BCI her name.

CHAPTER 29

From all outward appearances, Dawn Silvernail might have appeared to be a harmless country girl, a little rough around the edges, sure, maybe even manly, tomboyish and a little bit on the white trash side of the tracks. But, in truth, Dawn had graduated from Hunter-Tannersville Central School in Tannersville, New York, in 1967. She went on to earn a special endorsement in business. From 1967 to 1979, Dawn presided over the position of secretary to the principal of Hunter-Tannersville Central School. Beyond routine office work, she was responsible for preparing federal aid reports, handling confidential student records for well over four hundred pupils, as well as maintaining and ordering school supplies and books. To top it off, two days a week, Dawn was the school nurse.

Still, on the other side of this same coin was a person who went home at night and shot target practice in her backyard against one of the old oaks, which was loaded with bullet fragments.

Dawn moved to Nashville in 1979 and found work with a temp service. By 1982, she was working full-time as a clerk for the State of Tennessee Social Security Disability Services. Then she moved on to a job at a hospital.

Relocating back to New York in 1986, she found a job as a secretary to the director of personnel at the Rensselaer-Columbia Green, a private school. Shortly after that, Dawn landed a job as office manager of the garage Jim Karic would see her at from time to time.

Dawn Silvernail's life on paper was hardly that of a cold-blooded killer; she didn't seem like that bad of a person. "There was always something about Dawn," one former acquaintance later told me, "that I didn't like. Something about her that was cold. With most people, you can make some sort of connection . . . but with Dawn, no way. There was no way to 'connect.' Very weird person. Quiet and cold—like a sociopath, actually. No feeling behind her eyes."

On the day Fred Andros accused Dawn of murdering Susan Fassett, Dawn was working as a production supervisor and job coach for a maintenance company out of Kingston, New York. She had eight "coaches" working under her and also supervised a crew of twelve handicapped persons who were responsible for cleaning the Malden Travel Plaza in Saugerties, one of the places she and Fred sometimes met to discuss business.

"She would cry at times when it was appropriate," said a former friend. "But that was just it—she'd turn it on when she had to." She was quite manipulative, that same friend suggested. Dawn reacted to those things in which she believed she needed to, in order to get what she wanted.

Dawn the chameleon.

It was almost as if Dawn were two people wrapped in one. Her work history certainly spoke of a woman who was determined, professional, well-educated and liked. She worked hard to support her family. No one could deny Dawn that credit. Even friends later said how dedicated she was to her work—especially with the mentally challenged people she supervised.

"I never met a person who was more family-oriented," said one of Dawn's cousins. "Dawn has been a good friend and has been there in times of need. As a relative, she would do anything to protect you."

So how did Fred Andros fit into Dawn's life—or, rather, her double life? Where was Fred all those years? How did he come to know Dawn?

"It is difficult to understand," Dawn's lawyer, D. James "Jim" O'Neil, later said, "why Dawn Silvernail, a . . . woman with no criminal record, who has always been employed and by all accounts has strong family ties, could ever be put in a position to do what Fred Andros wanted her to do."

This was what BCI was looking at as it began to look at the possibility that Dawn Silvernail murdered Susan, and that Fred Andros had hired her to do the job.

CHAPTER 30

Jim Karic had seen senseless murders throughout his career with BCI. But the Susan Fassett murder, Karic so astutely observed later, had a domino effect on so many different lives. "It was one of the most disturbing aspects of this entire case to me." The idea that Jason Fassett and his brother would remember their mom in this manner twisted Karic's insides. "In fact," Karic added, "to show you how interconnected this case came to be, we soon found out that Jason Fassett had actually *worked* for Fred Andros."

Jason admitted later that being held at Troop K and the ordeal throughout that night, when his mother was murdered, was "the most traumatic event that has ever happened in my life. Yet, as much as I could sit here and say bad things about cops—all cops—the New York State Police broke this case and, well, did everything to find my mom's killers."

When Jason was kicked out of school after getting caught selling drugs, he was ordered to do community service. That led him into the web of Fred Andros, as he did his sentence under Fred in the Town of Poughkeepsie Water Department, which Susan had, of course, played a part in working out for her son. When school was over, and Jason was beating around town deciding what to do with his life, he went to the water department. Seeing that Jason knew how to do everything already, Fred hired him on as a full-time employee.

The thing Jason learned right away while working for Fred was that if you got on Fred's good side, he'd bend over backward to take care of you. Not without, however, letting you know that he was doing you favors and taking care of things for you.

"Everything Fred did," Jason said, "had an element of shadiness to it."

Fred was slaphappy when it came to power. For example, he'd announce in front of several of his employees that he needed to talk to a specific person, making a stink about it, so everyone would hear. "Hey, you, in my office—right now!"

Inside the office, however, he'd say something rather common or unimportant.

"It was a way for Fred to show us," Jason said, "that he was in control. He wanted to look all-powerful, like we should stand up and 'know' who Fred Andros is because he's important."

A common saying about Fred around Town Hall, and inside the small circle of people who ran with him, was "No one says no to Fred Andros."

It was more a way of thinking that began to develop among contractors going to Fred to get approval for projects around town. Without Fred signing off on the project, work would stop. Companies needed water. If Fred Andros didn't approve of the way a certain contractor was laying water lines, or where they were digging, there would be big problems. Or, if Fred was satisfied with how much a contractor was paying him on the side, forget about a permit.

"People probably at one time joked about it," Jason

explained. "'Oh, boy, you better not say no to Freddy.' But that joke became a way of life for people, and Fred fed into it."

In other words, if BCI was looking for a motive where Fred was concerned, there it was: Susan Fassett might have said no to Fred. *"No, it's over. No, I don't love you anymore. No, we cannot see each other again."*

And Fred wouldn't accept the rejection.

Basil Raucci, who was involved in the same corruption problem, but ended up dead after committing suicide, was Jason's boss at one time. "Basil was this nice old guy," Jason said, "but you just knew that he was involved in some really shady stuff."

The difference between Fred and Basil, Jason realized quickly, was that "Fred wanted you to know that he was this pseudogangster, whereas Basil was quiet about things. That's why we all suspected Basil of being involved in corruption. Fred walked around touting himself, letting people know he was this powerful person, when we knew he was a nobody. Fred was the epitome of 'short-guy complex, Napoleon syndrome.'"

Everything Fred was became birthed from his own hype. Still, Fred ran that water department as if it were *his* department, many who worked for him later said.

Small things turned into big things as Fred began to misappropriate town funds and skim off the bottom line. One of Fred's sons got into paintball, but, according to one source, the kid didn't have anyone to play with. So Fred gave several of his younger workers as much overtime as they wanted under the agreement that they would purchase paintball equipment and play with the kid.

As long as the things that happened within the water department made Fred Andros look good, a former employee said, it didn't matter what employees did. "He didn't care what you did, whether you slept for four hours in your truck parked in back of a building, or you stole overtime. If you made *him* look good, you got away with it."

Fred could also flip on a dime. The minute something went wrong and he needed to send someone down the road, he was out looking for a head to put on the chopping block. He had a filthy mouth and would snap when pushed. "He swore all the time," an employee said. "He had no problem degrading people in front of others. He was very, very overly sexual where it pertained to women. He could not speak to a woman without somehow making a sexual advance or remark."

He thought he was as smooth as the man he absolutely idolized more than anything else in his life: Elvis. Fred Andros was obsessed with Elvis Presley. Not only did Fred try to keep his hair in a pompadour like Elvis's, with that short little curl in the front, but he tried to walk like "the King" and talk to women as if he were somehow channeling the popular singer.

"Fred tried to be this little, tiny, tough Italian Elvis-like gangster," one former employee said.

Part of what made Fred so successful with women—something no one could later understand—was a certain cocky confidence he had around them. It was, claimed one former friend, the same mentality surrounding "that high-school theme of 'why do the hot girls like the a-holes?'" Why don't girls go for the nice guys? "It's the confidence. The cockiness."

The same was true for Fred. It drew women to him. Add to that the idea that if you shoot one hundred arrows at a target, sooner or later, one of those will strike a bull's-eye.

One of the most important pieces of the puzzle Fred Andros had related to the FBI when Agent O'Connor interviewed him in White Plains convinced the BCI that Dawn Silvernail and Fred Andros had, indeed, been involved in Susan's murder. *How* they were involved would become a sticky issue in the coming days as Fred began to pin the murder all on Dawn—suggesting that Dawn and Susan were lovers and the murder had been a lover's quarrel turned deadly.

As for convincing BCI—something Fred had said was extremely vital to the investigation. During the FBI interview, Fred described a telephone call he had received from Dawn on November 1, 1999, a few days after the murder.

"I told you not to call me," Fred screamed at Dawn.

"I did it," she said. "I shot her five or six times with my .45 semiautomatic."

"What?" Fred had said, playing stupid, as if he'd had nothing to do with it.

Cleverly, BCI had never released to the media or press the type of weapon used in the murder. Thus, only the murderer could have known.

During that same interview, Fred also told O'Connor that he had, in fact, seen Dawn driving a "champagne-colored station wagon, possibly a Ford," from time to time. Again, the fact that a station wagon was spotted leaving the crime scene was never made public.

Fred Andros, it appeared, knew details about Susan's murder that only someone involved in it could have known. What role he played would be, however, the next major hurdle for BCI—that is, after investigators went after Dawn Silvernail.

CHAPTER 31

BCI ran a quick records check on handguns sold in the region just to see if by chance Dawn Silvernail had registered a handgun in her own name. The chances of Dawn using a gun she had registered to commit a murder were slim to none, but one never knows how murderers think, so checking the obvious is always a good idea.

On her pistol permit, issued by New York State, sure enough, Dawn listed a Ruger .45-caliber handgun. BCI had the serial number.

"That's incredible," Jim Karic said, showing Boyko the report.

"Unbelievable."

According to the Department of Motor Vehicles, Dawn's husband Ed had a two-tone tan station wagon registered to his name.

"Things seem to be coming together," said one investigator as BCI began to think about who was going to question Dawn Silvernail.

When Jim Karic first heard the name Dawn Silvernail, he put it together right away. *Dawn Silvernail, this woman must have married Eddy Silvernail. I know these people.*

BCI Troop K made arrangements with BCI in the

Catskills to use their facility when—and if—they needed
to bring Dawn or Ed in. With Fred's admission, and the
fact that Dawn owned a registered .45 and had access to
a station wagon, Judge George Marlow signed a search
warrant on December 23, 1999, thus putting the kibosh
on any Bing Crosby "White Christmas" holiday that Ed
and Dawn Silvernail might have had planned.

With several of his BCI colleagues, Jim Karic drove up
to Earlton, in Greene County, where Dawn now lived
with Big Ed. The plan was to get Dawn and Ed out of the
house and into the confines of the Catskill barracks, on
BCI turf.

Karic and three of his colleagues rolled up on Dawn and
Ed's modest small white ranch (with blue shutters) out in
the middle of, Dawn later told me, "nowheresville," which
was located on the doorstep of the Catskill Mountains.

No one had called. It was a surprise visit.

Jim Karic rang the doorbell and Big Ed answered a
few moments later.

"Hey, Ed, you remember me? Jim Karic, from the old
neighborhood." Karic was using his friendly demeanor.
There was no reason to go barging into the house like mar-
shals on some sort of *Cops* TV show. Take it slow. Ed was a
monster of a guy. They wanted Dawn to open up and talk.

"Oh, man," Ed said right away. "Jimmy Karic. How the
hell are you doing?" Ed didn't put it together immediately, but then he looked around the door and saw the
others with Karic and put it together that Karic was with
the state police. ("He started to get a bit antsy and nervous," Karic later said.)

"I'm OK, Ed. . . ."

"Come on in," Ed invited.

Dawn came into the room as they all walked in and entered the kitchen area. Karic spoke first. "Listen, we hate

to bother you two, but we have a situation here and what we're hoping is that you're going to be able to help us out."

Ed began to pace the room. Karic sat down at the kitchen table across from Dawn. "Will you relax, Eddy," she said. "They just need our help with something."

With Ed pacing and sort of stomping around the house, Karic became a little nervous, he later admitted. "I know Ed," Karic mused. "He is not only a big guy, but he can be very aggressive. Ed had a reputation among some of us. He could hurt people. We knew that. And I thought that if Ed went off, someone was going to get hurt—and it would have likely been us. You'd need an elephant gun, for crying out loud, to take the guy down."

Karic started talking to Dawn as the rest of the team kept an eye on Ed. He started with light stuff. "How's your boy, Dawn? Don't you have a son from a previous marriage?"

"Yes, yes," Dawn said. "He's fine. Thanks." She seemed relaxed. Easy to speak to.

"Eddy," Karic said, turning toward Ed, who was now standing nearby, "how's your mom and dad? Geez, I haven't seen them for quite a few years now."

"OK. They're livin' just down the road here now."

"Listen," Karic said after they chatted some more about family and friends, "what we have here, maybe you can help us out. We're working on this case, that, ah, a woman in Poughkeepsie was killed and we're looking at anybody who owns a .45-caliber." Karic didn't want to play his hand. He wanted to generalize the search, the interview. Place Dawn into a "pool" of .45-caliber owners and see how she reacted.

"Sure, sure," Dawn said right away, quite cordially. "I have one, as you know."

"Great," Karic said. "Can I have a look at it?"

"No problem. Come on."

Karic stood up and followed Dawn into her bedroom, where she had the gun still sitting inside her drawer underneath the water bed. "Here," she said, handing it to Karic.

"Hey, thanks so much, Dawn," he said.

Ed was in the other room, arms folded, now pacing quickly back and forth. Karic took a look at him and didn't like Ed's body language. ("I didn't know *what* he was going to do.")

Ed finally spoke up. "Listen here, Jim, what's this all about? What's going on here?"

Dawn walked over. "Eddy, now just stop it. Sit down and relax." Dawn looked over toward Karic. "Sorry 'bout him . . ."

Karic began to consider the idea that perhaps Ed had something to do with the murder. Dawn seemed so calm. So cool. She wanted to help as much as she could.

"What's going on?" Ed said again.

"Just sit down, shut up and let them talk, Eddy," Dawn said.

Karic asked Dawn to sit down at the table. "There's a number of people involved in this thing, and it's really getting complicated. We need to clear up some things. Would you mind, Dawn, coming down to Catskill with us? That's where we have all the computers, typewriters and that sort of stuff. Maybe you can clear this all up for us."

Dawn didn't hesitate. "Sure. No problem, Detective."

Ed wanted to change his clothes. He was wearing a wife-beater T-shirt. He walked into the bedroom, out of sight, to slip on another shirt. While he was gone, Karic whispered to Dawn, "I want to get you away from Ed. I don't want him to know certain things. Some allegations have been made about you. Do you know Freddy Andros?"

"Well, yeah, of course. I've known Freddy for a long time."

"Listen, Fred's made some statements. We don't know if they're true, or what to believe." Karic sounded like Dawn's friend. Very reassuring. Like he wanted to help her. "He kind of threw your name out there and I really need to cover some territory. It's really personal stuff, you know what I mean." Karic raised his eyebrows. "I don't want to say anything about this stuff in front of Eddy."

"I understand," Dawn said. "We can talk about it all down at the station house."

Karic was thrown off his tightwire a bit. He had expected to go there and meet up with opposition from Dawn. Denials. *Get out of here! I didn't do that! Are you out of your mind?* But, instead, she was cooperative and rather cordial. He wondered if she'd had anything to do with the murder at all. Maybe Fred was, once again, lying.

It was Ed, it turned out, who was the troublesome one. As they made their way out to the cruisers to travel down to the Catskill barracks, the other members of BCI kept a close eye on Big Ed, who was acting strangely once again.

As they walked, one of the investigators, a big guy himself at about six feet, two hundred pounds, slipped on some ice and started to fall backward. Big Ed, however, was right there, following behind, and everyone was stunned at his strength when he caught the investigator, lifted him up and straightened him out as if he were a mannequin.

Down at Troop F, in the Catskills, BCI separated Ed and Dawn. Several investigators sat with Ed in one room and talked things through—the guy didn't know anything about the Susan Fassett murder, that was clear right away with a few questions.

Karic sat with Dawn in another room. She was still

completely composed. Karic allowed her to smoke as they sat together and began to go over things.

Karic could tell right away that Dawn was smarter than she looked. She understood how things worked. She was able to articulate her stories in a way that impressed the seasoned interrogator.

"It was very easy to talk to her," Karic said later. "You didn't have to bring the language down at all, or talk in circles. She knew what was going on. She knew exactly what I was saying at all times and was able to respond."

Karic asked Dawn to start at the beginning. How she and Fred had met. He was curious, as were several of his colleagues, as to how Fred Andros and Dawn Silver-nail had hooked up.

And the story Dawn told surely didn't disappoint.

Located in Dutchess County, New York, on the outskirts of the Catskill Mountains, the quaint town of Pleasant Valley is a flawless postcard of mostly farming real estate.

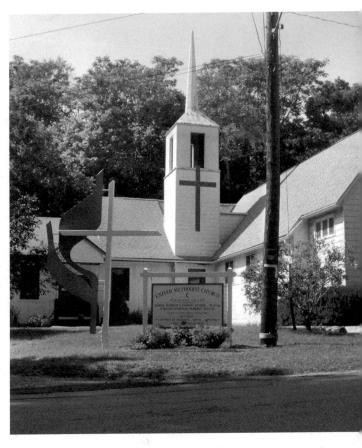

Northeast of Poughkeepsie, New York, the United Methodist Church in downtown Pleasant Valley was a great source of comfort for Susan Fassett, a devout Christian.

Susan Fassett and her sister grew up in Pawling, east of Pleasant Valley near the Connecticut border. *(Courtesy Jason Fassett)*

Although she suffered emotionally, rarely was there a day when Susan didn't smile for her two kids and husband. *(Courtesy Jason Fassett)*

Married for more than two decades, Susan was rebuilding her life and marriage when she was gunned down on October 28, 1999.
(Courtesy Jason Fassett)

After leaving choir practice, Susan walked out of this side door leading into the United Methodist Church parking lot and was gunned down.

New York State Police investigator Arthur Boyko, one of the first on the scene, points to the area across the street from the church where Susan was shot at point blank range while sitting in her vehicle.

Another view of the gravel parking lot where Susan was murdered.

New York State
Police investigator
Arthur Boyko.

New York State
Police investigator
Thomas Martin.

This memorial was made by church members just yards away
from where Susan Fassett was gunned down.

New York State Police Troop K barracks, in Pleasant Valley, became the center for the Susan Fassett murder investigation.

Stumped for months with a case going nowhere, investigators learned that Susan's killer had initially tried to sneak up on Susan while she was inside her home eating dinner with her husband and kids.

This view of the Fassett home shows where Susan's killer was spotted walking up the driveway before quickly running away.

After murdering Susan, her killer ditched the murder weapon, a ski mask and other items in a wooded area near the scene of the crime.

Later that night, the murderer's accomplice came by and grabbed the murder weapon and other articles used in the murder from this wooded area.

Susan worked for the Town of Poughkeepsie, where she met Fred Andros, with whom she began an affair four years prior to her murder.

Fred Andros in 2000, before he disfigured himself severely. *(Courtesy of the New York State Police Department)*

The house in Hyde Park, New York, where Fred Andros lived with his fourth wife.

This is the garage in back of Andros's house, where he videotaped Susan Fassett and another woman engaging in sexual relations.

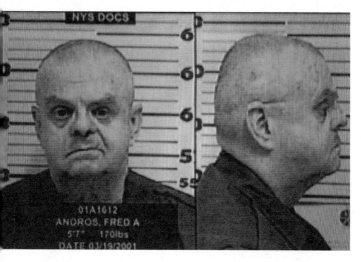

As Arthur Boyko and other New York State Police investigators
moved in to arrest Andros on suspicion of murder charges,
he tried committing suicide by shooting himself in the face.
(Courtesy of the New York State Police Department)

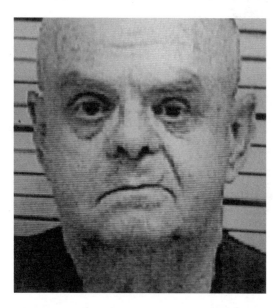

Smiling for her first booking photo, Dawn Silvernail believed she was going to walk away from her role in the murder of Susan Fassett. *(Courtesy of the New York State Police Department)*

After being booked on murder charges, Dawn Silvernail wasn't smiling anymore. *(Courtesy of the New York State Police Department)*

The courthouse in Poughkeepsie, just a block from where Susan and Fred met and worked, and where Fred was tried and found guilty of murder.

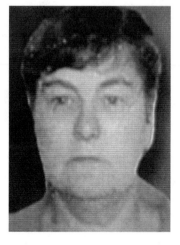

Time had changed Dawn Silvernail; here she is in 2001, one year after her arrest. *(Courtesy of the New York State Police Department)*

Jason Fassett remembers his mother Susan, forty-eight years old when she was murdered, as one of the best friends he's ever had in his life—someone he could talk to about anything.
(Courtesy of Jason Fassett)

CHAPTER 32

How Fred Andros and Dawn Silvernail met seems almost appropriate to how their lives would turn out some twenty or so years later. Born in 1949, Dawn grew up and lived in Tannersville, New York. Tannersville is located in the heart of the Catskills' "Borscht Belt" region. Winter weekends bring in the young Manhattanites to ski and eat and drink. When the snows melt, however, Tannersville becomes a quiet refuge for the locals and their easy way of life.

When Dawn lived in town, Tannersville was even more remote and secluded than it is today. The 2000 census reported 448 residents; back during Dawn's day, the town supported perhaps half of those people.

The 1970s were a time of radical social change, not to mention the decade of the gadget and the fad. Among the most popular were *Star Wars,* mopeds, the 8-track player, platform shoes, dashboard hula girls and the CB radio.

The CB during the 1970s was as popular as the iPod or Internet is today. The most successful of the trucker tunes was "Convoy," released in 1975, which epitomized CB lingo: *"Ah, breaker one-nine, this here's the Rubber Duck."*

A few simple words that were more familiar than the opening of the Pledge of Allegiance.

Being so isolated in the woods, Dawn got lonely and bored. So she used the CB radio to communicate with the outside world. For many, the CB was a way to escape—i.e., how instant messaging or e-mailing might be construed today. You could hide behind the lollipop microphone attached to the CB and be someone else.

As Dawn familiarized herself with the CB and started meeting people, she hooked up with Fred, who was living way down in Hyde Park, married, and cruising the CB airwaves, looking for new friends.

"This is Neptune, you out there, Delta?" Fred would say.

Dawn would be home, in another room. She'd run to her CB.

Dawn's handle, or CB name, was "Delta Dawn," obviously taken from the popular song of the same title by 1970s stalwart Helen Reddy. At the time, 1977, Dawn followed a local country band, Jerry and the New Prairie Ramblers, who frequently stopped at a bar she hung out at, the Golden Rooster. One of the songs the band routinely belted out for the crowds was "Delta Dawn." Because she loved that song so much, patrons in the bar and friends started calling her Delta Dawn. The other handle Fred knew her by was "Footloose."

Dawn lived on top of Hunter Mountain. "Geographically," she later told me, "where I was perched in my house trailer, the location was such that I faced in three directions into the three valleys through the Catskills. So I could pick up people down in Margaretville, Kingston and Poughkeepsie, or Hyde Park, where Fred lived."

At first, they chitchatted about what kind of radio equipment they both used. Casual stuff. Both were married. Both were happy. It was a friendship. Dawn's first husband would even sit and speak with Fred, just as Dawn would often talk with Fred's first wife.

"Eventually it evolved into more personal conversation between me and Fred," Dawn recalled.

Fred just happened to have a cabin in nearby Acra, New York, west of Hudson, at the base of the Catskills. One time Fred and his wife and two friends were heading up to the cabin for a weekend. Dawn was home at the time. Walking by the CB radio, she heard Fred calling out her handle.

"Go ahead," Dawn said.

"Hey," Fred replied, "we're heading up to the camp. If you give me directions, we'll take a side trip and stop by and meet up with you and [Dawn's first husband]."

Dawn thought about it. She had never met Fred before. It was only recently that they'd started talking on the telephone.

"Sure," she said. *What the heck.*

That first time Dawn actually met Fred in person, she was surprised by how short and small in stature he was, but overlooking that, he and his wife and friends were "quite nice," she recalled. "The four of them came, we had a drink. We talked about this and that. They left. And Fred and I just continued, as the weeks and months went by, to talk on the CB radio."

The first time Dawn realized that Fred wanted more than a simple friendship was during Christmas the year after they met. Fred invited Dawn and her husband down to Hyde Park to a Christmas party at his house. It was festive: lots of people, drinks, good food, good conversation. "It was a general social gathering," she said.

Nothing sexual happened on that night, but Fred had made several comments that led Dawn to believe that he was interested in more than being friends. In the days that followed, "he started calling me more and more on the phone," she offered. "And one thing led to another."

Fred was a charmer, according to Dawn. She said he told her exactly what she wanted to hear. She loved her husband, but there was something missing. Fred realized what that vulnerability was and worked it. Dawn was quick to say that "it takes two." She didn't want to place all the blame on Fred, but he used their earlier friendship as a means to talk her into bed.

"That was the first time I had sex with Fred," Dawn told Jim Karic when he interviewed her. "He came up to meet me after we talked on the radios and we went up to his camp and had sex."

It was one of those situations, Dawn later said, "where you get yourself caught up and you cannot get out. I cannot say it's through no fault of my own. Things could have gone differently, had I not been put in the position I was in."

Throughout their "friendship," Dawn said later, as she and her first husband and son continued to meet up with Fred and his wife and children for dinner parties, they'd play it off between them as if they were "buddies," the entire time sneaking around, behind everyone's back, having wild, experimental sex.

"Fred liked using toys," Dawn said later.

As their relationship turned from friends with benefits to merely friends, and Fred grew tired of Dawn sexually, they remained close. It was here, during the late 1970s and early 1980s, when Fred began to lend Dawn money and do her favors. Whenever Dawn was in a jam, she'd call on Fred, who she had been led to believe over the years was some sort of major "player" in Poughkeepsie, a local wiseguy. Fred would brag about his tough-guy exploits to Dawn—and she said she bought it all. None of it, however, held the least amount of truth. Fred was just another town worker trying to establish himself.

"He was able to get things done," Dawn told Karic. "Fred knew people."

Dawn went on to say that for her, Fred was a great friend. He rarely asked her for anything. Was always there when she needed him. And became a shoulder for her to air her marital problems.

"I don't really like sex," she said later. "Never did. Really have no interest in it whatsoever. I had relations with my husband, but it was never mutually satisfying."

One of Dawn's problems with sex, she claimed, was that she had gone through menopause in her early thirties, which turned her off sex entirely. Since that time, she said she had no "sexual sensation."

She said later, "I did it to satisfy my husbands, and Fred. But it wasn't my thing."

CHAPTER 33

It was the night before Christmas Eve and getting late. Dawn seemed to be itching to get back home and get out of the hot seat Jim Karic and his BCI colleague had her in at the Catskill barracks. Dawn seemed a bit frazzled as the interview carried on toward midnight.

"Let's go through this once more," Karic suggested. It was that old interrogator tactic of making a suspect tell his or her story front to back, back to front, sideways and upside down. The thought behind this practice was that if you were telling the truth, it wouldn't matter how you told it: two and two always made four.

Dawn put her head in her hands. Took a deep breath. "What do you want to know?" She was exhausted.

Karic kind of rolled his eyes. "Come on, Dawn, you know what we're talking about here. When was the last time you spoke to Fred Andros?"

"Past few weeks."

"When, exactly?"

"I don't know. . . . I went to see him in October about purchasing a generator he had for sale. In fact, while I was there, I met someone by the name of . . . I think . . . Sue, or something like that."

Now we're getting somewhere, Karic thought. "What about your .45, when was the last time you shot it?"

Dawn explained that she had just recently shot at a barrel behind her house. "Eddy reloads all of the ammunition I use."

Karic decided to inject a bit of reality into the interview. "Listen, Dawn, I need to read something to you before we go any further. Do you understand?"

"Sure," Dawn said, looking around. She seemed defeated. Lost. Ready to crack.

"You have the right to remain silent . . . ," Karic began, reading Dawn her Miranda rights. When he was finished, he asked, "Do you understand each of these rights?"

"Yes," Dawn said, letting out a deep breath, running her hands through her hair.

"Are you still willing to speak with us?"

Dawn thought about it. "Yes," she said.

Karic asked if she knew anyone in the Town of Poughkeepsie besides Fred.

"My sister works in engineering," Dawn replied.

"Relax," Karic assured Dawn, who was shifting in her seat, acting overly nervous, "everything will be OK."

Dawn told a story her sister had related to her about Fred. She qualified the story by saying that she was always scared of Fred and what he could "get done." She explained that Fred's first wife, after they divorced, was driving in town one day when a town truck swerved into the lane she was in and had a "narrow miss" with her car. "Fred arranged that," Dawn suggested.

Karic shook his head, agreeing with Dawn.

Dawn further said that she drove down to her sister's house in "late October" and had gone shopping on that same night at a nearby Kmart and that she left Kmart and stopped at Dunkin' Donuts and "swung back by" her sister's house around nine o'clock.

"There were no lights on inside the house, so I continued home," Dawn said.

"OK," Karic said. "I should say that Fred Andros made a statement to the effect that you told him how you personally shot and killed Susan Fassett—"

But Dawn wouldn't let him finish, lashing out, "That's totally untrue!"

"Oh, OK . . . ," Karic responded. "Why would Fred come out and say that, then?"

"I have no idea what he's talking about." Dawn was more heated and visibly upset than she had been all night. She paused, then, in a softer voice, said, "I could never harm another human being."

Dawn went through some of the details of that "late October" night, which Karic was able to establish from her was October 28, 1999, the night Susan was murdered. Locking Dawn down to a story was important. When they caught her lying—and they soon would—she would be forced to explain herself.

"Dawn, I have to tell you," Karic said, "Fred claims that you and Susan were lesbian lovers."

Dawn shot right back: "No way!" She was obviously shaken by the accusation. "That sort of behavior repulses me," she said. "My husband wanted me to do that a long time ago, but I refused to comply. I've had no other sexual partner besides my husband, Fred or otherwise."

As it happened, Dawn said she spoke to Fred the previous morning, explaining the conversation as pretty straightforward and casual. Fred said his father had fallen and broken his hip. "He's in a nursing home now." Dawn stated that there was nothing "unusual" about Fred. The "information," he relayed, "was generic." She had no idea why he would accuse her of such a thing as murder. It made no sense.

Karic and his colleague left the room for a while

and conversed with their boss about where to take the interview next. Karic agreed that the best thing to do was cut Dawn and Ed loose. Let them think about things over the Christmas holiday and then drag Dawn back in a few days after Christmas. A tail could be put on Dawn. See what she did. How she reacted to being brought in for questioning. Maybe she'd try to talk with Fred, meet him or show up at his house.

Karic drove Dawn home. As they made their way down the interstate, the state police were tearing through Dawn's house under the auspices of a search warrant.

Ed was sitting in the backseat as Karic pulled up to his house. Dawn spotted the vans and cruisers.

"What's this?"

"Search warrant, Dawn."

She was speechless.

"Thanks for your cooperation," Karic said. "We'll be in touch."

Karic drove back to the Catskill barracks after dropping Ed and Dawn off at their home. When he walked in, one of the troopers was on the phone with Dawn. She was livid. "I could hear a woman's voice while standing next to the trooper," Karic recalled. "She was swearing, cursing."

Apparently, Dawn was upset because the state police had opened all of the Christmas presents under her tree.

"She was irate."

Later, Dawn said, "Well, they trashed my house. They dumped the garbage pails all over the floor. They destroyed everything."

Dawn eventually hung up on the trooper.

Karic didn't quite know how to read Dawn's reaction to the troopers opening her presents. *Here she is,* he thought while driving back to Troop K that night, *being questioned for murder, we believe she did it, and she's going crazy because we opened her Christmas presents.*

CHAPTER 34

BCI's ballistics expert Craig Grazier, a cop Karic knew from years ago as a fellow firearms instructor, called Karic after having a look at Dawn's .45 Ruger. Grazier had some news. He wasn't finished with the testing just yet, but something was rather obvious to him immediately.

"Jim, listen," Grazier explained during the telephone call, "I need to run some more tests, but someone has really went to work on the barrel of this gun."

Karic's interest was piqued. "No kidding. How so?"

"It appears someone took an electric grinder or drill and tried to grind out the lands and grooves inside the barrel."

This was an interesting turn of events, Karic knew. Someone had tried to damage the inside of the weapon so ballistics would have a hard time matching projectiles to the barrel.

After hanging up, Karic went to one of his partners. "We need to go see Dawn and get her back down to the Catskill barracks."

On December 28, near one o'clock that afternoon, Jim Karic and a colleague, Bill Gray, once again showed up unannounced at Dawn's.

"There's a problem with your gun," Karic said to Dawn, standing in her living room. "We need to cover some more stuff with you. Can you come back down to the Catskill barracks with us?"

So once again, Dawn and Ed piled into Karic's cruiser and headed back down to the Catskill barracks, where Dawn was taken into a room by herself and asked more questions.

In the car, during the ride, Dawn seemed like a different person. More relaxed and laid-back, especially since that fiery telephone call she had made on the day BCI tore her house apart. She appeared to be thinking about things deeply. Contemplating scenarios.

"What about the gun?" Dawn asked Karic worriedly. They were pulling into the driveway of the Catskill barracks.

"Well, I don't really know," he said, playing dumb. "Forensics do all these technical things and, well, I guess we'll find out when *you* do. It's probably nothing."

Inside the barracks, Karic and Investigator Bill Gray began by reading Dawn her Miranda rights. She waived them, saying, "Listen, three or four months ago, Fred called me with an offer." Karic had mentioned that they were still waiting for the reports on the gun. It would take a while. But it wouldn't hurt to begin on another topic. So Dawn just came out with talking about Fred and Susan. She seemed eager to get something off her chest.

Karic and Gray never played good cop/bad cop with Dawn. They had always come across as her friend, there to help her out of whatever jam she had gotten into. This tactic made Dawn feel comfortable, willing to open up. ("They were great," Dawn told me later. "They never once pressured me or played strong-arm with me. I appreciated that.")

"We're all ears here, Dawn," Karic said comfortingly. "You wanted to say something about Fred and Susan?"

"OK," Dawn said before breaking into what was one of the more scandalous stories BCI had heard in quite some time.

CHAPTER 35

According to Dawn, Fred sounded rather needy on the day he called and mentioned he wanted to see her in person about "something." Dawn was curious, she explained to Karic and Gray. So she asked him, "What is it, Fred?"

"Just come down and see me."

A few days later, Dawn traveled south from work and met up with Fred at his house in Hyde Park.

"I have a lady friend named Sue," Fred explained. "You know we've been dating a long time."

"Yeah," Dawn said.

For a few years leading up to this moment, Dawn said later, she and Fred hadn't seen each other much. Fred was always busy. "I didn't even know Fred was remarried," Dawn explained. "He never told me. Every time I went to see him at the house, he was alone."

On this day, Fred had something different in mind for Dawn, she later explained to me.

"Sue," Fred said to Dawn, "a young lady I've been seeing, fantasizes about having sex with another woman." He then asked Dawn if she was interested. ("At this time," Dawn recalled, "I never even knew that Susan was married, or had kids, or anything. It was the first I had heard of her.")

"I don't know. . . ." Dawn answered Fred. She was taken aback by the offer. She'd had relations with several of Fred's friends, but they were all males and it was for no other reason than the money. This thing with Susan that Fred was suggesting seemed more intimate. More emotionally invested. Dawn never got involved with her various lovers. She owed Fred money and worked it off by sleeping with a few of his friends. It was pretty cut-and-dry.

"Sue and I have been talking about it," Fred said, pleading with Dawn, "you know, this fantasy that she has about being with another woman. You know how I feel about health issues and such." There was always an agreement between Dawn and Fred that they kept things clean. They cheated on their respective others, but only between themselves. Dawn had no idea that Fred was a whoremonger, picking up hookers whenever the feeling struck him, or that he was sleeping with any woman he met. Dawn, on the other hand, slept only with those friends of Fred's that he could guarantee were clean.

"Fred . . . I don't know about this," Dawn said again. It seemed strange. Her husband, Ed, had wanted to do it, but she refused. Why would she get involved with it now?

"She wants to be with someone else," Fred repeated. "I thought of you. Sue wants a healthy person."

Dawn was silent.

"It would involve the both of us," Fred offered.

"I've never done anything like that before, Fred."

"I just wanted to throw it out there. I'll make it worth your while. Three hundred and fifty dollars," Fred promised. "For *each* time."

"OK."

"You think about it and you call me."

Dawn left.

A few days later, she said, "I thought about it." *What the heck. It couldn't be all that terrible. Let me try it out and see.* In addition, she could use the money. After all, it would just be sex. No intimacy. No feelings. Just casual lesbian sex. What would it hurt?

She picked up the telephone and called Fred.

"Let me come down and see," Dawn said. "I'll make up my mind then. I want to meet this person first."

Fred made a date. "Meet me at my house."

Dawn drove down. Fred's wife was working. It was the middle of the day during the week. Dawn walked in. Fred and Susan were upstairs in Fred's bedroom, waiting.

"We talked about generalities," Dawn explained to me later. "Nothing especially."

Fred and Susan were naked, Dawn said.

"How do you feel about this?" Dawn said Susan asked her as she got undressed.

Dawn shrugged. She didn't really know.

"I should have known at that moment," Dawn recalled, looking back on that first time, "that it was all Fred's idea. I could tell from the way Susan was acting. She impressed me as being withdrawn from the situation, as if she was doing Fred the favor. She wasn't eager to do this. She wasn't excited about it." Dawn and Susan were like two kidnap victims under Fred's spell, caught up in his world of manipulation, believing whatever this man said. "Sue was shy. She was not at all the type of person who would instigate something such as a lesbian affair."

Susan wouldn't look Dawn in the eyes as they began to touch each other and kiss. Fred was the one pushing them both to "perform," if you will. "She was embarrassed, no doubt about it," Dawn said. "It was like she was goaded into something she wasn't hot about doing. And that was not at all what he led me to believe going into it."

The get-togethers between Fred, Susan and Dawn

would generally take place on weekday mornings. As Dawn later explained it to me, she said on one particular day, she pulled up to Fred's house and he was waiting in his car outside. Susan was sitting next to him.

"Follow me," Fred yelled.

And off they went.

It took about fifteen minutes. The two cars—Fred leading the way with Susan, Dawn following behind—filed into one of the water-pumping stations in Poughkeepsie and parked off the beaten path in a small lot. As Dawn got out of her car, she looked at the building, which was set inside a few acres of land by itself with a high chain-link fence encircling it. The windows of the building were semiopaque so no one could see in. As you walked in, there were several large red pipes that fed into the massive water pumps. Toward the back of the building, inside, there was a stairway that walked down into what would be considered a basement, where large valves and pipes were surrounded by concrete walls.

No one was around. Fred had likely set it up—seeing that he was still in charge of the water department then—so that none of his employees would walk in on them or be anywhere near the station.

"For the most part," Dawn later said, "the basement was the better choice because it was belowground. No one could see us. And if someone walked in, we'd hear."

Dawn entered behind Fred and Susan. It was chilly inside the building, quite colder than it was outside, not to mention loud with all the equipment running. Fred had laid out a moving blanket on the concrete floor in the basement.

"You think about it, Fred was spending upward of two hundred dollars a day on hookers," a former friend later observed, "and he couldn't even swing for a motel room for this three-way affair. It's incredible. He called himself classy and cool. But here he was with two ladies in the water department pumping station. It shows how truly disgusting Fred Andros was."

More than that, Dawn later said, she always believed how "clean" Fred was; it was one of the reasons why she agreed to get involved with Susan and the threesome to begin with. "I never saw any of Fred's dirtiness," Dawn later said. "I never knew he had hookers and other women he picked up in bars. He was always so worried—so concerned—about being healthy. He told me Susan was healthy. Clean. We always talked about sexually transmitted diseases."

So not only was Fred putting Dawn at risk, but Susan too.

Fred took off his clothes and put on a fluffy robe shortly after they entered the basement of the building, and Dawn and Susan got started. After they were finished downstairs, Fred said, "Let's go back upstairs. I have something to set up."

Upstairs, Fred had a video camera on a tripod a few yards away from a window. He said something about the lighting from the window would help clarity, that's why they couldn't do it downstairs.

Dawn didn't much care for the idea of the video camera, but what was she to do? she later explained. She had agreed to the ménage à trois. And here she was: Taking part. Being filmed. Doing whatever Fred wanted.

"For all I know, he could have set that camera up without any film in it. I have no idea," Dawn said later. "He focused the camera in on the blanket where we were all going to be, walked away from it, joined us and never went back to it until after we were done."

Fred was the lead, Dawn explained, when it came to sex acts. He was the one telling the girls what to do and how to do it. Susan was especially shy. She really didn't want anything to do with it, but Dawn could tell she was going through with it for Fred's benefit, for his sake entirely.

"Come on, Sue," Fred had said that day he was filming, "now go with it."

Susan just stared at him.

"Everything will be fine," Fred said. "You enjoy it."

As Dawn stood by, fully naked, she could easily tell that it was "never Susan's idea to do this. Fred cajoled her all the way. Now, when I look back, I know this thing was never her idea—it was Fred's."

Fred wasn't belligerent or angry in his direction, Dawn explained. He was nice. "Like he was trying to coax a child into trying a new food for the first time."

Furthermore, Dawn could tell, Susan was inexperienced in the actual lesbian sex acts. She didn't know what to do, which spoke to how it was without a doubt her first time.

"Of course," Dawn recalled, "I had never been with another woman, either. So this was new ground for me, too. But we figured it out."

When it was over, Fred walked Dawn to the door and showed her out. With $50 bills, and a smile on his face, he counted out $350. "Thanks, honey," he said, kissing her on the cheek, "I'll be in touch."

CHAPTER 36

When Dawn was finished admitting to Jim Karic and Bill Gray that she'd had sex with Susan and Fred on numerous occasions, she made sure to add, "Look, this was not retaliation for what my husband did (having an affair). Nor was there any emotional involvement between me and Sue."

"What did Fred do with those videotapes, Dawn?" Karic wondered.

She shrugged. "I don't know. He said he was making them for Sue." Later, Dawn recalled that she was under the impression that "Fred and Susan wanted the tapes for their own private enjoyment. That's what I believed. I don't know that for certain. Fred had told me that he and Susan liked to watch the tapes together."

"How many times did you meet with Fred and Susan?"

According to a report of the interview, Dawn said, "Four or five more times throughout the summer. Fred only videotaped the first time, though."

By now, it was getting well into the late afternoon. Dawn asked for some water. She had poured her soul out, admitting to some rather shameful behavior. Although talking about it didn't seem to rattle her much, it was clear that Dawn had more to divulge. Karic and Gray could see it on her face.

How could Dawn account for murdering Susan? She'd admittedly had sex with Susan on a number of occasions, and now Fred Andros was saying she had murdered Susan in some sort of jealous rage. Fred was saying that he was there, participating in the sex, yes, but this was a relationship between Susan and Dawn. He never set them up. They had taken it upon themselves to hook up. They had fallen in love and Dawn snapped and killed Susan in a jealous fit of rage.

What did Dawn have to say about that theory?

As she talked her way through her relationship with Fred and Susan, Dawn's stories were not falling together so cohesively. After going over what she did on the night of October 28, 1999, backward and forward, Karic explained, "She'd leave out certain parts of the night." She tell it once and leave out the beginning; a second time, and leave out the end; a third, and forget to add the middle.

Karic and Gray could tell Dawn was nervous. Nerves, they knew from experience, made people say and do strange things. The walls were beginning to close in on Dawn Silvernail, and the pressure of lying so much was beginning to unravel her emotionally.

"Can we go through this again?" Karic asked at one point. "We know you're not the bad person here, Dawn."

"I didn't do anything," Dawn continually said. "I didn't kill that woman."

Not getting anywhere, Gray and Karic excused themselves and talked about their lack of progress outside in the hallway. What was their next move? They essentially had to roll the dice. They weren't getting very far, as it was. The ballistics information worked at getting Dawn down to the barracks, but now she didn't seem to care about admitting anything more than having sexual relations with Susan.

It had been a while since Dawn had smoked or had any coffee. There comes a point where a good interrogator deprives his suspect of those nonessential luxuries. Not water or food, mind you, but cigarettes and coffee. So as Dawn started to get anxious after not smoking for a long spell, Karic and Gray spoke with their boss about maybe bringing Ed into the interview. They knew Dawn didn't want to disappoint Ed. They knew she generally cared about him. They could use that against her now. Maybe Ed could get things stirred up. There was a risk involved, but it was worth it.

Karic went in and spoke with Ed, saying, "Listen, Dawn knows more about this than she's telling us." Karic wasn't confrontational or pushy. He sounded more earnest than anything else. "I'm absolutely certain of it. I need you to help me out here, Eddy. Can you do that?"

Ed looked shocked. *What's going on here?* How had his life gone from living in the serene country of the Catskills with his wife to spending the afternoon down at the state police barracks discussing the murder of a woman he didn't even know?

At this time, Ed knew nothing about Dawn's sexual activity with Fred or Susan. BCI didn't want him to know. It was up to Dawn, they decided, to tell him . . . if she wanted. Moreover, BCI was confident by now that Ed had had nothing whatsoever to do with Susan's murder.

Ed looked at Karic. They had known each other a long time. There was an unspoken trust there between them. "I'd like you to go in," Karic said, "and explain to Dawn what's happening."

Ed stood up from his seat. "Absolutely," he said without hesitating. "Let me in and I'll talk to her."

So Ed walked into the room where Dawn was waiting,

Karic and Gray behind him, and told Dawn that the state police wanted to work with her. Karic had explained to Ed that they were willing to work things out and speak with the district attorney (DA) on Dawn's behalf. They couldn't make any promises, but they could vouch for Dawn and Ed. How helpful they had been.

"If you know something about this murder," Ed said to Dawn, "please tell them." Karic was standing nearby, listening. "I love you, Dawn. I'll be by your side," Ed added. "We'll make the best deal we can. Just please, please talk to them."

Ed started walking toward the door. He had said what he needed to say. Dawn was sitting down, with her head in her hands. Karic and Gray were standing. Before Ed left the room, he looked over at Dawn and said one last thing: "Hey . . . now you *buck* up and be a Silvernail!"

Then Ed left the room.

About an hour after Ed walked out, as Karic and Gray spoke with Dawn, Karic noticed Dawn's shoulders had begun to droop. Her face had taken on a somber hue of paleness. Was she finally ready?

Within a few moments of just sitting silent and thinking, Dawn broke down and explained that she wanted to talk about what really happened that night.

"Proceed," Karic said.

Dawn said Fred had telephoned one day and asked for a "big favor"—he wanted her to kill Susan for him because she was going to bury him when it came time for his federal corruption case to go to court. Susan, Fred insisted, was causing him and the "big guy," meaning William Paroli, problems with the corruption probe.

So she needed to go away.

Dawn said she offered to speak to Susan on Fred's behalf. But Fred insisted: "No. She must go!"

After a period of days, and some resistance on her part, Dawn explained, Fred started threatening her family. He turned up the pressure, so she started thinking more seriously about what he had suggested.

From there, she explained how Fred had convinced her to drive to Pleasant Valley that night and meet him at the Kmart shopping mall. "So Fred told me," Dawn explained to Karic and Gray, "to leave the gun in my car and go into Kmart that night and shop for a while. When I came back out, the gun was gone."

"Dawn, did you have the magazine with the gun at that time?" Karic asked.

"Ah, no. I didn't have the magazine then."

"So what you're telling us is, someone took your gun, and just happened to have a magazine and bullets to fit it, shot Susan Fassett, and somehow you got it back?"

Dawn was still talking in circles. It appeared that she didn't really want to come entirely clean. She was turning the case into a classic "he said/she said." Dawn was now trying to take the blame off her shoulders completely and place it *all* on Fred.

She became quiet when Karic caught her lying. "Dawn, we're on your side in this," Karic said with comfort. "We know who the bad guy is here. We know it's not you. Help us out."

Dawn was not a woman of tears. There was no change in her demeanor or posture from one moment to the next. She simply raised her head, shrugged off any anxiety and said rather matter-of-factly, "I shot that poor woman . . . I shot that poor woman . . . I shot that poor woman." And then she broke into her version of events, which, in the end, put Fred Andros at the center of a conspiracy to murder Susan Fassett.

It was odd that it had taken so long for Dawn to come around and give the state police a complete statement from her point of view. Murder for hire, in New York State, at the time, was a capital crime, punishable by the death penalty.

As she told it, Dawn truly believed that Fred was a major player in New York politics. She liked the idea of living in the shadow of what she believed was a powerful man, someone who she thought could get things done with a telephone call. But when the walls crumbled around Fred Andros, Dawn Silvernail slowly began to realize that Fred was no more powerful than the rubble left behind. Fred was just another two-bit con man who wanted people to think he was somebody he was not.

CHAPTER 37

There were no shell casings found at the scene of Susan's murder, BCI learned, because Dawn Silvernail sat in her vehicle when she fired the rounds and not once did a shell casing fall outside her car. Still, maybe BCI could find a few in Dawn's Taurus station wagon.

No luck, she explained. Ed had cleaned out the car. On top of that, Ed reloaded all the shells himself.

As the days progressed, BCI began building its case against Dawn and Fred, who was at home, stewing, wondering what was going on. Fred had been talking crazy lately. He'd been telling those close to him that he was feeling depressed again. Thinking of suicide. Yet, as far as Dawn was concerned, she was in a holding cell in nearby Claverack, beginning to contemplate what in the world she was going to do now that she'd dropped a dime on old Freddy Boy. Her lawyer, Jim O'Neil, was working with the district attorney's office on figuring out a deal. If Dawn could provide evidence against Fred, she wasn't looking at life. With good time, she could possibly even be out one day.

After that second interview with Dawn proved productive, BCI amended the search warrant so troopers could go back into Dawn's house and look for any tools she might have used to mangle the barrel of her gun and anything else that might help them build a case.

As investigators went door to door to see what neighbors could say about Dawn and Ed, something came up.

"They're good neighbors," one woman said, "but I have to call my kids in the house from time to time because they're out there in the backyard firing their weapons at the tree stump."

Forensics was called in and, lo and behold, investigators found several rounds of ammunition in the tree stump that ballistics could, in turn, use to match up against Dawn's .45 and, ultimately, one of the rounds found inside Susan Fassett.

One BCI investigator had been assigned to interview Ed's father, where something even more incriminating turned up.

The Taurus Dawn had purportedly used in the murder had been given to Ed and Dawn by his parents. Ed's parents didn't have much use for Dawn. "They hated her from day one," a former friend recalled. "Maybe it was Dawn's tomboyish ways, or the fact that Dawn controlled things in the house."

What came out of the interview with Ed's parents turned out to be an important piece of the puzzle. "We're very upset with Dawn," Ed's father said. "We gave them that damn car and Dawn turned around and changed the tires. Perfectly good tires! She had them taken off one day for no reason."

The investigator asked when she'd had it done.

"End of October, I believe. Maybe beginning of November."

BCI took the lead and started looking for tire-changing service stations in and around where Dawn worked, figuring she'd drop it off on the way into work. Within a few days, they came up with a tire station a few miles from her job that produced a receipt. Dawn had had her tires changed the day after the murder.

So they went back and asked her about it.

"Fred paid for that," she said.

CHAPTER 38

Things weren't looking too good for Fred Andros. He had to know that once he gave up Dawn's name, she would likely turn around and finger him. At one point the previous night, while Dawn was confessing to the crime, she took the hand of Dutchess County chief assistant DA William O'Neil. He had been brought in to make sure Dawn's rights were protected. Staring at O'Neil, Dawn said, "I'm so sorry . . . so, so sorry. What a dope I am. What an idiot I am to have done such a thing."

On December 29, 1999, a day later, Dawn was still at BCI headquarters in Pleasant Valley. She was waiting with Investigator Darren Forbes and Trooper Scott Rifenburgh, who were there keeping an eye on her. The plan was for Dawn to take a ride with the two troopers and show them exactly where she went after the murder.

"The route you traveled," Forbes said.

"Sure," Dawn agreed. "Let's go."

When they arrived at the parking lot of the United Methodist Church, Dawn was sitting in the front seat with Trooper Rifenburgh, who was driving. From the backseat, Forbes asked, "Where did you go, exactly, after

killing Mrs. Fassett?" He had a notebook in his hand.
"Show us."

"Right up that way," Dawn said, pointing.

For the next twenty minutes, Dawn talked her way
through each step after murdering Susan. It was chilling
to listen to her describe each incident, sounding as if she
were simply talking about a trip to the market.

When they got back to Troop K, investigators asked
Dawn if she was willing to make a telephone call to Fred.
It hadn't been reported yet in the media that Dawn had
been arrested. Investigators wanted to wait, for obvious
reasons. Maybe the call from Dawn could help to implicate Fred and make things a lot easier on everyone.

"They coerced me the night before," Dawn said, "into
calling Fred at two-thirty in the morning. Twenty-five
years I had known that man and never, ever would I have
called him at that time. But I did and he didn't answer."

When she tried again, Fred's son answered. "Yeah."

"Fred . . . there? It's an emergency."

The kid recognized who it was. "I don't give a damn
if it's an emergency or not, I am not getting him." He
hung up.

The investigator said, "Dawn, try again."

When she called back, the kid picked up the telephone
and hung it back up quickly.

When she called a third time, the boy had taken the
telephone off the hook—the line was busy.

Based on the information Dawn had provided BCI,
a search warrant for Fred's house in Hyde Park was
drafted and was waiting to be signed off by a judge.

From the moment Dawn had given up Fred, BCI put
a surveillance team on Fred's house to make sure of his
whereabouts at all times. Art Boyko, who had led the

charge against Fred, knew BCI had enough now to go straight after him.

Fred knew this, too, of course. He was well aware that the case was unraveling before him. How could he not? He had given up Dawn. Did he think it wasn't going to come back to him?

Fred was holed up in his house. BCI had to consider that he had a small stockpile of weapons. It was a volatile situation at the least. When faced with the end, there was no telling how Fred would react.

"Fred had provided Dawn's name," Art Boyko later said. "Obviously, he knew that we were going to speak to her and she was going to say, 'Yeah, you may have me, but go back after him for *these* reasons.'"

So the questions became: Why would Fred even bring Dawn's name into the mix? Why would he give Dawn up, knowing it was going to come back to him in the end?

"We always wondered that," Boyko added. "But he had to. He had a cooperation agreement with the government, so he's got to come up with *something*."

The bottom line was that Fred Andros was not quite as smart as he might have liked to have led people to believe.

Boyko, along with three other members of BCI, showed up in the neighborhood where Fred lived at about 8:00 A.M. on December 30, 1999. Before heading over to Fred's house, Boyko checked with the surveillance team to get a status report.

"He hasn't left," one of the troopers watching the house told Boyko. "We're confident he's in the house."

Boyko shook his head. "All right. Thanks."

Whenever Boyko had gone over to Fred's to talk to him, it had always been just Boyko and, at times, another investigator. This time it was different: Boyko was with three others. They were wearing raid jackets. They had a game plan set up for what they were going to do. It was not another friendly visit to Fred Andros's house to talk things through. BCI needed answers now from Fred— and there was a good chance he wasn't leaving his house without wearing handcuffs.

"One way or another," Boyko said, "we were there to arrest Fred this time. Whether or not he decided to give us a statement, he *was* going to jail. We also wanted Fred to talk to us. It would have been helpful if Fred answered the door, let us in and spoke openly."

That would have been the simple route. But as Boyko was about to learn, Fred wasn't interested in talking on this day.

Boyko and his three colleagues surrounded Fred's house. Knowing Fred fairly well, Boyko knocked on the front door.

No answer.

Fred understood Boyko had always called before he came over. But here was Boyko standing outside the house, knocking on the door, with three other investigators standing at various locations around the house. Surely, Fred knew it was not another friendly visit from Investigator Boyko.

With no answer at the front, Boyko walked over to a side door, which led down into the basement area of the house.

He knocked again. There was some movement inside.

"What is it?" a voice said from behind the door.

It took a while, but Fred's teenage son opened the door.

"Is your dad here?" Boyko asked the kid.

"No!" he shot back angrily. "What do *you* want?"

"You sure?" Boyko could tell the kid had just woken up. He looked sleepy. His hair was matted and unkempt. He was blinking his eyes quickly, adjusting his vision to the outside light.

"No, I said. He's not here."

"How do you know? Looks like you were sleeping."

"Look, he's *not* here!"

"Go check out the house, would you, and come back and let me know," Boyko suggested.

"OK."

The boy walked away from the door while Boyko and his two colleagues waited. There was one investigator still standing by the front door, just in case Fred decided to make a dash for it.

A minute later: "No, no, no. I told you, he's not here."

"OK," Boyko said, "you won't mind then if I have a look myself."

"No, I don't want you coming in here."

"Well, I'm trying to be polite here. We have a search warrant and I'm coming in."

"You can't."

"Yes, I can."

For BCI it was rather simple: the surveillance team indicated that Fred was in the house. But now they had a kid saying he wasn't. This made Boyko and his colleagues even more protective. It had turned into a semihostile environment. The boy had made it such by lying and not cooperating.

Boyko had one of his colleagues pull the kid out of the house as he and the other investigator went in through the basement area where the kid had answered the door. The boy had had a friend sleep over and BCI pulled him out of the house, too.

After not finding anyone in the basement area, Boyko and his partners walked up the stairs into the main floor of the house, where Boyko had been many times already talking to Fred in the dining area.

Guns drawn. Raid mode. "Fred, it's Boyko, you around?" he said, walking slowly up the stairs.

Nothing.

"Fred, it's Art Boyko from BCI, you in here?" he said as he entered the main floor from the basement stairs.

Not a word.

As Boyko and the others were making their way around the main floor, Boyko spotted a set of car keys, pager, wallet, an open newspaper and a coffee mug sitting on the countertop. He could tell someone had just been there. It felt as if someone was having breakfast and had just abandoned the area abruptly.

On the main floor, there was a set of stairs leading up to the third floor (counting the basement), which led to another set of stairs that filed up to an attic area.

"Fred, it's Investigator Boyko!" he said, standing near the bottom of the stairs. "We need to talk to you, Fred. Come on."

Boyko motioned to the others with a head nod that he believed Fred was upstairs. In fact, he seriously thought Fred was hiding out in a closet somewhere, unwilling to face the fact that he was under arrest. It was clear Fred was home. He wasn't answering purposely. "Fred knows," Boyko said later, "at this time that the game is up."

They decided that one investigator would stay on the main floor, while Boyko and the other one (the fourth was still outside with the kids) would head up the stairs slowly, guns leading the way.

Again, as Boyko walked up the stairs, his colleague behind him, he yelled, "Fred? Fred? We're coming up."

They cleared a few bedrooms and failed to locate Fred; then they checked in the closets and under the beds.

No sign of him.

Boyko went into the front bedroom, the room facing the street. All the blinds in the room were closed except for the one blind in the window facing the surveillance team, which was bent up so someone could peek out of it.

Boyko looked toward the bed. On top of the bedsheet

was a long zoom lens. Then he spotted one closet in the room and motioned for his colleague to step to the side of the doorjamb so he could take the other side.

Fred had to be in there.

With his gun in one hand, Boyko carefully opened the door.

Both of them couldn't believe Fred wasn't inside the closet.

They looked at each other. *Where else could he be?*

CHAPTER 39

Investigator Boyko and his colleague returned to the common area of the third floor, near where the stairs brought you up to the landing, and stood for a moment wondering where Fred Andros could be hiding. He had to be in the house. There was no way he could have jumped out a window. But they had looked everywhere.

Or so they thought.

Boyko began scouting the immediate area where he and his colleague were standing and noticed one door they hadn't checked. It was open just a crack. There was a window on the top of the door. The sun had just poked its gaze up and through this particular window and was beating a path down in through the room at the top of the stairs, just beyond the door.

Boyko walked over and, being over six feet tall himself, was able to look up and into the room. As he looked toward the rays of sunlight, he saw dust particles moving about in one direction—as if someone had just walked through the path of the sunlight and stirred up the dust in the room.

"It was a cloud of dust that just moved," Boyko recalled.

The door led to a stairwell that led to the attic.

Damn, he's up there, Boyko thought, looking up the stairs.

Boyko opened the door outward. The stairwell was steep. He looked upward and didn't see anyone. There was room for only one man of his size at a time to walk up the stairs.

"Fred . . . listen, you know why we're here," Boyko yelled up the stairs. "You know what this is about. I need to talk to you about what you did to Susan."

They waited.

Several seconds went by.

No response.

"I'm comin' up, Fred," Boyko said, taking the first step.

As he walked, Boyko heard a creak on the other side of the wall—and then, without warning, a quick pop.

A gunshot.

Bang!

Boyko bolted as fast as he could down the stairs, his partner in front of him. They were back on the second (main) floor again in a few seconds.

No one had been hit. It hadn't sounded like a normal gunshot, either. It was muffled and soft, with just the whisper of a faint thud afterward.

While they were deciphering what had happened, someone called in "shots fired," which mobilized the troops and sent scores of officers heading into Fred's house.

The investigator downstairs and the one outside with the kids hadn't even heard the shot.

Boyko stood at the bottom of the stairs, still wondering what had happened.

"Shh . . . ," he said. Then, "You hear that?"

It was movement. Moaning. Someone was gasping for air.

"Fred?"

Was it a ploy? Had Fred fired at Boyko and missed?

Those investigators standing at the bottom of the stairs had all wondered—especially Boyko.

"Fred, are you up there?" Boyko yelled. "Can you hear me, Fred? Are you hurt?"

No answer.

"Fred, I want you to moan if you're hurt and can hear me."

Boyko heard a weak-sounding groan.

He looked at his colleagues. "He's hurt."

Had Fred shot himself? Was that the sound of his gun going off?

"Fred, I want to come up and help you," Boyko said, "moan if you'd like me to come up and help you."

A slight whine.

Boyko could tell Fred was trying to talk but couldn't.

"Make sure the gun isn't anywhere near you."

Even a semiconscious man with a gun can be dangerous. Fred was moving around on the ground. They could hear him.

"Fred, I'm coming up now and my purpose is to help you. Make sure the gun is not in your hand or anywhere near you. I'd have to interpret the gun in your hand as an aggressive action and take action, Fred. Do you understand me?"

Another faint moaning sound.

Several BCI investigators went up the stairs. When Boyko came around the corner of the attic stairs, he saw Fred lying on his back, the gun a few feet from him. There was a large pool of blood by Fred's side. It appeared he had tried to shoot himself in the head, underneath his chin, but had misfired and shot the bottom of his jaw off, instead.

Near the top of the stairs, on the side of the wall, Boyko noticed where the bullet had lodged into the wall.

He had been standing not a foot from where the bullet had entered the wall.

But how? he wondered, staring at it. If Fred had held the gun underneath his chin and fired, the bullet, if anywhere, would have lodged itself in the ceiling of the room he was standing in.

The bullet had entered Fred's face below his chin, traveled up through the inside of his mouth, shattering his jaw, into his nasal cavity, but then it ricocheted off the inside bone of his upper nose, thus taking a complete ninety-degree turn, traveling out of his body on an east-to-west plane and entering the wall near Boyko's head.

CHAPTER 40

"Whenever someone shoots themselves," Art Boyko later surmised, "he or she is in serious need of medical help. Rarely does a person survive a self-inflicted gunshot wound to the head."

Except, maybe, for Fred Andros—apparently, the luckiest man alive.

"Fred needed our help," Boyko later said. That was their first task. Making sure the guy lived. Didn't matter what Fred had allegedly been involved in; he was in need of medical assistance . . . fast.

Investigator Tom Martin, of forensics, had shown up with a team to collect evidence and was upstairs with Boyko, surveying what they could do for Fred.

"Call an ambulance was about it," Boyko said. "Not much else."

So Boyko and another investigator carried Fred down the stairs and placed him on a stretcher. He was in a tremendous amount of pain.

"He's not going to make it," Boyko said. "I should probably go with him in the ambulance."

Was Fred going to give a deathbed confession? Boyko wanted to make himself available if he did.

As they traveled toward the hospital, Boyko held Fred's hand. By this point, medics had fitted Fred with a neck brace. Boyko could clearly see where the bullet had exited the bridge of Fred's nose and where it had entered and shattered Fred's jaw. There was no way Fred could talk. Moan, sure, he did a lot of that. But words? Not a chance.

The hospital was about ten minutes from Fred's house. Once there, Boyko wouldn't be able to get a crack at Fred anymore. As it was, the medics hadn't really given Fred much in the form of pain medication, so although he had shot himself and was slipping away, his mind was still working.

"Fred, listen," Boyko said as the ambulance raced down the road, "we spoke to Dawn and we know what happened to Susan. Did you want to give your side of the story?"

Fred was staring at Boyko. His eyes open. He certainly understood what Boyko was asking.

Fred started grabbing at the neck brace, whispering best he could, "Get this . . . off . . . me . . . right now."

Boyko had to strain to hear him, but had no trouble understanding what Fred was trying to say. "You can get off your chest whatever you want to, Fred," Boyko said.

No matter what Fred was trying to say, Boyko wanted to later make clear, "I wasn't going to interfere with them if they needed to save him. . . . His life certainly came before me trying to get a confession out of him."

BCI had enough to arrest Fred if he survived, and didn't confess.

"And that would have been enough," Boyko added, "but we still wanted to hear from his *mouth*, 'I did it. You got me. I'm guilty.'"

Fred wouldn't say anything in the ambulance. When they arrived at the hospital, emergency personnel took him away and Boyko was left without a confession, not knowing if Fred was going to live or die. The hospital, in fact, thought Fred was in such bad shape that it wound up airlifting him to a larger hospital in Westchester County, where Fred was stabilized.

He had survived.

When Boyko found out hours later that Fred was going to live, he knew then that he'd be driving to Westchester County within the next few days to make a formal arrest.

CHAPTER 41

The senior assistant DA of Dutchess County, Edward "Ned" McLoughlin, wasn't a hard-nosed public official looking to the DA's office as a stepping-stone toward a political career. Ned was on the job solely representing the victims of crime. He liked putting away criminals, whether vicious and predatory, such as the case of Dawn Silvernail and Fred Andros, or a simple drunk driver, who had put the entire community in jeopardy.

Ned looked more like a college professor than a trial attorney, yet he was one of the best the county had. His boss, District Attorney William Grady, echoed Ned's sentiments where victims were concerned, releasing a statement once that said, "My staff and I are committed to insuring that offenders are held accountable for their criminal conduct. We are also committed to assuring that the voices of victims are heard and that their experiences with the criminal justice system are as safe and convenient as possible."

With Dawn, Ned had a decision to make: offer the woman a deal and use her to prosecute Fred, or go after both of them separately.

Dawn was officially charged with first-degree murder

and arraigned during the first week of January 2000. The role she would eventually play for Ned and the prosecution would have to be worked out later. Right now, Dawn was facing life behind bars if she was found guilty.

Since Fred had shot himself, several things came to light. For one, the chief assistant U.S. attorney in White Plains, Andrew C. McCarthy, came out and released a statement to quell any rumors that Susan had been murdered because of her role in Fred's federal case. "Sue Fassett was not a witness or prospective government witness in the Paroli case," the U.S. attorney said. "I cannot say anything further."

With former Republican Elections Committee chair William Paroli's name being tossed around in the same light with Fred Andros, Paroli also came out and spoke up for himself, telling the *Poughkeepsie Journal* in early January that he *never talked to Fassett about his case or Andros.* When the newspaper pressured Paroli for a "theory," however, regarding what might have happened, Paroli seemed to say what everyone else in town was thinking: *He . . . believed Fassett may have been trying "to get away from Andros and may have threatened to talk to federal authorities about some of his alleged dealings in the town. Anything Sue had to say (to federal investigators) would have been favorable to my situation and would have shown what a liar Fred Andros was."*

Jim Karic was on fairly good terms with Dawn. He had questioned her for hours with his partner back in December and had visited Dawn in jail several times to see what else she might be willing to divulge. BCI knew that Dawn and Fred were still holding out. With Fred still recuperating from his wounds, Dawn was the only one who could provide information. It was good for Karic to keep the communication line open with Dawn and Big Ed in case Dawn decided to talk and Ned decided to offer her some sort of plea deal to testify against Fred.

By this point, Fred had brought in Noel Tepper and Mary Jo Whateley, two of Poughkeepsie's more expensive and well-known defense attorneys. Tepper, in fact, had had his moment in the spotlight once. Decades before taking on Fred's case, Tepper represented none other than American writer and psychedelic drug advocate Timothy Leary, the "Lord of LSD," who insisted the use of the drug had not only therapeutic but spiritual benefits.

One of the last times Karic went to see Dawn in prison, he asked her about Susan. BCI had heard that Fred was going to go with the story that the three-way was Susan's idea from the get-go—that she had wanted it.

"No, no, no," Dawn said. "She wasn't into it. She was no more into it than I was. It was *all* for Fred."

Fred Andros was a bastard when he wanted to be. As the Town of Poughkeepsie water superintendent, Fred ran the show. During the mid-to-late 1990s, there was a mini building-boom taking place along Route 9 in Poughkeepsie. Commercial buildings were going up all over the place. Strip malls. Offices. Stores. You name it.

And every building, if its owner wanted water, had to be zoned and OK'd through Fred Andros.

Fred was suave about it. He'd allow the permits for a builder to get started on a project. Then he'd go to the site a few weeks into it and start bothering the contractor. "Hey, those lines cannot go there."

"What do you mean?" one builder asked him.

"I said those water lines are in the wrong place!"

"You OK'd this, however."

"That's what I want," Fred raged, walking around the site, his stumpy little arms flinging in the air as he spoke loudly, "and you'll do it."

"Or what?"

"Or this building will sit here unfinished without the right permits."

The builder broke things down, rearranged the lines the way Fred wanted them and asked Fred to have another look.

He OK'd it.

Then he'd let the guy finish the job, and before the water was turned on, Fred would go to him and say, "You know, it still doesn't look right. I need you to change it back."

The builder was furious.

Then the shakedown: "Well, you could leave it the way it is, but you'll have to begin paying me."

CHAPTER 42

D. James O'Neil, or just Jim, as his friends called him, had been an assistant district attorney in Poughkeepsie from 1977 to 1989, when he went into private practice. Jim's primary function as a practicing private attorney is criminal. In early January, O'Neil received a call from someone of "importance" at the courthouse who explained to him that there was an extremely fragile case that had the potential to be very high-profile. It involved a cop's wife, who had been murdered; a former town official; some scandalous sex; and a Catskill housewife turned killer, who needed a lawyer.

"I'll take it," Jim said without hesitation. He thought it would be interesting. He had seen newspaper stories about the crime.

Dawn was still being housed at the Dutchess County Jail in downtown Poughkeepsie, not too far from Jim's office. He went down to sit and talk with Dawn immediately. He needed to get her side of the story.

"She was scared," Jim later said. "Dawn had made admissions to the police and she was concerned about what she had said."

BCI investigators had told Dawn they were on her

side. If she cooperated, she could depend on the DA's office to at least hear her out and maybe work on a plea bargain. It had been days, however, since Dawn had admitted her role and she still hadn't heard anything. According to what Dawn was telling Jim, BCI said "things were going to work out."

Jim's first order of business was to find out exactly what Dawn had said and how he could possibly get those statements tossed out of the case. If he could do that, the DA *had* no case. "First," Jim told me, "I needed to look at if there was proof sufficient enough to sustain the charges. Sometime it's scientific evidence. Sometimes it's circumstantial evidence. Other times it's based in part on a confession. When it's a confession, as in Dawn's case, automatically, as a lawyer, you begin to assess the circumstances of the taking of the confession."

Were Miranda rights offered? Was the suspect threatened in any way? Made promises? What could you do as a lawyer to suppress the admissions?

Of course, BCI had been very careful not to repudiate Dawn's rights. As Jim read Dawn's statements over a few days, he was certain that Dawn had slit her own throat, but he was going to do everything in his power to see that those statements were tossed out, or an offer, which had been talked about as part of her confession, was put on the table.

Art Boyko made his way to White Plains and stepped into Fred Andros's hospital room, hoping to sit and talk with Fred. However, Fred wasn't in such good shape. If Fred had looked the least bit homely before his suicide attempt, he now had the face of a bulldog or Pekinese, a pushed-in and disfigured jawline, to the point of being grotesque. But he was still alive—which was all BCI and Art Boyko were concerned about at the moment.

BCI had placed a 24/7 watch at Fred's door. He was in police custody and under arrest, even though he was struggling to heal after such a devastating injury and emergency reconstructive surgery.

Fred was in a tremendous amount of pain. Fully medicated. But Boyko still wanted to hear from him. Considering it was a head injury, Fred's face and brain had swelled. Gases from the bullet had caused an infection.

After a while of getting no response from him, Boyko handed Fred a piece of paper.

He scribbled something. It was hard to read.

Lawyer, maybe. *I can't talk,* perhaps. Boyko had a hard time making any of it out. So he walked out. Fred barely knew his own name. There was no way he could answer any questions.

The following morning, however, Boyko went back. First thing he did was Mirandize Fred and make him aware of his rights. Fred acted as though he was having difficulty communicating, and probably was, considering all the tubes coming out of his face.

"I need to ask you some questions, Fred," Boyko said.

Fred still wasn't able to verbalize his thoughts. The tubes in his mouth were draining the fluids from his head. So Boyko established a way for the two of them to communicate. Boyko's right hand became a "yes" for Fred, he explained. His left was obviously "no." All Fred had to do was squeeze either hand to indicate his answers to the questions.

To make sure they understood each other, Boyko had Fred answer a few basic questions they both knew to be true: name, town, age.

Fred proved he was clear on everything.

After several questions about Dawn, the gun and the

murder, Boyko realized he wasn't going to get anywhere. Fred wasn't interested in answering.

"Are you at least sorry for what you did to Susan?" Boyko asked at one point, hoping to get Fred to show a bit of mercy or compassion. The question, Boyko could immediately tell, got Fred's attention. He perked up. Looked at the investigator sharply.

But he still wouldn't answer.

Boyko then moved in closer, leaning in to Fred's ear. "Listen, can't you at least say that you're sorry for what you did to Susan, Fred?"

Fred turned. Took Boyko's "yes" hand, placed it over his heart, held it with both of his hands crossed over and nodded his head in agreement.

There was no telling if Fred was actually sorry for what he had done, or just trying to maybe sneak his way into heaven. But to Boyko, the only part of the conversation that mattered was that Fred had admitted he was sorry for killing Susan—and thus, in Boyko's mind, admitted he had participated in murder.

CHAPTER 43

Jim O'Neil knew it was not going to be easy to represent Dawn Silvernail, which was maybe one of the reasons why he had agreed to take on the case to begin with. Jim grew up in Hudson, New York, an hour or so north of Poughkeepsie, where he had moved to and settled in 1969 in order to attend Marist College. As Jim was going through college, he interned at the Dutchess County District Attorney's Office, which he was now facing off against as Dawn's attorney. After graduation Jim went north and attended Vermont Law School, where he graduated in 1977.

"I decided that the DA's office was what I wanted to do," Jim later said, reflecting on those years right after law school. "The day after I graduated, I went to work for the DA."

Jim saw his share of bizarre and interesting cases over the years while working for the DA; his first trial—which he won—was for a misdemeanor charge, a $25 fine a guy didn't want to pay.

Throughout the years, Jim said, he has tried between seventeen and twenty murder cases. As the years went by, Jim watched a lot of his colleagues in the DA's office leave to go into private practice, using the connection

with the DA as a way to build up clientele. It was the
thrill of starting from scratch and beginning all over
again that bit Jim ten years into his tenure at the DA's
office. So he left, too.

The difference, Jim said, between his own practice
and working in the DA's office became the creativity involved on the defensive end of justice. "As a defense
lawyer," he said, "you have to be creative. It's challenging
to try to figure out different ways of defending people.
In the DA's office, number one, you're *expected* to win.
If you take on a case as a DA and decide to prosecute it,
you did it because you *believed* the person was guilty and
you could convict him. If you didn't think he was guilty,
why would you even take on the case to begin with?"
Working as a defense attorney, Jim added, "The cards
are stacked against you in most cases."

Jim's philosophy (and task) in defending those accused of murder is pretty simple: "What can I do to help
my client?" It seemed Dawn had dug a hole for herself—
looking at the file against her, Jim knew it was going to
be extremely difficult for her to get out of it. "There appeared to be a lot of evidence on top of a confession."
Furthermore, reading the confession Dawn had signed,
Jim believed it would be sustained—that the court was
going to hold it up and rule in the DA's favor, admitting it if Dawn took her case to trial.

After weighing their options carefully, Jim went to
Dawn and asked her if she wanted to cooperate with the
DA's office. She had already expressed interest.

As Jim was going through their options, the DA's office
just happened to call and ask about making a deal to nail
Fred. The problem with Dawn was that she was under the
impression that if she gave BCI a confession and cooperated, she was *not* going to receive a substantial sentence,
anyway—which was untrue. No one had ever promised

Dawn no or little jail time. It had never been discussed. What investigators had said to Dawn as they interrogated her was, *"You help us and we'll try to help you."*

The first offer came in as twenty-two years to life.

Dawn blew a gasket. "Twenty-two to life? Are they crazy?"

"No," Jim told Ned McLoughlin over the telephone a few days after receiving the offer. "My client won't take that."

And so negotiations between them were on.

CHAPTER 44

On Thursday, February 17, 2000, Fred Andros was well enough to show his new face for the first time in public as he appeared before Judge Thomas J. Dolan to answer charges of second-degree murder. Fred wore a dark blue, two-piece suit against a white shirt; however, it was the shiny shackles dangling and clanking around his wrists and waist that stood out more than his chosen garb.

Fred stood next to Noel Tepper for most of the eight-minute proceeding, which was nothing more than a mere formality. Fred had been moved from Westchester County Medical Center just a few weeks ago to Dutchess County Jail in Poughkeepsie. On the day Fred was placed in the jail, Dawn was moved also, to Putnam County Jail in Carmel, thirty miles south of Poughkeepsie, so she wouldn't be under the same roof with Fred.

The main reason for Fred's appearance was to plead not guilty, which he did without equivocation, almost smugly, with a sharp attitude and a "how dare you all accuse me of this crime" inflection. Fred was taking his case to trial. There was no way, he told friends and family, he was going down for something Dawn Silvernail had done on her own. From this day on, Fred's defense

would be that Dawn and Susan had a lesbian relationship between them, and Dawn had become enraged at
Susan after she spoke of ending it and thus took it upon
herself to murder Susan in an act of revenge.

"When they searched my house," Dawn told me later,
"they took my computer, address books, personal letters,
and there was nothing, I mean nothing, that tied Susan
and [me] together. Fred was, well, being Fred—passing
the buck once again."

One would think Dawn and Susan would have
e-mailed each other, or called each other. Or that Dawn
would have a note from Susan, her telephone number,
or something tying the two of them together.

But there was nothing.

"Fred was miffed at Susan," Dawn said, "because for
once in his life, he had been dumped. He had always
played the dumper in the relationship. Now Susan [was]
the dumper—and Fred *couldn't* take that type of rejection. So he asked me to kill her."

Dawn explained that when she went off to Tennessee
soon after they had started a sexual relationship, back in
the early 1980s, one reason why she left was to get away
from Fred. That was why she never told him she was leaving, or where she had moved.

But Fred found her.

"He called me," she recalled, "out of the blue one day.
I had moved around the state for six years, many, many
different times. There was *no* way he could have kept
track because we didn't speak. Then he calls me one day."
She was convinced that the call was his way of saying, "No
one walks out on Fred Andros."

What was clear after Noel Tepper finished addressing
reporters out in front of the courthouse after Fred

pleaded not guilty was that Fred Andros was in no shape
to stand trial at the moment. Once a fairly fit man, full
of vigor and sexual cravings and thirst for life, Fred was
still suffering from the injuries he had inflicted upon
himself. Tepper said Fred was "moderately depressed,"
adding that he still had a tube in his stomach, which was
going to have to be removed soon. "He has severe,
severe headaches," Tepper announced, "and he also has
major memory lapses. If he were to stand trial tomorrow,
I would be reluctant to have him attend the trial."

The judge continued Fred's case until March 3, 2000.
Ned McLoughlin said he'd be prepared.

When March 3 came, Fred's case was continued once
again. Rumors swirling about town were that Dawn Silvernail had cut a sweet deal with the prosecution to testify against Fred. It was shaping up to be a "he said/she
said" murder trial the likes of which Poughkeepsie had
never seen. But getting Dawn to the point where she was
ready to go up against Noel Tepper, however, was going
to be another matter entirely. What trial watchers and reporters didn't know was that the backroom talks Dawn
had entered into with the DA's office had become somewhat of a circus—and Dawn herself would sustain a devastating physical injury in the coming days.

CHAPTER 45

Dawn Silvernail, Jim O'Neil, Art Boyko, Jim Karic, DA Ned McLoughlin and a few additional investigators, as well as Ed Silvernail, were all together in the DA's office one afternoon discussing Dawn's plea deal. The previous day, Ed Silvernail had visited Dawn in jail and referred to her to the guards as "Trigger." In doing so, the guard had asked Ed, "What are you talking about? There's no Trigger here."

Ed laughed, a source at the jail reported later, and said rather matter-of-factly, "That one that killed the woman, the trigger girl, Dawn."

From that day on, everyone called Dawn "Trigger." She'd walk by a group of inmates and they'd all stick out their hands and make an impression of a gun, like kids playing cops and robbers. "Hey, it's Trigger!"

"They'd do this and act like I was some sort of hero, as if they were proud of me," Dawn said, breaking down as she recalled the memory, "and I was no hero. I wasn't proud of me. Not at all."

Standing in the DA's office that afternoon, however, Ed Silvernail was not laughing anymore. During the conversation Dawn was having with the DA, she had mentioned something about the fact that she and Susan had a lesbian affair.

"What's that about? What does that mean?" Ed asked.

Everyone looked perplexed: *He doesn't know yet?*

"It's nothing, Eddy," Dawn said, "I'll tell you about it later."

Dawn couldn't seem to find her way behind bars. As the weeks wore on, with Ed finally hearing about what she and Susan had done for Fred Andros, Ed had all but written her off. He felt slighted. Maybe not because Dawn had had a lesbian tryst—but more so because it seemed that everyone except him had known about it.

Yet things would get worse for Dawn before they got better. There was one day before she was transferred when Dawn was helping out with moving some things around the common room. "Dawn liked [the jail]," a former friend said, "the food was good, it was clean, and she could smoke."

Being a big gal, Dawn had volunteered to help with moving what was a divider that ran from one end of the room to the other. It was one of those fanlike accordion dividers that open auditoriums install to separate what is a large room into two smaller rooms.

As they were moving the divider across the room, Dawn had a firm grip on one end, but it started to roll toward the other side quickly and she could not get her entire hand out of the way before the momentum created by its own weight slammed it closed. As it met the opposite end of the room, the heavy partition dug into Dawn's middle finger—and when she reacted to the pain by pulling the finger out from between the wall and the door, she peeled off the skin on her finger, leaving just the bare bone exposed, like stripping a piece of coating off copper wire.

Dawn screamed. Went down.

The tip of her finger, from the first knuckle, was gone.

CHAPTER 46

The DA felt he had a solid case against Dawn if he decided to take it to trial, which was one of the main reasons why Dawn had been offered a deal of twenty-two to life. After all, beyond a strong case, the DA wanted Dawn to pay for what she had done with some serious time in the slammer.

Dawn, of course, thought otherwise.

Jim O'Neil was hoping for a manslaughter charge, which carried a term of eight to twenty-five. Dawn would be out in ten. But Dawn hadn't been in a drunken stupor and run Susan over with her car. Nor had she mistakenly killed her by some other "accident." No, Dawn had left her house that evening with the *intention* of murdering Susan Fassett. Charging Dawn with manslaughter would be to spit on Susan's grave. The Fassett family wouldn't stand for such a thing. Dawn had *murdered* Susan.

Jim and Dawn's problem was that there was no chance of the DA offering a manslaughter charge, and there was no chance of Dawn agreeing to twenty years to life. They were at an impasse: no side wanted to budge.

After a few weeks, Dawn reconsidered her options. And as she did that, the DA's office called with "eighteen to life." Without saying as much, Jim O'Neil understood it was the DA's *final* offer.

In the state of New York, an inmate serves the minimum amount of time sentenced, which meant Dawn, with good behavior, could be out of prison, after deliberately and intentionally murdering Susan Fassett, in eighteen years.

With that, knowing the DA was not going to come down, Dawn took the deal. In court, on March 27, 2000, she made it all official. At fifty years old, a gray-haired woman who had made a mess of what had been a simple life of living in the Catskill Mountains with her husband, working with the disabled, now stood in front of the judge. Dawn looked weak in her blue denim skirt and long-sleeved white shirt. Jim O'Neil stood by Dawn's side, comforting her as best he could as she wept.

During the proceeding, Dawn said, she was on anti-anxiety medication and also pain medication for the injury she had received to her finger, which was still wrapped in a bandage.

"I understand the consequences of my plea," Dawn acknowledged.

The judge had DA Ned McLoughlin go through and ask Dawn a series of questions, beginning with if she recalled being in the parking lot of the church on the night of October 28, 1999.

"Yes," she answered somberly.

"And did there come a time when you came into contact with a woman named Susan Fassett?" McLoughlin wanted to know next.

"I knew her as Sue, or Susan," Silvernail said.

"And what did you do on that night?" McLoughlin queried.

"I pointed my .45-caliber Ruger pistol and shot the lady six times," Dawn replied.

It was here where Dawn began to break down and cry louder and more animatedly.

Then the money question: "Was Fred Andros involved in the crime?"

"Yes," Dawn gladly said.

"Did Fred Andros request and demand that you kill Susan Fassett?" McLoughlin asked.

"Yes, he did," Dawn said stoically.

It took an additional month for a grand jury to indict Fred Andros, but the DA's office released a statement on April 26, 2000, that Fred was facing new charges in the death of Susan Fassett. He was indicted under second-degree conspiracy charges, as well as the original accusation of second-degree murder. With Dawn prepared to testify against Fred, the DA believed there was no way Fred Andros was going to get out of this one. He might have pushed people around his entire life, and made himself out to be some sort of big shot, but Fred Andros was staring down the barrel of a life sentence—considering he was sixty years old.

CHAPTER 47

Dawn's primary function for the DA's office was to explain exactly what she knew about Fred's role in the murder of Susan Fassett, beyond adding every minor detail she could recall. It was time for Dawn to set the record straight and lay it all out on the table—and, in turn, help the DA build a case against Fred Andros.

By now, seventy-one-year-old William Paroli had pleaded guilty in federal court to one count of conspiracy to commit extortion. He was scheduled to be sentenced after Fred's federal case concluded. Fred had been next in line for the feds—that is, until he was charged with murder. He was set to appear in front of the judge on extortion and corruption charges. In the span of one year, Fred Andros's life had made a complete about-face. As he sat in Dutchess County Jail, still recovering from the self-inflicted gunshot wound to the face, his fourth wife, Diana, set in motion the wheels to divorce him. It would be the third divorce for Fred (his third wife died of breast cancer). Reportedly, Fred had been making $72,000 a year when he was tossed out of the water department. Not a bad salary for a guy who had never gone to college and had been skimming off the top for a number of years without getting caught. But now, as Dawn began to explain how Fred planned and executed the murder of Susan Fassett, Fred's corruption case seemed like a misdemeanor compared to what he could get if convicted of conspiracy to commit murder.

For hours at a time, Dawn sat while DA Ned McLoughlin drilled her with questions. Ned needed to prepare Dawn best he could for Noel Tepper, who he knew could be intimidating in the courtroom. What Ned got, however, no one expected.

Out of nowhere one day, Dawn said, "There was another person involved in the murder."

Dawn viewed Ned as a "very riotous prosecutor," she later told me. "He was really into what he was doing. It got to the point where . . . I'm being shuffled back and forth from the jail to his office in shackles and chains, and it got to be a drag. One day I was kind of annoyed because Ned had tried to pull my husband into this thing. At one time, Ned seemed to think that I was protecting Ed. That Ed had helped me and maybe backed out, or whatever. He also thought Ed might have had something to do with disfiguring the gun barrel."

This upset Dawn. So, on one particular afternoon, as Art Boyko and Jim Karic, Dawn's attorney Jim O'Neil and several others sat in the room, listening, taking notes, she decided to get Ned back for all the "bullshit" he had put her through.

After Dawn said there had been someone else involved, she believed they all sat up and thought, *Aha! It was Ed!*

And she enjoyed the moment.

"What? There was someone else there?" Ned asked, according to several in the room that day.

"Yeah. Some guy I just met at a bar," Dawn said. "I brought him along."

"You're kidding?"

"No. He was involved as well."

One person in the room later told me, "Honestly, I still have questions about the validity of the stories, as provided by Fred and Dawn. I don't know that Dawn ever gave a one hundred percent accurate account. I'm sure it was self-serving."

"What if," Dawn said, speaking to Ned again, "I told you somebody I knew actually altered the gun?"

Jim O'Neil looked over toward Dawn with his mouth agape, and Ned's "whole demeanor changed," Dawn said.

"What are you saying? What are you saying?" Ned asked.

No one could believe it. Dawn sat there and went into great detail about where she met the guy and how she convinced him to participate in the murder. She described the guy down to what he was wearing, his facial expressions, what he had said.

For the next three sessions (days), Dawn and Ned went back and forth about this new suspect. According to two sources in the room, the DA's office was captivated and, at the same time, befuddled and stunned. Dawn was transfixed by the discussion, totally absorbed in bringing out this new person. She sounded sincere. Articulate. Poised. Seemingly sure of each and every detail she could add to the case.

At one point, Dawn said she had never gone over to Susan's house on the night of the murder, that the person in the Fassett driveway Jef and Jason Fassett saw walking up the dirt path wasn't her.

"No," she said. "That was not me."

"Are you sure?" Ned asked. He was befuddled. It was as if everything he thought he knew about the case was now untrue.

"Absolutely. Not me. Never happened. You're talking

about somebody else entirely." Dawn waved her arms around. "I'm telling ya, it *wasn't* me."

Ned became upset at one point, and according to Dawn, he threatened to take the plea deal off the table. He then sent her back to her prison cell and let her sit there for a few more days.

Sometime later, about halfway into a new discussion about the guy she met and took with her to the murder scene, Dawn paused for a moment, smiled and said, "I'm just messing with you, Ned. None of what I've said is true."

"What? What do you mean?"

She laughed. "I made it all up. That was me in the driveway. There was no one else involved."

Dawn had wasted everybody's time. She had been playing games with the DA's office, having a little fun at everyone's expense. "As much as they had messed with me," Dawn said later, "this was my payback. You must understand, this was an extremely stressful situation for me. It was my first arrest. The first time I had ever been in any trouble. I didn't know what to expect. Sometimes, my self-protection when dealing with stress is putting on a flip front, if you know what I mean. You see, after I did this (lied to Ned), they all stopped badgering me. So it worked. . . . What it boiled down to was that Ned made me mad by trying to drag my husband into this. So I got him back."

CHAPTER 48

By the first of April, Ed Silvernail had had enough of reading the newspapers about his wife's affair with another woman, which had culminated in murder. Ed and Dawn's life had become a punch line—some sort of joke for the people in the bar and at the diner and around town to laugh at and make fun of. For those who knew them as the hokey couple who loved to hunt and hang out together and shoot the trees in their backyard, to think that Dawn had been running around with the troll of Dutchess County—Fred Andros—*and* the woman Dawn murdered was not only a shock, but disgraceful, embarrassing and, of course, unbelievable.

Dawn and Ed owned a thirty-two-foot boat they had loved to sail up and down the Hudson River together. With the thaw of April, Ed had gotten the boat ready early and prepared to take a long trip. The papers had been drawn up and he filed for divorce; although, Ed admitted later, he "still loved" his wife. When the *Poughkeepsie Journal* caught up with Ed near this time, he said he couldn't believe what had happened. That person who had admitted to the murder and lesbian tryst wasn't the woman he had been married to for the past twelve years.

Ed told the reporter Dawn was the *"kind of woman who would bring homeless people home and give them dinner."* He said Dawn had a tough time swatting flies.

But murder? Lesbian sex? He couldn't believe it, as much as he accepted it.

Ed said he was taking the boat and sailing away. He was going to start in Long Island and wherever the water and wind took him was not far enough away from what was going on at home.

In conclusion, the *Journal* asked Ed what he thought of Fred Andros. *"I'd like to watch him burn."*

By the end of June 2000, Fred Andros faced a federal judge and was sentenced to thirty-three months in prison for his role in the Poughkeepsie corruption scandal. Fred could have received upward of five years and fines near a quarter of a million dollars. Yet the judge was lenient, which no one could quite understand. In any event, Fred addressed Judge Barrington Parker in a quiet, solemn voice, saying rather defiantly, "I've nothing to say. Thank you."

Barrington explained how Fred had manipulated his position of power and taken advantage of people, causing "such a profound damage to the community."

Many on hand sat quietly, shaking their heads, realizing the judge's words were an understatement.

Fred shook his head, too, and sighed, as if he'd had nothing to do with what Barrington suggested.

What the community found most interesting about Fred's court appearance was what Assistant U.S. Attorney Mark Godsey explained to Judge Barrington: the fact that Fred, in conspiring to murder Susan Fassett, had undermined the government's case against William Paroli, who could have faced many years behind bars.

But since Fred had destroyed his credibility as a witness, the government had to cut its losses and cut a plea deal with Paroli.

"It had a very detrimental effect on our case against Mr. Paroli," Godsey told the judge in a defeated tone. "Fred Andros was our star witness! We dropped some counts against Mr. Paroli that we probably wouldn't have dropped."

Some later said this comment brought a faint smile to Fred's disfigured face.

Still, no matter how good (or bad) Fred Andros felt about bilking the town he had been employed by for over three decades, the fact that the government case was concluded had now opened the door for DA Ned McLoughlin to drag Fred back into court to face murder charges. This was where real prison time was at stake. Any potential juror following the Andros-Paroli corruption scandal, upset over how both men seemingly got slaps on the wrists, could get old Freddy Boy back when it came time for him to face the fact that the DA had an overwhelming amount of evidence to convict Fred on murder.

CHAPTER 49

With the summer of 2000 bearing down on Dutchess County, Fred's attorney Noel Tepper got to work on filing motions to suppress certain evidence the NYSP had collected. Fred's trial was slated to start in October or November, but for now, both sides were resigned to wait.

Tepper wanted a court-appointed psychiatrist to test Dawn to see if she was off her rocker, or ready to sit and testify.

The judge said no.

Fred's defense was saying that Dawn acted alone in murdering Susan Fassett; the two had had a lesbian affair and a lover's quarrel, and Dawn murdered Susan in a rage.

Dawn could only laugh when she heard. Moreover, the DA's office was certain Fred and Dawn and Susan's telephone records would explain the relationship in full.

Over the course of the summer, both sides hammered it out and finally agreed on what would make it into trial. For Noel Tepper, no one could knock the guy for trying to get everything that he could thrown out.

Perhaps the most incriminating of the statements Fred had made to Art Boyko was at Westchester Medical Center, when Boyko and Fred were communicating via hand signals. Tepper was appalled that a judge might consider such a gesture "evidence."

The judge set a suppression hearing for the beginning of December, noting that the trial was likely going to be postponed until after the 2000 holiday season and would begin sometime in 2001. During the first day of the hearing, Dutchess County court judge Thomas J. Dolan sat patiently as FBI Agent James O'Connor testified how he and several other agents questioned Fred near Christmas 1999 after the NYSP called to say they believed Fred was lying to them about his role in Susan's murder.

O'Connor explained how he "confronted" Fred with the inconsistencies in his story, telling the judge, "At first, he said he believed [Jef] Fassett might have done it. But he then changed his story and said . . . William Paroli had killed her."

When it was his turn, Noel Tepper stood and reminded O'Connor that Fred had made an agreement with the feds, asking, "Was he ever told that he'd had a right *not* to respond to questions?" Tepper's tone was accusatory, as if he were trying to shift the weight of the conversation back onto O'Connor's shoulders, implying that the feds had done something wrong.

"He was told that he had a *duty* to respond," O'Connor replied, not backing down.

Tepper wanted to know if Fred had been advised of his constitutional right to remain silent.

O'Connor laughed. "He was with his attorney."

As the hearing continued, Dawn Silvernail was making news herself. It seemed that Dawn had found a lawyer in New York City to sue the Town of Poughkeepsie for the finger she lost during the accident at the jail. Papers filed with the clerk indicated that Dawn was seeking $2 million

in damages for losing part of her finger. The suit placed
the blame on the corrections guard who was helping
Dawn close the folding divider. Dawn's lawyer made the
claim that Dawn was a secretary and that the loss of the
fingertip would severely hamper her typing skills, which
disallowed her to make an honest living after she was released.

In a murder case that seemed to have every plot twist
and sexy moment a hit soap opera had, nothing was over
the top. Here was a woman who admitted murdering a
woman in a church parking lot that she'd had lesbian
sex with on a number of occasions now suing the prison
holding her.

"To look at it on paper," a town resident said, "well, it
all just seemed too incredible to be true."

CHAPTER 50

Ned McLoughlin wanted to nail down a few more things with Dawn before the start of trial. He needed to speak with her again to make sure she knew what needed to be done. No surprises. No last-minute changes to her story. No strange behavior on her part while in the courtroom.

After clearing it with Jim O'Neil, Ned McLoughlin and Jim Karic took off one day before the trial and went to see Dawn at Putnam County Jail.

Dawn's injury wasn't quite as simple as maybe both men had thought after hearing about it. The way the accident had been described led Karic and Ned to believe that Dawn's finger had been snipped off rather quickly, like a pruned branch. That maybe beyond the immediate pain and shock, the accident wasn't all that traumatizing.

But that wasn't the case. The door had, in fact, peeled the skin off Dawn's middle finger. It was extremely painful and grotesque. The bone of the finger had stayed intact. It was not until the doctor snipped the bone off at the hospital that Dawn had lost the entire top of her finger.

When Ned and Jim Karic walked into the visiting area of the jail, Dawn was standing behind the glass partition.

She was smiling. She had her stub raised in the air at both men.

As the two of them sat down, Dawn addressed Ned specifically, saying, "I guess you've got your pound of flesh from me now, don't you!" while shoving her stub into the glass.

Dawn was still trying to coerce Ned into knocking off additional years, but the deal had been done. Ned had declined. She was lucky to have the eighteen.

"Listen," Ned said wryly, "you stalked this poor woman, you shot her, you took her away from her family, and you—"

Dawn interrupted. She was shaking her head. "But what about me? What about me, Ned?"

Jim Karic and Ned looked at each other. After a few more unimportant questions, they got up and left. In their mind, it was clear to them that Dawn Silvernail cared about one person.

Jury selection began on schedule on January 25, 2001, as Judge Dolan ruled that the statements Fred had made to Art Boyko while under the influence of prescribed medication were not going to be admissible during trial. It was a blow to the DA. Still, Ned McLoughlin was no neophyte; he understood how to take the good with the bad. He still had boxes full of evidence to present—most notably, an expert who was going to prove that Dawn and Susan didn't even know each other beyond the sexual rendezvous Fred had set up between them for his own sick benefit.

By January 29, at 11:00 A.M., according to the clerk's minutes of the day, Dutchess County court judge Thomas Dolan read his instructions to the jury and then nodded to Ned. "Proceed."

Ned McLoughlin stood from his seat inside the second-floor downtown Poughkeepsie courtroom and slowly walked toward jurors. The Dutchess County courtroom where Fred would soon learn his fate was smaller than most others in the region. Finished in a light-colored wood, there were roughly five rows of wooden pews on each side to sit trial watchers, reporters and family members. In keeping with custom, the prosecution sat on one side of the room, the defense on the other, while the judge watched over proceedings from the middle. The jury—nine men and three women—sat to the judge's left side, the court reporter to the right. As McLoughlin made his way toward jurors, no one could deny that the man was in deep thought, perhaps thinking about how to approach such a taboo subject of sexual promiscuity and a ménage à trois. He had obviously thought about his opening statement, long and hard, and now had to verbalize what he firmly believed: Fred Andros was essentially the mastermind of the brutally vicious murder of his lover solely because the woman had broken the relationship off. Susan Fassett had, effectively, said no to Fred. And if there was one thing McLoughlin knew, like most sitting in the courtroom, no one said no to Fred Andros without paying a price for it.

McLoughlin went through and introduced jurors to Susan and explained how she'd had an affair with Fred for "three to four years" and how she had, three weeks before her murder, told Fred she wanted to end it—that she'd decided to reconcile with her husband. Then he explained Fred's role in the federal corruption probe that, most likely, everyone in town had heard about by that point.

As Ned McLoughlin found his groove, speaking comfortably, with pauses for effect and raising his voice at certain times to make a point, he began to work Dawn, arguably his star witness, into focus, launching into a carefully written biography. Dawn was the DA's one true witness, he implied, who was going to sit in the witness's chair, point a finger at Fred and say: *"That man told me to do it. He threatened me. That eerily-looking, flawed, gross little man sitting there . . . he's the one who wanted Susan Fassett dead, not me."*

"In early 1999," McLoughlin told jurors in his best attorney's voice, "Fred Andros called on his friend Dawn Silvernail to have a sexual encounter with Susan Fassett. He arranged it. He filmed it. He joined in. And he compensated Dawn for her involvement."

There it was: the white elephant. McLoughlin had reminded everyone that his victim wasn't perfect. She had flaws, like the rest of us. She went to church, of course, but she had sinned. She was human. And through it all, naturally, the woman did not—no matter whom she hurt with her behavior—deserve to die. Her killer was evil and indignant. He knew not the person Susan was, only what his selfish desires mandated.

As most would soon find out, Susan and Fred's affair, along with Dawn's involvement, turned out to be the basis, as scandalous as it sounded, for the DA's case: Fred had arranged the sexual relationship and then called on Dawn to kill Susan. If she didn't do it, Fred would make sure, he had threatened, that Dawn's family paid a lethal price.

"He threatened her family," Ned McLoughlin said before he read all of the charges against Fred Andros, one by one.

"This is, in many ways, a complex story. Many seemingly unrelated events. But I ask you," McLoughlin pleaded with jurors, "and I would ask you in earnest to please not draw any conclusions until the end of the case, because it's really only then that a lot of things you hear that seem to have no relevance, I think, will be *relevant* to you."

Near the end of his opening, McLoughlin put it as plainly as he could, saying, "Ladies and gentlemen, this is not, as some other cases, a whodunit. We know whodunit. Dawn Silvernail. . . . This case is about, who *had* it done? That's where this case exists."

Before Noel Tepper got to his brief fifteen-minute opening, the jury was led out of the room. Tepper, quite obviously angered by something, stated into the record that he wanted to object to some of what Ned McLoughlin had argued.

Then he asked for a mistrial.

Then the judge quickly denied the request.

In his opening statement, Tepper warned jurors to watch out for what Dawn said when she came into the courtroom to testify. She was a woman with an agenda, he suggested, adding, "She has a *reason* to lie . . . because she has made a *deal* with the prosecution in this case."

The DA's first few witnesses described the scene on the night Susan was murdered. Friends of Susan's talked about attending choir practice and singing the praises of Jesus Christ one minute and then, the next, having to frantically call 911 after hearing "loud pops" from the parking lot. One choir member explained how he held Susan's head in his lap as she slipped away, bleeding to death not fifty feet from the cross that stood in front of United Methodist.

It was a nightmare, like something out of a movie of the week. These common people, churchgoing and rather mundane, had been drawn into what was an ugly crime inspired by hate and vengeance.

Near the end of the day, Jef Fassett took the stand and began to talk about his marriage to Susan and how he had caught her with Fred, and how he and Susan had reconciled shortly before her death. Jef was gravely affected by the words coming from his mouth. It all seemed so distant, yet had happened just over a year prior. Since Susan's murder, Jef and the kids had grown closer, like three buddies.

For Ned McLoughlin, Jef added support to one of his core arguments: Fred Andros couldn't take being rejected; he couldn't take the fact that Susan Fassett had chosen her husband over him. Fred Andros was a man who got what he wanted, no matter the cost. Fred made demands and people served him.

"I said," Jef Fassett explained to jurors, describing the night he had tape-recorded Susan and Fred on the telephone and confronted Susan with the evidence, "'You're busted. Get out.'"

Jef was not a man who displayed his irritation or discontent openly. He was not someone who blew up, or some sort of angry husband who would run over to Fred's house after learning about the affair and beat him up. He and Fred had had words, sure. But Jef Fassett was calm and collected: he caught his wife cheating and wanted her out of the house.

It should have been, well, the end of the story.

After answering a few more personal questions about his marriage, Jef said that he and Susan decided to re-unite and resolve their marital issues. They had talked and made up. They even decided to get new rings to honor the reunion. Jef said he picked up Susan's ring at the jewelry store soon after they decided to take a week off from work and make things right between them.

"When did you get your new ring?" McLoughlin asked.

Jef began to cry. Not loudly or animatedly. But it was clear the thought of Susan's final day had rattled a memory that wasn't pleasant to think about, regardless of how their lives had turned out. There he was back on that day, when their lives together seemed to be heading in the right direction.

"October 28, 1999," Jef said quietly, answering McLoughlin.

For the next half hour, Jef explained how he and the kids were waiting for Susan to come home from choir practice, but she never did. Instead, he said, things got really weird. He talked about the cops surrounding his house, how he made several calls to the church and the Poughkeepsie PD, but no one would tell him exactly what was going on.

"And that's when they took you into custody?" McLoughlin asked, skipping over the sticky issue of the Poughkeepsie PD handcuffing Jef and the kids and dragging them down to Troop K like common criminals.

Jef paused, then turned serious. "Yes," he replied. "For *sixteen* hours at Troop K headquarters."

The courtroom sat silent. Jurors were obviously taken aback by the sheer duration of time the guy withstood questioning on the night his wife was murdered. It seemed almost ludicrous that Jef and his kids and their girlfriends would be treated like common criminals. But Jef Fassett had left his house that night near seven-thirty and didn't return until near eight-thirty—which had given him time to murder his wife. There was a reason why Jef had been treated so unsympathetically.

* * *

The following afternoon, January 30, after Jef left the stand, the trial's first major bombshell—although not many in town, in the end, would be all that surprised by the allegation—was dropped.

Fred Andros had been loyal and dedicated to a local restaurateur in town. For two years, Fred walked in and out of a downtown Poughkeepsie diner almost daily. Fred became close with the owner, Leonidas Efstratiou, a Greek immigrant. In fact, Efstratiou testified, when Fred was ousted from his job at the water department, he became a near-permanent fixture inside the diner, which was when the two of them started talking more personally: about life, love and anything else that floated Fred's fancy.

Ned McLoughlin asked the diner owner to describe one particular conversation he'd had with Fred a few weeks before Susan was murdered. Efstratiou said Fred walked into the diner one day. Sat down at one of the tables and ordered his favorite beverage, a diet cola. On this day, Efstratiou recalled, Fred was "unusually serious." He didn't seem to be his bubbly old self. He definitely had something weighing heavily on his mind that he wanted to talk about. He looked depressed. Confused. Serious.

"What is it, Freddy?" Efstratiou asked his friend.

"I need to talk to you, Leon," Fred said gravely.

"OK, Freddy, what is it?"

"Someone is troubling me," Fred said, "I need something done. Do you know anyone from the Greek Mafia?"

Efstratiou thought it was a joke. "Is there such a thing in existence as the Greek Mafia, Freddy?" he asked, laughing.

Eventually, Efstratiou testified, he told Fred he knew a Greek man who had been deported from the United States back to Greece, insinuating that the man was shady.

Fred wanted the guy's name.

"Why'd you give him the name?" the senior assistant
DA asked Efstratiou, who answered, "I knew he was over-
seas, in Greece, and that Freddy couldn't reach him." It
was a way to get rid of Fred and his crazy idea, the diner
owner added. Nothing more.

When Tepper got a crack at Efstratiou, he brought out
the fact that Fred never mentioned Susan by name, or
what he wanted done, which might have been a fact.
However, it did little to change the meaning behind
what Fred wanted, especially considering the context of
the conversation, as it was put into the situation of how
Fred's life had played out over the next few weeks.

CHAPTER 51

Dawn was sitting in Dutchess County Jail, waiting to testify against her former lover and friend, Fred Andros. By now, Dawn was eager and ready and certainly willing to step in front of the jury and tell her stories about her and Fred's plan to murder Susan. The speculation that it was all Dawn's idea because she and Susan had been lovers was laughable. "I never even knew the woman," Dawn later told me, "except for those times we made love for Fred's enjoyment."

In order to protect Dawn, the DA's office had placed her in a segregated medical ward of the Dutchess County Jail, where she had been waiting to be called as a witness. She had no idea when, exactly, Ned McLoughlin was going to need her. It could be any day. But she was prepared.

Inside the medical unit one afternoon, Dawn sat by herself. Beside her was a mesh-type screen, which separated Dawn from about eight or nine, she later recalled, male prisoners in there for various medical reasons.

One of the guys sitting, waiting for a doctor, had looked through a crack in the mesh and saw Dawn. "Hey," he said quietly, "you're that Silvernail woman I saw on television, right?"

She hesitated at first. Then, "Yeah . . . ?"

"You're waiting to testify against Fred Andros, right?"

"Um, yeah," she said standoffishly. *What's going on?* she thought. *What is this?* Should she call a guard?

"I hope you hang that bastard," the inmate said.

"What are you talking about?"

"When he came back up here from Westchester," the inmate said, referring to the time when Fred was released from the hospital after shooting himself, "he told everyone on the cell block that you, Dawn Silvernail, would never live to testify against him."

For a moment, that old chill Dawn had remembered from years past when Fred used to threaten her came back in an instant. But then, she realized, here was Fred, locked up, half his face shot off, still playing that tired game of wannabe gangster. Was the guy serious?

CHAPTER 52

Several women who knew Fred personally testified throughout the second day of the trial that he was a good man and would never do anything to harm anyone. And in the days after Susan was murdered, Fred appeared to be awfully upset about it. Even broken up and depressed. Yet, there were other things bothering Fred, too.

One woman explained that he was particularly upset after he lost his job with the town and wanted to open up a hot dog cart in Hyde Park, but the town wouldn't give him a permit for the business.

Another woman, who worked across the street from Fred's house and saw him from time to time when he stopped in to say hello, said she couldn't believe how saddened he seemed that the police hadn't found Susan's killer by the beginning of December. The woman was, without realizing it, of course, painting a compassionate picture of Fred.

Here was this little man, sitting in the courtroom, facing off against the DA for an incredibly brutal, cold-blooded murder, full of hatred and vengeance. However, it wasn't the same Fred Andros, several witnesses testified, who seemed to be a kind, gentle and sweet man to them whenever they saw him.

Late into the morning of Wednesday, January 31, 2001, a large-framed woman wearing an orange jumpsuit, a silvery cap of natty gray hair, her skin pasty and pale, sauntered into the courtroom to square off against the man she had known since her early twenties. Dawn had seemed to age—remarkably, ten years inside of the year she had been incarcerated. She looked old, like a grandmother, weak and beaten down by the system. Conversely speaking, though, she wasn't the same easily manipulatable woman Fred had manhandled all those years. It was the way Dawn stared at Fred as she sat down, as if to imply through her glare, *"It's my turn to talk now."*

Fred looked up when Dawn found her seat, watching closely as she got herself situated.

Dawn had put on weight, but looked ready to do her duty and answer to her end of the plea bargain she had signed with the DA. When Ned McLoughlin asked why she had agreed to a plea, fifty-one-year-old Dawn Silvernail answered, "I'm here to testify, to tell the truth about the murder of Susan Fassett and those people that were involved in it."

"And were you indicted for the murder of Susan Fassett acting in concert with a person named Fred Andros?"

"Yes, sir."

"In exchange for at least eighteen years to life, and the plea of guilty to murder, can you tell the jury what you are expected to do?"

"To sit here and tell the truth about Fred Andros and my involvement in the planning and execution of Susan Fassett's murder."

McLoughlin led Dawn down a series of questions centered on the money she owed Fred and how much she had borrowed from him throughout the years, which appeared to be another motive for Dawn to partake in Fred's criminal behavior.

McLoughlin had Dawn answer a series of questions that walked jurors through her employment and married life: all straightforward testimony the prosecutor needed to get out of the way. As Dawn talked her way through her life, it was clear that she had led a fairly successful, productive life. She wasn't some sort of down-on-her-luck transient Fred could have easily manipulated; Dawn was in some respects smarter than Fred and probably should have known better.

At one point, the prosecutor asked Dawn about the type of vehicle she drove—the make, model and color. Then wondered if she owned any weapons.

"Yes, sir," Dawn answered sharply, "I have a license to carry a pistol."

He asked Dawn to describe it.

"A Ruger P90 .45-caliber."

As her testimony continued, Dawn pointed out Fred in the room and said she had known him for twenty-three years. She told the jury how they met. "His handle was Neptune," she said, adding that she, her husband and Fred and his wife were all friends, but that at one point, "we had a brief sexual relationship."

There had always been the insinuation that Dawn had performed sexual favors for a few of Fred's friends, but Dawn had never admitted to it publicly. On that topic, Ned McLoughlin asked, "Could you just briefly give the jury an idea how that occurred and what type of transaction it was?"

Dawn didn't hesitate. "Mr. Andros set up the meeting," she said, staring at Fred, "between a gentleman that works for the Water Department, whose name I don't know, and myself. And I drove down to Spackenkill water plant where his office was and he had a camping trailer in the yard at the water plant, and I met with the gentleman there."

"And did you know the person before you got there?"

"No."

"And what, if anything, did Mr. Andros give or do for you as a result of that?"

"He paid me one hundred dollars."

Dawn spent some time establishing how she and Fred communicated and how often she would meet him. It was clear that as the year 1999 began, Fred was talking to Dawn on a regular basis. Whenever Dawn needed extra money, she would always turn to Fred and he would oblige, whether she turned a trick for him or took the cash with a promise to pay him back.

Dawn explained that her financial situation in 1999 was bad; she owed everyone money and was falling into an abyss of debt.

But there was Freddy—always willing to come up with a solution.

The problem became, however—which Dawn was pretty good at putting on Fred's shoulders entirely—that Dawn had no way of paying Fred back. Thus, she was totally indebted to the guy and didn't know what to do.

"In September/October of 1999, how was your financial situation?" McLoughlin asked. "How had you been making payments to Mr. Andros and/or meeting your bills?"

"Since I couldn't keep up the monetary arrangement with Mr. Andros, he decided there was another way I could pay him back. He called me and told me that he had a lady friend who had a fantasy about having sex with another woman."

The courtroom sat stunned. Right here, in Pleasant Valley, in Dutchess County, New York, here were seemingly plain old-fashioned housewives involved in some sort of drama that might have appeared at one time impossible to fathom.

"Did there come a time when this transaction, like this, was arranged again?"

"Yes, sir."

"And who arranged that?"

"Mr. Andros."

"And how many times total was this set up?"

"I believe around five."

"And after the first occasion, were any of the next occasions filmed, as far as you know?"

"Not that I was aware of, no."

"And on all those occasions, were you given any money for your involvement?"

"No." (Dawn later said she was indeed paid in cash one time.)

"And were you remunerated or paid in any way?"

"Yes. By a reduction in my debt."

"How much was your debt reduction for the first event, the first time?"

"Three hundred fifty dollars."

"Did there come a time, the beginning of October 1999, that you had conversations over the phone with Fred Andros?"

"Yes," Dawn answered bitterly.

"And can you tell the jury what discussions or what issue was spoken about during those initial conversations?" The prosecutor sounded confident and poised. The jury sat captivated and, at the same time, horrified that a woman could murder another woman for so little money.

"The initial conversations had to do with my inability to pay."

"How did he act, or what did he say, more particularly, if you know?"

"He told me that we would have to come up with another way to 'take care of the situation.'" Fred's way of referring to the murder without coming out and saying as much.

"Did he ever tell you, during any of your discussions about your debt, what might be the result if you did not?"

"Yes. He said someone in my family could be hurt."

Fred was ten years Dawn's senior. Yet, sitting there with his shaved head and caved-in face, he looked as though he could have been her father.

"Here were two [strange] people," one man sitting in the courtroom later said, "facing off against each another in court as if it were a jousting match."

Dawn spoke with a direct affect, answering Ned McLoughlin's questions as succinctly as she could. She sounded rather articulate, considering the fact that many thought she was nothing more than white trash, some sort of mountain woman who had never left the woods.

In order for McLoughlin to prove that Dawn knew what she was talking about, the lawyer asked, "Did any of these transactions"—the sexual meetings—"or where did the *other* transactions take place?"

"At Mr. Andros's home."

"And where in his home, if you remember?"

"I believe it was the second-floor bedroom that he said was his bedroom." The same bed, in other words, Fred had slept in with his wife.

"Do you remember anything about that room?" Details were always a way to allow a witness to prove he or she was there. "Can you describe anything in that room?"

"Yes! It had a beautiful four-poster bed."

"Do you remember what material, if any, that it was made out of?"

"Looked like dark pine."

CHAPTER 53

As Dawn continued to tell her story, it was quite clear to jurors—if they believed her—that Fred had used every manipulative molecule of DNA he had in his system to implore this woman to carry out a deed he didn't have the guts to do himself. It was as if Dawn and Fred's lives together had been a slow promenade up to this one fatal moment. And it was only now, as Dawn sat in prison day after day, staring at the walls, going through her life line by line, that she could clearly see how gullible and willing she was to fall victim to Fred Andros, like so many other naïve women had.

Ned McLoughlin made sure to have Dawn explain to the jury that all of the sexual rendezvous between her and Susan had taken place before May 1999, when Fred was ousted as water superintendent.

"Did you ever see Susan Fassett outside the presence of Fred Andros?" the prosecutor asked.

"No."

"Anywhere in person?"

"Never."

"Did you ever speak to Susan Fassett on the phone in your life?"

"No."

"She *never* called you, you *never* called her?"

"No, sir."

"Did you ever set up any personal contact of any kind with Susan Fassett?"

"I did not."

This back-and-forth regarding Dawn and Susan having any personal relationship outside of that with Fred continued ad nauseam for about five more minutes before jurors were beginning to convey, with body gestures, *Enough already. We get it.*

There was always the question of why the sexual meetings ended so abruptly. Many wondered why, all of a sudden, Fred and Susan stopped meeting with Dawn, as did Dawn herself.

So she asked Fred one day.

"He told me," Dawn told jurors, "that Susan had had female problems and that she was out of commission for a while and could not engage in any kind of sexual activity."

This was, of course, untrue. Susan had been having second thoughts about her and Fred's relationship. Moreover, Fred was under a tremendous amount of stress because of what he had learned near this time about an imminent indictment. In addition to that, Fred didn't want Dawn to pay off her debt—that's why he had paid her cash only that one time in the pumping station. He needed Dawn to "owe him." After Susan indicated a desire to end the affair, Fred became enraged. How dare she break it off with me! He became stuck on revenge and payback: Susan was going to have to suffer for breaking up with him. It was the only way.

To keep Dawn under his thumb, Fred set up a few more sexual encounters for her with friends of his—and one could argue, to encourage Dawn to think that he was still in charge.

But then their relationship—Fred and Dawn's—kept coming back to Susan. It was during late summer 1999 when Fred began to bring Susan up into his conversations with Dawn once again.

"He told me that Susan had decided to go back and reconcile with her husband, and that she was sup[posed] to go down and meet with the FBI in Westchester and possibly testify about something to do with the corruption case he had been involved with at the beginning of that year."

Dawn had no idea how into the mud Fred was with the corruption probe. Fred had told her not to worry, it was nothing—that is, as long as Susan wasn't able to testify. Dawn recalled how she had run "bags" full of money for Fred that summer to various people. She'd walk into a diner, put an envelope of money inside a newspaper, place it on a table, then wait for a man to sit down. Next, without saying a word, he'd nod, then get up and leave.

"No drugs," she had once told Fred. "I'll help you as long as there are no drugs involved."

After all, Dawn later implied, she had morals. Drugs crossed a line.

CHAPTER 54

Saint Francis de Sales was a voracious letter writer, often detailing and preaching a better part of his Christian (Catholic) beliefs to friends and family. In one of those letters, de Sales wrote, rather passionately and profoundly, *The first inducement to attain . . . purification is a keen and lively apprehension of the great evils resulting from sin, by means of which we acquire a deep, hearty contrition.*[1]

Profound words that still ring true today.

Contrition, de Sales was certain, purged sin at any cost. No matter how grave. However vile. However dirty or wicked. If one paid penance—true penance, that is—one was forgiven in the eyes of Jesus Christ and de Sales's God.

This act of contrition on Dawn's part (testifying in front of a jury on behalf of the DA), in hope of putting away the true mastermind behind Susan's murder, drove Dawn as she sat and talked about the most intimate details and moments of her life. She was fueled by the good that could come out of her testimony—a reparation she understood wouldn't necessarily secure her a place in

---

[1] From *Introduction to the Devout Life* by Saint Francis de Sales (New York: Vintage Books, 2002), pp. 15–16.

paradise, but was a start, nonetheless, she later said. In fact, whatever she could do to pay any sort of penance to the Fassett family for what she had done, Dawn added, was too small a price to pay for taking Susan away from them. Dawn understood perfectly and took total responsibility for killing Susan. As she stared down Fred at times during her testimony, knowing him for as long as she did, she could read Fred's mind through his eye contact and facial expressions. What he told her was that there was no way he would ever admit his culpability in setting up and condoning the murder of Susan Fassett. It just wasn't in Fred's cold heart to admit his shortcomings or faults and offer his own act of penance—whatever that would be. Fred was a man of selfish morals, who thought about one person, and one person only.

After coaching Dawn through a period of her life where she and Susan stopped seeing each other under Fred's direction, Ned McLoughlin walked her down a pathway toward how the idea of murder had come about.

According to Dawn's testimony, the language Fred used in convincing her was no doubt the work of a man who knew exactly how to get people to do things they otherwise would not have thought about doing on their own.

"He told me," Dawn testified, "that he could not afford to go to prison and do a long prison time, and that sometimes your best friend can be your worst enemy, and Susan might inadvertently say something that might lead the FBI people to discover involvement he had in the corruption case that he had not admitted to, which would void his immunity deal he had with the FBI."

It was clear from Dawn's point of view that she believed Fred was afraid of a life behind bars, and that was motivating him to have Susan taken out of the picture.

There was one time when Fred had called Dawn, she said, and he was crying like a child who had been grounded by his parents. Weeping as if he had lost everything, "he told me . . . on the telephone that he received a phone call of a threatening nature, that he had been told that if he didn't keep his mouth shut about Bill Paroli, he could wind up like another gentleman (Basil Raucci) who had been found floating in the river."

This was Fred doing his best work: pleading to Dawn's sympathies. He knew Dawn cared, generally, about people—otherwise she would have never agreed to work with the handicapped or mentally challenged. He knew Dawn had never been in trouble in her entire life. His challenge was, then, to turn that otherwise decent person into a cold-blooded killer. But how to do such a thing?

Kill or be killed was what Dawn thought as she walked away from that telephone call. And if Fred Andros was killed, Dawn assumed, she would be next.

Dawn suggested at one time that Fred get one of his cronies to do the deed. After all, Dawn told Fred, "You're the big shot around town. You know *people*. Get your 'people' to do it."

Fred gave Dawn quite the story. And what an impact it had on jurors after just hearing from the witness himself. Fred had explained to Dawn when she suggested a hired hand "that he had tried to contact a 'friend' of his that usually took care of these kinds of things for him, but the gentleman was in Greece on holiday and he couldn't contact him. So he told me that he wanted me to consider helping him to eliminate Susan."

It had to be done now, Fred insisted, before Susan was able to make it to the FBI and hang the both of them.

Much of the morning of February 1's court day was passed by Dawn giving her version of the events leading up to the murder and the actual crime itself. As the morning came to an end, Ned McLoughlin walked Dawn through many lies Fred had told her in order to convince her—manipulate her, rather—to murder Susan. At one point, McLoughlin asked, "Beyond Mr. Andros's expressed concerns about Susan Fassett, did he ever express to you what if anything he needed to do about her or that situation?"

"Yes, he did."

"What did he say?"

"He said he needed her eliminated."

"Did he speak to you about what he meant by 'eliminate'?"

"Yes. He wanted her dead."

"Did he use that word?"

"Yes."

The prosecutor encouraged Dawn to talk a little bit about how she carried out the murder: the actual act and how it was done.

"I sat up and I pointed the gun in her direction and I pulled the trigger."

For the most part, Dawn sat poised, unaffected by the dark nature of what she was talking about. Then, "He told me to put my pistol under her chin and 'blow her f***ing brains out.'"

She talked about Fred's anger over her not completing the job one night when she promised she would.

She mentioned how scared of him she had become.

She talked about how Fred would refer to the murder in his own little way, one time saying, "I better take care of business." But on another day, it became the "final results."

McLoughlin wanted Dawn to explain to the jury how long it took her to exit the parking lot of the church after shooting Susan.

"It seemed like forever," she answered hastily, seemingly not wanting to talk about that part of the crime further. "Almost immediately."

In the end, she said, Fred was "pleased the murder had been committed."

Fred sat and shook his head at that comment. Rolled his eyes. Whispered something to his attorney Noel Tepper, who had been watching Dawn, taking notes, preparing to go after the one witness who had, beyond Fred himself, buried Fred's tarnished reputation so deep it was going to be nearly impossible to redeem.

CHAPTER 55

By 11:45 A.M., on February 1, 2001, Dawn was staring at Noel Tepper as he stood and began what she knew was going to be a heated cross-examination. *Tell the truth*, Dawn told herself as Tepper began to speak. *That's all I have to do.*

Tepper began with Dawn's supposed anxiety disorder.

"Two years," she said after being asked how long she'd been diagnosed.

Tepper shook his head slowly . . . as if to imply, *Right* . . .

Then he asked, "Are you on medication now?"

"Yes, I am."

"And you said Paxil?"

"That's correct."

They hashed out the dosage.

"And in October of 1999," Tepper wondered, "were you on Paxil?"

"Yes!"

Almost three times less the dosage than now, Dawn explained.

Then she talked about how "fine" she was when on the medication, but very "anxious" when not.

"You also get confused?" Tepper asked.

"Not so much, no."

"You have problems with memory, isn't that so?"

"Not aware that I do," Dawn answered flatly. Tepper had wanted a rise out of her, for sure; he didn't get it.

"Now, did you have an occasion to write to a fellow inmate who you referred to as 'Big Daddy'?"

"Yes."

"And was this in July of 2000?"

"Could be."

"And in your letter to him, did you indicate that without it (medication), [you are] 'a fruitcake'?"

"I don't remember what I wrote."

Tepper spent about thirty minutes trying to convince jurors that Dawn had lied to the DA during their pretrial conversations and that there was no real reason for anyone to believe her story now, considering the fact that she could lie so easily to a member of the justice system.

But Dawn fought back, saying she had no *reason* to lie about Fred's involvement and, furthermore, had no reason herself to kill Susan Fassett. It made no sense. The connection between Susan and Dawn was Tepper's client, Fred Andros. Yes, she'd had sex with Susan. Yes, she'd had sex with Fred's friends for money. Yes, she'd lied to her husband, Ed. Yes, she was full of anxiety and needed medication. And yes, she'd murdered Susan Fassett.

But no, she didn't do it on her own—it was Fred Andros who had convinced her.

When defense attorneys don't have much on a key witnesses, they sometimes try to trip them up on dates and get them to stumble, and through that litany of confusing bits of information, they can begin to beat them up a little bit and—maybe, just maybe—get them to stick their foot in their mouth.

But not Dawn. She stuck firm to her ground and never once winced or backed down to Noel Tepper.

After they discussed who taught Dawn how to hold a weapon ("my father"), Tepper had Dawn describe how she shot Susan, encouraging her to dredge up every detail she could recall. It was meaningless testimony that only saddened Susan's family members sitting in the courtroom: Dawn had admitted killing Susan. That wasn't the issue here.

But Tepper kept insisting on hearing the wicked details: "Did you look her in the eye?"

"No."

"Did you avoid looking her in the eye?"

"Yes!" Tears now. A bit of choking up on Dawn's part.

"You knew she was a mother, correct?"

"That's correct."

"You knew she was a wife, correct?"

"That's correct."

"And you testified you knew she had a warm, kind voice, didn't you?"

Jason Fassett, sitting, listening, threw up his hands, whispering to himself, "What is this bullshit?"

"And yet you proceeded?" Tepper continued.

"Sorry?"

"Yet you *proceeded*," he said again, raising his voice, "to do that which you did do?"

"Yes, I did."

"Now, ma'am, when you were spoken to . . . you indicated there was no way you could have been her lesbian lover, correct?"

"That's correct."

"You were told that Mr. Andros had told the police that he believed that you had killed her because you were her lesbian lover and that you were upset with her?"

"That's correct."

"And your reaction to the police was, *no way*?"

"That's right."

Where was Tepper going? Many of these facts had been established already.

"No way would you be a lesbian lover, correct?"

"Correct again!"

"You lied to the police."

"Yep."

"Yeah!" Tepper seethed. "To protect yourself and to help yourself?"

"And also because I didn't want to admit anything like that with my husband standing right there, yes."

"And you also said that you were repulsed by that sort of thing?"

"That's correct."

"Is that correct?"

"Yes."

"You are still repulsed?"

"Yes."

"You had sex with Susan five times and you are still repulsed by it?"

"Yes."

"Didn't you have any warm feelings toward Susan at some point in time?"

"I don't understand the question."

"Isn't it true that at some point in time you started loving or liking Susan very much?"

"No!" Dawn was appalled by the accusation. Sure, she'd had feelings for Susan enough to engage in the sexual acts, but the best part of the deal on her end was that she didn't have to invest emotionally in the affair. Fred had made a point to say that Susan was his, and his alone. Furthermore, Dawn loved her husband. The "dates" with Susan were something she did to scratch an itch and make some extra money—however vain and repulsive—to steal Tepper's word—the behavior may have been.

"You never liked her?" Tepper asked.

"I liked her as a person. I didn't like her as a lover."

"You didn't care for her physically, and yet you were able to do it five times with her?"

"Yes."

"Without any emotional reaction?"

"That's correct."

"Without any response?"

"Yes."

"Totally mechanically, without any caring?"

"That's correct."

"You also told the police that you had no recent sexual intimacy with Mr. Andros or anyone other than your husband—is that true?"

"Yes."

This back-and-forth between Dawn and Tepper about her sexual activity got old rather quickly. Any first-year law student sitting and watching proceedings could see that Dawn wasn't going to back down from her story, and all Noel Tepper was doing was alienating his client from the jury even further by insisting on staying on the topic.

Dawn sounded believable—a lot of that had to do with Ned McLoughlin's expert direct examination, in which he was able to extract from Dawn the reasons behind her motivation for the murder.

For the next hour, Tepper went through all the "lies" Dawn had told police before she had admitted to the crime. Dawn reacted by saying—generally—that, sure, she had lied through her teeth over and over to try to get out of the position she was in—at the time.

CHAPTER 56

After a long lunch break, Dawn was back on the stand answering more of Tepper's questions, which seemed to grow more tired as the afternoon wore on and on. Jurors, especially, looked drained and burned out from all the different questions regarding Dawn's credibility. What it came down to was: you either believed Dawn or you believed Fred. Nothing else really mattered at this point.

Beyond accusing Dawn of telling multiple lies, all of which she had no trouble admitting to, Tepper didn't have much more. He went through and asked her a few basic questions, trying to once again trip her up on times and dates, but was unsuccessful. Concluding, Tepper finally said, "Isn't it true that you called Mr. Andros and asked him why Susan didn't want to get together with you anymore?"

"No."

"You *didn't*?"

"No, I didn't. I called Mr. Andros and I asked him, what had happened with Susan that he wasn't calling me anymore?"

Ned quickly conducted his redirect. "Miss Silvernail, did you ever go out to lunch with Susan Fassett?"

"No, sir, I didn't."

"Ever go shopping?"

"No."

"Ever talk on the phone?"

"No."

"Go to a movie?"

Fred squirmed as he watched his freedom slowly slipping away.

"Never!" Dawn answered.

After a few more questions, which took about five minutes, Dawn was excused and the next witness was sworn in.

Judge Dolan had a reputation for running a tight courtroom, not allowing things to run off on tangents, and Fred's trial was falling into that mold. Jason Fassett had sat in the courtroom every day. "I needed to be there," he said. Still, for Jason, the trial couldn't end soon enough. He wanted to see the man he had worked for—the one he was sure had masterminded his mother's murder—found guilty and sent to prison. It was tough for Jason to have to sit and listen to a narrative of his mother's final moments as she struggled for life, or was rushed away from the church on a stretcher, gasping for breath, or the lesbian affair she had been involved in. It was *so not* the person, the mother, the Christian, Jason had come to know throughout his life as his loving mother. He had never let go and cried out loud in court, but every once in a while, a tear trickled down the side of his face slowly and he'd have to leave the room.

"In my mind, I didn't need Fred to come out and admit what he did," Jason said later. "The pieces all fit together for me as I sat there and listened to testimony. As soon as you put Fred into the scenario of what each person testified to, it all made sense."

Indeed it had.

Sitting by Jason was his aunt and grandmother.

For the immediate Fassett family (Jason, Jef and Christopher), they knew the person Fred Andros was, Jason explained. So it wasn't hard to see how Fred could have been involved, or how he could sit and lie and tell stories through his attorney that had absolutely nothing whatsoever to do with the reality that had become his sad life story.

"If he was a complete stranger," Jason mused later, "well, it might have been different. But because we knew the person Fred Andros [was], we also knew he would never have the guts to say he was involved and live up to his responsibilities. He was a coward."

This was one of the reasons why the small courtroom was packed to capacity on February 2: to hear more evidence *against* Fred. For Jason, the smoking gun—literally—that lay next to Fred's face on the day he shot himself was enough to convict. Why would an innocent man try to end his life? It didn't add up.

Still, there was Fred, sitting next to his lawyers, taking notes, smiling at times, all with the hope he could reach just *one* juror.

CHAPTER 57

Diana Andros, Fred's fourth wife, was still waiting on divorce papers to come through, so she could finally rid herself—at least legally—of Fred's disgusting ways and move on with her life. By all accounts, Diana was a kind and loving woman who had perhaps naïvely fallen in love with the wrong man, and because she had such a big heart, she allowed herself to stay in a marriage that her gut was telling her had been doomed since the day she spoke her vows. Even so, Diana was willing to testify about what she knew, which spoke to her fine moral character.

On the morning of February 2, Diana took the stand, looking troubled, probably born more out of the difficulty of having to testify than having a problem with telling the truth. All who knew her later said Diana was thoughtful and loving, and just one more innocent victim to add to Fred's long list. Not a bad bone in her body. It wasn't her fault she had gotten mixed up with a lothario in the flesh.

But then, love can do strange things to people, can't it?

The courtroom sat in shock, naturally, when Diana announced her maiden name into the record: Diana *Taber* Andros. Wasn't "Taber" also Susan Fassett's maiden name?

Indeed, it was. But Diana and Susan were not in the least bit related. It was a coincidence. Nothing more.

"Dee," as friends called her, said she and Fred were married in 1995 but had been legally separated ever since the winter of 1999, when her life caved in on her *and* her husband was suspected of killing his longtime lover.

Ned McLoughlin had Dee talk about the telephone lines in the house, where they were located and how often Fred used different lines for different reasons. From her testimony, it seemed Fred was always talking to someone about something that his wife didn't need to know about.

Through Dee's testimony regarding the telephone lines, McLoughlin was laying the groundwork for future testimony that would ultimately show how often Dawn and Fred communicated during those crucial days leading up to the murder. This was one of the most important pieces of circumstantial evidence the DA had at his disposal.

At one point, Dee described Fred's fascination with cameras and photography, telling jurors that he had developed a passion for the hobby with his first wife. Through that, she talked about a long zoom lens Fred liked to use.

For the first time, jurors heard that Fred was a diabetic, although it was much too late by this point to draw any sympathy for him having suffered from the disease.

Dee described Susan Fassett as a "family friend"—that is, before she learned that she was sleeping with her husband.

After about a half hour of questioning with regard to telephone numbers and pagers, McLoughlin asked Dee if Fred had taken a telephone call at about eleven forty-five on the night of Susan Fassett's death. They had been sleeping, Dee explained, for about an hour, when the telephone startled her awake.

"And was that, in general, from federal authorities?" Ned queried.

"Yes," Dee said tersely.

"And can you tell the jury, generally, what did you learn?"

"That Susan Fassett was murdered," she said matter-of-factly, without as much as a quaver. It was Agent O'Connor, from the FBI, telling Fred that his lover had been murdered earlier that night.

"Ma'am, I direct your attention now to three-thirty later that night, actually, October 29 of 1999, about three hours and forty-five minutes after that telephone call (from the FBI). Did there come a time that *other* authorities came to your house?"

"Yes," she said.

"And which authorities were those?"

"State police."

It was Art Boyko.

"And how did news that Susan Fassett had been murdered that you received at eleven forty-five, affect you?" Ned asked.

"I felt very bad," she answered. "Very bad about it."

"Can you tell this jury what you saw Mr. Andros do between eleven forty-five and three-thirty?"

"Sleep."

And so Fred got the news of Susan's murder, Ned McLoughlin pointed out for the jury through Dee's gratifying testimony, and then quickly went back to sleep—as if he had just been told not to come in to work the next morning. It meant nothing to him that she had been killed. He didn't break down, admit his affair and explain to Dee that his lover of four years had been murdered (oh, my God!)—as anyone with at least a drop of emotional connection with that person would have done.

How cold Fred seemed, given the fact that if he didn't have anything to do with the crime, as he himself had been saying, he still felt *nothing* for the woman he had claimed (to Art Boyko) to have loved up until the moment she was killed.

* * *

Tepper tried to compartmentalize Fred's reaction to the FBI's 11:45 P.M. telephone call by asking Dee if he had, in fact, "held his head in his hands and went silent" after the call. Wasn't that what happened? Didn't Fred also "gasp" when he heard what the FBI had to say?

"No," Dee said sharply. Was there anything more to add? It wasn't about being the scorned wife anymore for Diana Taber. Her testimony wasn't about revenge or getting Fred back for the hell and embarrassment he had put her through. Dee was over it all, moving on with her life. It was about stating facts. No matter how Tepper framed it, Fred had little or no reaction to Susan's death, as if, one could only guess, he *expected* it to happen when it did.

As the day wore on, one of Fred's good friends, Ralph Stevens, explained how he saw Fred the following day, after Susan's murder, and said sarcastically, "What did you do, Freddy, have Susan killed?"

But, Stevens said, Fred "appeared upset and said he had not arranged the killing. He cried."

More incriminating than it should have sounded, Stevens told jurors that during the same conversation, however, Fred had said, "Why would I have Susan murdered? I loved her."

Stevens wasn't on the stand to talk about his conversations with Fred—they were all a plus for Ned. Instead, Stevens told jurors that he owned an auto repair shop that often towed vehicles, saying that Fred had asked him about a week prior to Susan's death if he could spare an extra set of license plates. "He needed a set of plates to move a car, he told me. He asked me, did I have any he could borrow? I told him I didn't think I did."

It was devastating testimony—seeing that Dawn had testified that Fred had promised her that he'd get a pair of spare plates to put on her car. And, in truth, Fred had delivered on that promise, handing Dawn a pair of brand-new plates on the afternoon of the night of the murder.

CHAPTER 58

The next few days of proceedings seemed to be rocked by one contingency after another. First, on February 5, the trial was postponed due to an incredible snowstorm that nearly shut the entire region down. Then, the following day, one of the jurors became ill and called in sick.

By Wednesday, February 7, however, the trial was back on track as Ned McLoughlin continued calling witnesses in order to impeach Fred's dwindling story of Dawn acting on her own behalf. As each witness testified, it was clear that subtle things Fred had done or said *after* the murder were going to now come back and influence the jury.

At 2:20 P.M., McLoughlin called Investigator Derek Brockhoff, who had put together, for the most part, a telephone call trail that clearly outlined the cusp of the prosecution's case: Fred Andros was the mastermind, Dawn Silvernail his pawn. Before Brockhoff, McLoughlin had called a few reps from various telephone companies to explain, in part, an overwhelming bundle of over 3,200 pages of telephone records the prosecution had submitted as evidence—a long paper trail showing how Fred and Dawn communicated throughout the course of planning Susan's murder. It had taken the NYSP months to sit down and sift through the mountain of telephone records and establish the connection between Fred and Susan, and Dawn and Fred—or if there was, in fact, a link between Susan and Dawn. If, as Fred had been saying all along, Susan and Dawn were in a "relationship" of some sort, there would undoubtedly be a cell and landline telephone and/or pager trail to prove that a relationship existed. There would have to be some sort of established communication between Dawn and Susan. Otherwise, how in the world could they have had any sort of relationship?

The second part of the question became how did Dawn's telephone calls to Fred fit into a timeline with the telephone calls Fred and Susan had made between them? When one looked at all the records together, it appeared to be a paper maze of which there was no way out. There were hundreds and hundreds of telephone calls. How could an investigator sit down and decipher which was which, who called whom and how those individuals corresponded and were connected to one another?

Because of the vast number of calls and the fact that the NYSP was looking for a concrete link between three different people, Investigator Tom Martin, who had worked the forensic side of the Susan Fassett case, reached out to the National Law Enforcement and Corrections Technology Center (NLECTC) and its Law Enforcement Analysis Facility (LEAF) network, a group that specialized in analyzing audio, video and electronic evidence. Part of what LEAF was implored to do in the case included entering all of the call records into a unique Web program called Web Enabled Timeline Analysis System (WebTAS), which amounted to nothing more than a computerized program developed by the Air Force Research Laboratory/Information Directorate in Rome, New York.

Through a tedious process over what was reported to

be six weeks, however, a significant piece of new evidence emerged in WebTAS's deduction and study of the records: there had been "no independent communication" between Dawn and Susan, thus substantiating further Dawn's story that Fred had paid and enticed her to have sex with Susan for money. When one looked at the results, the evidence proved Dawn and Susan had *never* telephoned each other. It was always Dawn calling Fred, or Fred calling Dawn, or Susan calling Fred, or Fred calling Susan. Not once did Susan call Dawn, or vice versa. It didn't prove what was said during each telephone call, certainly not. But it spoke volumes where beyond a reasonable doubt was concerned—screaming to the fact that the *only* connection between Dawn Silvernail and Susan Fassett was Fred Andros.

While on the stand, Derek Brockhoff explained how Fred's E-ZPass records, from his travels along the interstate up to where Dawn worked and lived, indicated that someone driving his car—presumably Fred—had gone to see Dawn on the days and approximate times she had claimed.

"With E-ZPass," Brockhoff later told me, "we were able to establish not only when Fred went on and off the thruway, but we were able to coordinate all the times to show how long he spent at each place."

This was important information. When Fred met Dawn that day shortly after the murder to pick up the garbage bag full of evidence (those "fish" Fred said he had for Dawn), after averaging out the time it would take to drive back and forth using E-ZPass to gage when Fred drove north and south, the times matched perfectly.

Dawn was telling the truth. Her memory—if in this instance only—appeared to be flawless.

"Fred was not a very good person," Brockhoff later explained to me. Brockhoff had also interviewed Dawn on several occasions with Jim Karic. He got to know her fairly well. "She liked Fred. Not at the time we met up with her, but I mean before that. At that point, she realized she had been used by Fred, which was his MO with just about everybody he ever came in contact with. She thought she had a strong and powerful boyfriend of sorts."

Of all the bad people investigators from Troop K had looked into over the years, Brockhoff said, "Fred Andros is right up there. A real master manipulator. Probably the only guy who was manipulating people from the time he was a small kid, not doing anything good for anybody."

Surprising as it may seem considering his size, Fred was known as a bully growing up. The kind of kid who would kick the neighborhood dog and laugh at it walking away. As a youth, he ran with a crowd of burglars and stole and cheated people out of money any way he could. He took advantage of everyone, whenever he could, Brockhoff explained.

One thing Brockhoff wanted to make clear, suffice it to say, where the investigation into Susan Fassett's murder was concerned, is that although cases sometimes might seem like the work of three or four key investigators, "it's a family effort all the way. All of us from Troop K Major Crimes chipped in on this one," he said.

At one point, Ned McLoughlin asked Brockhoff how many times Fred had contacted Dawn via pager or telephone during the month of October, leading up to Susan's murder. "Thirty-seven," Brockhoff answered curtly. On the opposite side of that coin, Dawn had contacted Fred, Brockhoff added, twenty-one times over the same time period. Susan had contacted Fred nearly forty times through the course of October, Brockhoff went on to say; but the most shocking, perhaps most damaging, testimony from Brockhoff regarding Fred's list of telephone call buddies included the fact that Fred called Dawn—on the day of the murder—on at least nine separate occasions. The calls ranged from the hours Dawn was at her job until later on that night when Dawn was in Pleasant Valley and after the murder. Even worse for Fred was that Brockhoff said he proved with the telephone records that someone— it might not have been Dawn, but Dawn had claimed it was—had telephoned Fred's private telephone line and pager twice from the A&P parking lot in Pleasant Valley "on the night Susan was murdered." Calls that came in at 7:28 and again at 7:46 P.M., said Brockhoff, which Dawn claimed was only moments after the murder.

When the records were put side by side with Dawn's statements, the times and locations matched perfectly. There was no way around Fred explaining any of these circumstances without implicating someone else.

Just for the record, McLoughlin had Brockhoff answer the question that would become one of the most important ones of the trial thus far: how many times, during that same month, or at *any* time, for that matter, did Dawn contact Susan, or Susan contact Dawn?

"Not once."

"How many calls were there between those two?"

"There were none."

After Brockhoff was excused from the witness stand the following day, admitting to Noel Tepper at one point that he had indeed "made assumptions" regarding some of the telephone calls (because, when it comes down to it, a paper trail proves the calls were made, but does not prove by whom), jurors were quite clear about a few important pieces of the prosecution's puzzle. For one, Fred Andros had lied about Dawn and Susan hooking up without him. It had never happened. And two, Fred had better be able to pull some sort of magic evidence out of his hat, or he was going to prison for the rest of his natural life.

CHAPTER 59

Senior Investigator Tom Martin took the stand on Friday, February 9, in the middle of the afternoon. Martin had played a pivotal role in the execution of the forensic side of the Susan Fassett murder investigation. Assistant District Attorney (ADA) Frank Chase, McLoughlin's prosecuting partner, had Martin move quickly from October 28, the day Susan was murdered, to the following afternoon, when he met up with Dr. Michael Baden at St. Francis Hospital to take part in the autopsy.

Jason Fassett was sitting with his grandmother. He looked pale. Tired and anxious. The next few days of testimony were going to be brutal on the soul, Jason knew. After Tom Martin, Baden was going to be taking the stand to talk about his findings. The autopsy was an ugly, inevitable part of the prosecution's case, detailing the graphic forensic pathology side of the crime. It was a road, however, Ned McLoughlin needed to go down if he wanted to show the jury the true results of what he believed was Fred's evil nature. After all, a woman had been viciously murdered—shot to death while sitting in her car. The *how* of the crime could not be overshadowed, or toned down. Up until this point, Susan had been a

woman cheating on her husband; someone who was
having lesbian sex with one of Fred's girlfriends; a town
worker, like Fred; a confused woman with marital problems. Being a victim of murder had to take its expected
place in the trial. It was the state's responsibility to place
the cruelty of the crime front and center at some point.

Martin described how he had taken most of the photographs during the autopsy, adding, "I also assist with a
little note taking. Mostly . . . evidence collection. Anything that's removed from the body by the doctor, I
would help out with packaging and labeling and eventually forwarding up to the crime laboratory."

For the next few moments, he talked about the jewelry
he had taken off Susan. Here, in this moment, the prosecution's case was coming full circle: the ring Jef Fassett
had talked about was part of what Martin had marked as
evidence.

"And could you tell the jury," ADA Chase asked several questions later, "generally about those [other items]
you removed?"

"Yes," Martin said, staring down at his notes, "we recovered four projectiles or bullets from the victim's body."

At that response, Jason blinked quickly. Bowed his
head. He couldn't believe what he was hearing. His
mother's life had come down to being shot dead after
leaving church choir practice. It still didn't seem real. *Is
this actually happening?* he pondered. Was he actually sitting there listening to this? Jason felt as if the past fifteen
months since his mother's death had been a blur—some
sort of slow-motion walk in water that mimicked someone else's life. At first, he later said, things moved fast:
everything passing him by as if a blur. Nothing mattered.
Noting seemed important. Nothing overshadowed "the
murder." But now, with Susan's life being played out in

front of everyone, Jason was on a treadmill, running and running and running . . . only to stand still.

ADA Chase asked Martin about biological evidence, especially the procedures he and Baden had followed.

Jason shifted in his seat. He didn't want to hear it, but then he did. That's why he was there: to hear the truth.

All of it.

No matter how ghastly, how vile and hurtful. It was the only way through the pain.

Martin described the kits they used, saying at one point, "Dr. Baden would have actually taken these samples and handed them to me to be packaged and recorded. Envelopes are there for everything as [a way to] control hair and [forensic] samples of the victim, maybe foreign hairs or substances that might be in or around the victim's body. We would also have envelopes that would contain"—and he paused a moment, hesitating—"different swabbings, oral, anal and vaginal, as well as controlled blood samples from the blood of the victim."

ADA Chase left it there. He didn't have his witness explain further what they actually found: among other things, a sample of semen in Susan's vagina that turned out to be Fred's.

From there, Martin moved on to talk about uncovering a bullet fragment in the door frame of Susan's Jeep Cherokee.

"Sir, did there come a time when you removed that projectile?" Chase asked.

"Yes, sir."

"How many projectiles did you remove from both the car and Mrs. Fassett?" Chase wondered a few questions later.

Martin held up his hand. "A total of five."

Next he discussed a trip he took to Dawn's house in the Catskills under a search warrant. He described a reloading room Dawn and Ed had set up in the house, which was a room they had devoted to reloading gunpowder into shell casings. Then it was on to Fred's house and several photographs Martin had taken inside. For about ten minutes, using a series of photos, Martin took the jury on a tour through Fred's house: the metal shavings in the basement—presumably where Fred had drilled out Dawn's weapon—on the floor, and the gun on the table upstairs, and the binoculars on the bed next to a zoom lens. It was all there. For what intention, of course, was left to each juror to decide.

"Did you collect metal shavings from both the Andros and Silvernail home?" ADA Chase asked.

"Yes, sir, I did."

"Same kind of shavings?"

"Yes, sir."

Near 3:00 P.M. that same day, after a sidebar conference, Martin was asked to step down so the court could accommodate Ned's next witness, Dr. Michael Baden, the renowned forensic pathologist and television personality anyone in the courtroom who had watched TV recognized almost immediately. Baden is a tall man, over six foot two. He has a presence about him that speaks to his vast knowledge of forensics and intelligence for solving the forensic crimes.

Watching Baden walk in, Jason said to his grandmother, "What's this? What's happening?"

It was decided that Martin would be recalled at a later date, the judge explained, so Tepper could cross-examine him. Dr. Baden was in high demand as a pathologist, overall forensic expert and crime-television pundit. He was always being hired to investigate and testify in cases across the country. Both sides agreed that he could begin his testimony on this day and conclude, perhaps, on the following morning, so as to free himself up for other obligations.

"This is ridiculous," Jason snapped. "What did this guy do, anyway?" Jason didn't understand Baden's role in the entire process, that Baden was one of the medical examiners the state police used in homicide cases. Jason felt Baden was nothing more than a show-off and egotistical television star. He failed to see that Baden actually conducted autopsies—tens of thousands of them, actually—and had helped the state police solve cases and convict killers for decades. In fact, when punk rocker Sid Vicious, the Sex Pistols' crazy front man, died from a heroin overdose on February 2, 1979, it was Baden who went out in the middle of the night to pronounce him dead and investigate what turned out to be a lethal injection of the drug given to Sid by his own mother.

Ned McLoughlin stood up from his table in front of the judge and said, "At this time, Your Honor, the people call Dr. Baden. Thank you, Your Honor, I know Dr. Baden has a very busy schedule."

That comment served to only infuriate Jason further. He snapped, "This is totally ridiculous."

Baden began by running through his rather long list of credentials—an opening byline Baden had recited hundreds of times while sitting in courtrooms from California to Alaska to New York. He had been a full-time medical examiner for New York City since 1965, thirty-six years and counting. The guy was a machine.

At some point, as Baden spoke, Noel Tepper interrupted and asked, "I would stipulate to his expertise."

It was a fair argument. Baden had done so much throughout his career it was hard to keep track of exactly what he had done in the Fassett case and what division of the state police he was actually testifying for.

Chase spoke for Baden, saying, "Dr. Baden will be recognized as an expert in forensic pathology."

For the next few minutes, Baden explained his job and the focus of the Fassett case. When he first met Susan, she was on an EMT backboard, Baden said. "She had been brought to the St. Francis Hospital morgue area still on a backboard with evidence of CPR having been attempted, still wearing clothing that had been cut through."

According to Baden, Susan was six foot one inch. "So she was tall," he said. "And I . . . the most significant findings were multiple gunshot wounds of the body, centrally coming from the left side of the body, which I was able to determine represented six gunshot tracks. There were six," Baden said, looking at his report, "gunshot tracks in the body."

Further, he explained that whenever there were multiple gunshot wounds on a victim, pathologists refer to them as tracks, and number them from the top down, seeing that they cannot tell from looking at them which shot was first or last. "So that bullet track number one," Baden explained, "is the highest, and as we go down, the lowest one is the last bullet track. But that should not be taken as indicating the sequence of how they were delivered. . . ."

As Baden continued talking about the wounds Susan sustained during her death, it became clear that the DA was making sure the testimony fit the description that Dawn had given in her testimony and statements already. Not only was Baden proving how Susan died, but also the details of her last few moments. "The first [shot] goes from left to right and it went through the neck," he said, "and transected both carotid arteries."

What some found most intriguing, but again, Jason Fassett could have done without, was Baden's description of the actual pain involved. From his years of experience, interviewing people and examining them, Baden described what it was like to get shot. "In general, bullets don't cause much pain. The pain is the skin. There is pain when the bullet pierces the skin because it's like a needle puncture. But once the bullet's inside the body, there aren't very many nerve fibers inside the body that give pain."

With that comment, however, Jason perked up. It was clear, if the good doctor was correct, that Susan hadn't suffered much. She was shot and went unconscious in about ten seconds, Baden said. The brain only has about ten seconds reserve oxygen, so if it is cut off at any point beyond ten seconds, you pass out. With the bullet going straight through Susan's neck, puncturing both carotid arteries at the same time, she had passed out quickly and never knew, effectively, that she was dying.

CHAPTER 60

Dr. Michael Baden was well-versed in how to handle himself in a courtroom, not to mention how to establish a rapport with the jury. Baden knew jurors were open and willing to hear his opinions, as well as his findings, but he had to keep focused on how he viewed the evidence he had collected. Baden had always conducted himself under the auspices of looking at all of the evidence to determine a possible outcome. Meaning, simply, that along with his autopsy results, Baden relied on interviews with suspects and witnesses he had access to, along with police reports, other statements, and any other important pieces of the puzzle. His professional opinion wasn't based on his autopsies alone; it was a culmination of many different pieces of pertinent evidence.

"People," Baden explained as the afternoon of February 9 turned into early evening, "don't know when they are shot . . . because the pain is just like a needle stick. So it isn't much pain." He had prefaced the argument with a reference to the assassination attempt on former president Ronald Reagan, "who didn't know he was shot until he started coughing up blood."

Baden said that most bullets, traveling toward a target,

begin to wobble as they spiral through the air, like a football. The amount a bullet wobbles dictates how large or small a hole will be left in the skin. One of the bullets that struck Susan's neck had made a larger than normal hole, "even though it's a big bullet (.45-caliber) to begin with . . . it's my opinion it struck something before it struck her, and the obvious thing would be the glass."

Susan's window was up. When the bullet broke through the glass, it started to wobble more than normal and eventually caused a larger wound.

For the first time, many of the other injuries Susan had sustained were discussed. One bullet struck the left side of her left shoulder and then ricocheted off the bone and headed north, going through her fifth rib on the left side of her chest, through her left lung, diaphragm, pancreas, stomach, until it ended up in her right kidney.

"There was extensive bleeding from that injury," Baden said.

When it came out, it sounded redundant and quite gratuitous, but DA Chase had to ask the doctor the obvious next question. There was no way around it. The jury needed to hear the answer from Baden. "Doctor," Chase said slowly, sounding almost apologetic, "based on your autopsy examination and your expertise in the field of forensic medicine, are you able to form an opinion, to a reasonable degree of medical certainty, as to the cause of death of Susan Fassett?"

"Yes," Baden said without hesitation. "The cause of death I attributed on October 29, 1999, which is still my opinion today, is that she died of multiple gunshot wounds to the body and internal organs with internal hemorrhage."

Jason cried as the doctor continued describing how Susan likely died. It all seemed so immediate and real now—but, at the same time, unbelievable. *How, in the hell had her life come to this?* Jason wondered, sitting there, listening to the final moments of his mother's life unfold, like some sort of Court TV special. Jason stared at the back of Fred's head. Fred had never turned to look at his former employee—the boy whose mother he allegedly had murdered. Instead, for the entire time, Fred Andros, the one person everyone in the room had gathered together for, sat with a look in his eyes that only Fred could manage. "Fred could look you in the eye," one former acquaintance later said, echoing what a dozen others had reiterated in some form or fashion, "and lie like he was telling the truth. And here he was, on trial for the rest of his life, acting as though he'd had nothing to do with any of it."

Jason's girlfriend, Sarah, later said that her life was never the same after that moment Susan walked out the door, never to return again. "In the short year that I knew Susan Fassett," Sarah later told me, "she was a loving mother and caretaker. She was kind and considerate and made me immediately feel like I was part of her family. She obviously made some bad choices and associated with the wrong people, but she never deserved to die the cruel and heartless way she did. This tragedy affected people in so many devastating ways that some of us will never fully recover. . . ."

For the next ten minutes, Chase and Baden reenacted how the shooting had "likely" taken place. Baden played the part of victim while Chase played the shooter. Chase wanted to give the jury a visual of the crime to latch onto and take into the jury room. What better witness than Baden to give that image.

Chase then began to hand Baden each piece of evidence he had uncovered from Susan's body, asking him to explain what it was and how he and Tom Martin had extracted it, tagged and bagged it.

Jurors were, of course, captivated by Baden—if not for

his expertise and knowledge of forensic medicine, then for the celebrity he brought to the room. Michael Baden had investigated some of the most famous cases in history, sitting as chairman of the Forensic Pathology Panel of the U.S. Congress Select Committee on Assassinations, ultimately reinvestigating the deaths of JFK and Dr. Martin Luther King Jr. He was part of a team that traveled to Russia to examine the remains of Tsar Nicholas II, Alexandra and the Romanov family in Siberia in the 1990s. More than that, however, most important to the Susan Fassett case, Baden had testified as an expert witness for prosecutors and defense attorneys in the cases of Medgar Evers, John Belushi and O. J. Simpson. The man was well-respected and had a knack for charming juries, who wanted to like him the moment he sat down.

The detail that Chase had Baden talk about regarding the bullets and gunshot wounds seemed to carry on and on, which meant that the jury was probably getting tired of all the talk about ballistics from a pathologist. In fact, at one point earlier in his testimony, Baden had even said, "I'm not a ballistics expert." But Chase kept pounding the idea of bullet trajectory, which Baden was certainly qualified to talk about. He wanted to make sure the jury understood exactly how many times Susan was shot at point-blank range and where those bullets ended up.

Finally, after scouring through his notes one last time for a few brief moments, Chase looked up at Baden and said, "Thank you, Doctor." In total, Baden had been on the stand for an hour and ten minutes.

It was 4:10 P.M. Baden was in a rush—as was usual for him—to get out of there and on to his next case, but Noel Tepper still had plenty of time left in the day to begin his cross-examination. There was a lot to talk about—several questions left unanswered. For example, it was clear how Susan Fassett died and how her killer had managed to shoot her so many times in such a short time frame. But how did any of it fit into the context of Fred Andros, Tepper's client? Tepper was curious how any of Baden's testimony had reflected back on Fred, who wasn't even at the murder scene.

CHAPTER 61

The judge called for a brief recess after Baden's direct testimony. When everyone returned, Noel Tepper stood, took one last look at his notes and began to address Baden, who beat him to the punch, saying, "Good afternoon, Mr. Tepper."

Tepper smiled. "Good afternoon . . . couple of, just a few areas I'm interested in. One, sir, is my understanding is that one of the bullets fractured her wrist?"

"Yes, sir."

And for the next few minutes, Tepper seemed to be "interested" in the injury Susan sustained on her wrist, but for what reason no one actually seemed to know. It was as if Tepper wanted to insinuate that Susan couldn't have opened the door to her Jeep with her left hand if she had been shot in the wrist. But then, what did that matter, really, in the grand scheme of the crime? Susan had managed to open the door. So what?

Perhaps Tepper had nothing to trip Baden up on. So why not waste everyone's time by talking about an insignificant point? It was certainly better—and looked a lot more inconspicuous—than simply standing after the direct examination and saying, "I have nothing, Your Honor."

After the wrist argument, Tepper moved on to the bullet found in the door frame and asked if Baden knew for sure which trajectory the bullet had traveled, by looking at the way it was lodged in the metal.

Again, the questioning was a diversion from the fact that he had nothing else to argue.

Then he asked Baden how close the shooter was at the time of the murder. Baden explained, rather convincingly, that if a person is shot at close range—meaning eighteen inches or less—there are generally powder burns on the victim's clothing and on her skin tissue. With Susan, there were neither.

Not to be outdone by the district attorney, Tepper had his associate, Mary Jo Whateley, act out a scenario with Baden, which also could have happened. But again, no one in the courtroom could understand what significance it made to the case.

By 4:45 P.M., Tepper was finished. Chase stood and had a few redirect questions for Baden that amounted to nothing, and Baden was released from his obligation.

The Monday of the following week was a holiday, so the jury was excused until Tuesday, which came and went without the case moving forward because of another ill juror. Then on Wednesday it was Mary Jo Whateley's turn to be sick and the trial was postponed until the following day, Thursday, February 15, when Senior Investigator Tom Martin returned to the stand to resume his direct testimony.

Martin first talked about several photographs he took of Fred's basement, indicating that Fred had a second, private telephone line downstairs in the basement of his house inside his workshop. Then he broke into a discussion over how he extracted the bullet from the door frame of Susan's Jeep. When he finished, Chase asked Martin about some of the machinery Fred had downstairs.

"As I recall," Tom said, "there were six drills and one drill press."

Martin described what type of drills they were, saying, "Power equipment."

"What else did you remove besides the drills?"

"We removed numerous drill bits, as well as some metal shavings in and around the workbench area and on the floor."

The strategy, through the questioning by ADA Frank Chase, was to get those metal shavings into the record and allow jurors to think about them. In the end, BCI couldn't prove that the metal shavings were from Dawn's .45-caliber weapon. But why not drop that notion into the jury's mind-set, anyway?

Noel Tepper stood and went right at Tom Martin. "Were you in charge of the investigation, or at least the collection of evidence?"

"The crime scene aspect of it, yes, sir."

"Now," Tepper said, "the crime scene was Martin Road, correct?" He was looking down at his notes, then looking up.

"Yes, sir."

"And you are a *senior*"—he emphasized the word so as to sound sarcastic—"investigator *Martin*?"

"Coincidence only," Martin said, explaining away Tepper's contention that perhaps he was related to the person whom the road was named after.

"No relation? Did you also make a determination that as part of the choir there was a William Paroli Jr.?"

This was a surprise to many in the courtroom. William Paroli Sr. was the man Fred had been indicted in connection with in the federal corruption probe. Tepper was trying to say that his son, Paroli Jr., was part of Susan's choir. This was something BCI had never heard.

"I'm sorry, sir?" Martin answered, quite confused by the mention of Paroli's name.

"Did you determine or learn that a member of the choir was a William Paroli Jr.?"

"No, sir. First I heard of *that.*"

"You don't know who was in the choir or not?"

"No, sir, not at all."

"Now, when you viewed the scene," Tepper said, moving on, "for the first time, were you able to denote where the glass was located at that time?"

For the next few moments, Tepper kept on asking questions about the glass from Susan's driver's-side window and how Tom Martin had collected it. Then he moved on to the bullets and bullet casings. Of course, Tepper knew what everyone else knew: there were no casings found at the scene.

"And you were unable to recover any casings?"

"There were no casings at the scene, correct."

"And how far did you look around?" Tepper asked, almost making the leap that it was Martin's fault for not finding any.

"Pretty extensively, and we used metal detectors also."

"In your experience, for every bullet, there is a casing?"

"You are right, yes, sir."

"And you were also in charge of recovery from both vehicles that were involved, or *supposedly* involved in this incident, correct?"

Tepper had a way of stopping and starting his questions to try to accentuate the points he wanted to make. He was quite good at making something out of nothing. Somehow, by asking the questions—rather common, insignificant questions at that—Tepper made them seem important. And, truly, that was his job: to beckon reasonable doubt. Try to get his client a fair trial by making the jury think about every single aspect of the case: don't just assume something is either accurate or true because a police officer said so.

Question everything. Take nothing for granted.

"Which vehicles?" Martin asked. He wanted to be sure he and Tepper were on the same page. A good law enforcement witness, experienced in testifying, was aware of the tactics defense lawyers—especially high-profile lawyers like Tepper—used to try to draw reasonable doubt into an otherwise airtight case.

"Talking about . . . ," Tepper said slowly, deliberately and rather sharply, ". . . the Jeep Cherokee and the Ford Taurus."

"Yes, sir."

"And you searched both vehicles, both the undercarriage and inside thoroughly for casings?"

"Myself and/or members of my staff, yes, sir."

"And are you aware of the fact that the so-called *killer,* or the *person* who said that she shot the gun, only claimed that she found *four* casings?"

"That rings a bell," Martin said. "It rings a bell, yes, sir."

"And there was concerns about locating the additional two casings?"

"Yes."

"And you were unable to do so after trying?"

"That's correct. Yes, sir."

Over the course of the morning, Tepper tried to make it appear as if there could have been another shooter. Sure, Dawn had admitted it—but she had also claimed that Fred Andros had made her do it. So Tepper had to bring in a sense of mystery to the trial and ask the jury to at least consider other alternatives.

In the end, however, the evidence spoke for itself. No matter what he said, or didn't say, Tom Martin couldn't change the facts of the case.

Throughout the remainder of the afternoon, Chase and McLoughlin called in their ballistics experts to confirm the fact that Dawn's gun, proven to be the murder weapon, had been tampered with.

At one point, McLoughlin asked Craig Grazier, who had tested the weapon, what his opinion was regarding why the weapon was disfigured. "To try and to destroy the identification of the lands and grooves in the inside of the barrel," Grazier said. It was as simple as that. What other purpose would someone have for destroying what was a perfectly fine weapon?

In what turned out to be an important point, Grazier further testified that they could tell the gun was tampered with after the murder because the bullets recovered from Susan's body were unhampered and contained markings made by the lands and grooves of a perfectly normal gun barrel.

Art Boyko told the jury about all the times he questioned Fred at his house and how Fred shot himself in the face on the day BCI served a search warrant. Then Special Agent James O'Connor followed with his version of Fred fingering Dawn as the shooter.

After that, the trial broke for the weekend. When everyone returned on Tuesday, February 20, Jim Karic testified, along with Investigator Kevin Rosa, who was the DA's final witness.

When Tepper called his first witness shortly before lunch recess, rumor inside the building was that Fred

Andros was going to testify next. No one was sure if Fred was bold enough to do it, or if Tepper was going to allow his client to become fair game for the DA, but whispers in the hallway outside the courtroom were that Fred's ego would not allow him to keep his mouth shut.

CHAPTER 62

Dressed in a light green, firmly pressed business suit, white dress shirt and emerald tie, sixty-one-year-old Fred Andros was sworn in at 1:35 P.M. on Tuesday afternoon, February 20, 2001. Fred stood and pledged an oath to tell the truth—but then, most everyone sitting, anticipating this pinnacle moment of the trial, knew that Fred Andros was likely never going to tell the truth about his role in Susan's death, or possibly anything else in his life. By now, Fred was not the powerhouse political player he had once thought he was, leading up to Susan's murder. He was a broken man, stained by his own hand, charged with conspiracy to commit murder, and was an admitted corrupt former city official who had been indicted on bribery and extortion charges. When it came down to it, Fred Andros had no credibility left with anyone but his lawyers.

When Fred left his job at the Water Department in May 1999, he went begrudgingly, and not under his own free will. It was a forced resignation—although, reading his initial letter to the board and his supervisor, one would be left with the impression that it was Fred's health that led him to make a *decision* to leave. *Due to major medical concerns,* Fred had written, doctors had *advised* him to *take immediate action* in controlling his *health problems.* He said he had discussed the situation with his doctors and members of his family and, *with deep regret,* was being forced to *submit this letter as a notice of my intent to retire . . . effective May 26, 1999.*

Sometime later, however, a second letter emerged, in which Fred wrote, *From around 1994 up until April of 1999, I agreed with other town officials and with . . . William Paroli Sr., to do a variety of illegal things.* From there, he explained how he and Paroli had approached *contractors working in the Town of Poughkeepsie and used our official power to extort bribes.* There were two occasions specifically, Fred mentioned, where he personally *picked up more than $5,000 in cash from contractors.*

During a hearing before his trial, another evil part of Fred's true nature was unveiled by a former coworker who had heard Fred make a threat one day on someone's life. The man in the Water Department who had taken over Fred's position had been, according to Fred, giving Fred's son, who kept his job after Fred was forced out, a "hard time." One of Fred's former coworkers testified during a pretrial hearing that Fred had talked about "hiring a hit man" to whack the guy if he didn't start treating his son any better.

"He seemed like he was agitated," the man testified during the hearing, speaking of a conversation he'd had with Fred in August 1999, a few months before Susan's murder.

"If [that guy] doesn't leave my son alone," Fred told his coworker, "I am going to take him down with me in the federal case. If the feds don't take him, I'll have him *hit!*"

Ending the conversation, Fred had said, "I can have anybody hit for about five grand."

* * *

The courtroom was pin-drop quiet as Noel Tepper stood and began questioning his client. It seemed the entire town—if not the entire building, of which Susan and Fred had at one time worked in and knew many of the same people still roaming the hallways and sitting in on the trial—wanted to hear Fred's side of what was a seemingly sordid tale of sex, betrayal and murder. What would Fred say? How much would he admit? What new revelations was he going to divulge in an already scandalous case? It was almost as if a live soap opera everyone in town had been following for two years was finally coming to an end—and here was the main scriptwriter, the man behind the curtain, ready to release the end of the saga.

For the first few moments, Tepper had Fred explain where he grew up and how his health had declined over several years. In between, Tepper was sure to bring out the fact that Fred had a son who had cancer and a former wife who died of cancer. Not that the information had anything to do with the trial, but it was always a good move to play the sympathy card.

"You indicated," Tepper asked at one point, "that you were depressed in the spring of 1999?"

"Yes."

"Was that connected to anything that was happening in your life?"

Fred paused a moment, as if calling on tears, but relinquished the emotional display for a quick answer. "Yes, that was directly connected to the investigation of the Town of Poughkeepsie corruption."

"And what was your role in that investigation?"

"I was a suspect in that investigation."

"And isn't it true that you do have a federal conviction?"

"It is true."

From there, Fred went on to tell a rags-to-riches story of how he had worked his way up through the Water Department without a college education.

"And when you finally resigned," Tepper asked, "what position did you hold?"

"Superintendent."

"Was that the highest position in the Water Department?"

"Yes, it was."

Then came the invitation to discuss Dawn as Tepper asked Fred if he recalled when they first met—"twenty, twenty-five years ago," Fred said—and "under what circumstances."

Fred explained that he and Dawn were CB radio fans and connected through the CB one night. He and his wife ended up meeting Dawn and her husband for a drink somewhere not too long after. The way he spun it, Fred made it sound as if the four of them were great friends who got together all the time for dinner and drinks and fun nights out. But then, Tepper asked if the relationship ever became "more than just a social friendship."

"Yes," Fred answered stoically, as if beaten, "I was restoring an old Mack truck that I had got, and I needed a Klaxon horn for it. And one of the people in Hunter, New York, had that type of horn. And I was going to pick it up and I was talking to her on the CB radio and she said, 'Well, why don't you stop at the house before you go back.' I said, 'OK, I will.' So I did."

"And did you have a sexual relationship at that moment, at that time?"

"Yes, I did."

"Did you continue having a sexual relationship with her?"

"I wouldn't think more than twice, and that was early on. After that, no."

Fred went on to give his interpretation of the relationship he had with Dawn—that is, after the initial sexual
encounters began, when he and Dawn were more or less
just friends who talked a lot.

"And what was it that you spoke about on the conversations at the time?"

"Oh, God," Fred said with a queer sort of nostalgia in
his voice, "many, many things." He made it sound as if
the thought was comforting; as if he was a sounding
board for Dawn back then. "The one important thing
that we spoke about is that she was leaving her husband
and going to Tennessee with some boyfriend she had
met up there. And I tried to talk her out of that. I said,
'You know, you got a young son'—I think the boy was
two years old at the time. But I was unsuccessful, and she
went, anyway."

Dawn never denied that Fred was once a good friend.
She never said he wasn't a good listener, either, nor that
he hadn't given her fitting advice on occasion regarding
family problems she was having. If anything, Dawn was
suggesting that this was one of the reasons why Fred felt
he could later confide in her and threaten her family
and demand she kill Susan—because he had known her
so darn well.

"Did you have any discussions about your own marital
problems, too?" Tepper wanted to know next.

"We discussed it, yeah," Fred said defeatedly. "I was
having a few problems, too, and not to the point I was
going to Tennessee, but certainly I had marital problems
at that time. It was just something we talked about."

Apparently, by Fred's estimation, sleeping with Dawn
outside his marriage fell under the "few problems"
column of life's domestic ills.

CHAPTER 63

The courtroom would not have to wait long for an answer to the question of how honest and open Fred Andros was going to be on the witness stand. Sure, talking about his and Dawn's early relationship was a breeze. He could rattle on all day long about how much he was "there" for Dawn when she needed money, or how he became a shoulder for her to cry on, or maybe called upon to give her some sage advice about her messed-up life. Heck, Fred could even slap around Dawn's reputation a little by degrading her.

"Did you notice any change in Dawn . . . ?"

"Yes," Fred answered instantly, smiling at the thought. "She had gained weight and she had her hair cut shorter. And she had a gruff exterior. I would say she was not lady-like or timid, like she was before she left." They were discussing how Dawn was when she returned from her little rendezvous in Tennessee with the man she thought was the love of her life.

Fred had tried desperately to sound like the guy next door, the country-bumpkin type, who lived a wholesome Gomer Pyle–like existence. When Tepper asked him to describe a few "discussions" he'd had with Dawn, just casual stuff, to show how close they were, Fred responded with: "Oh, my golly . . . in what period of time?"

Then came the contradictions to Dawn's story: one after the other.

"Did you ever have occasion to take photographs, or have photographs taken, of any of [Dawn's] relatives?"

"No." Fred smiled as if the question was ridiculous.

"Did you ever show her any photographs of her relatives?"

"No."

"Did you ever possess any photographs of any of Dawn's relatives?"

"No."

"Did you ever threaten Dawn harm to any of her relatives?"

"No."

"Was there ever a situation in which you demanded payment, repayment of money from her?"

"No." Fred shuffled in his seat a bit, shaking his head in disgust of the question.

"What is the most she ever owed you at any one point in time?"

"Four hundred dollars." (Quite the discrepancy: Dawn had testified, Tepper pointed out, that she had owed Fred upward of $17,000 at some point.)

Many had wondered how Susan and Fred had hooked up, to begin with, besides the fact that they had worked in the same building and, for about twenty years, had run into each other quite often. In Fred's own way, he nearly admitted that he manipulated Susan into beginning an affair. "My wife had recently died," Fred said, referring to the year 1995, when he and Susan started seeing each other romantically. "Susan was helping me with insurance forms and stuff like that. I was extremely upset about it. And she was helpful, extremely helpful to me. She talked to me. She was in a consoling kind of way. And I came to see her nearly every single day. And one thing just led to another. And we realized it was more than just friendship."

That was one way to describe it. But others claimed Fred had badgered Susan—had called and called and called her, using the death of his wife as a means to both draw on Susan's inherent sympathetic nature and, at the same time, worm his way into her good graces.

"Did you understand she was married?" Tepper asked.

"Yes, I did."

"Did that have any effect on the relationship?"

"It did not." Fred went on to note that the intimate sexual aspect of the affair wasn't what drove either of their feelings, explaining, "The main part of the relationship is that we realized how close we were and how much we loved each other. And it was talking, holding each other, crying on each other's shoulders a lot. But certainly, the sexual thing was secondary." (Indeed, Fred had a series of regular hookers who took care of those needs for him.)

It got to the point where many sitting in the courtroom who knew Fred and Susan personally began to wonder if Fred was talking about the same relationship they had witnessed. Jason Fassett, especially. He sat and shook his head as Fred described the relationship he'd had with his mother, as if the two had had some sort of connection of the soul. It disgusted Jason to sit and hear Fred talk about his mother as though the two of them had led some sort of secret, dreamy life out of an old Hollywood romance film. The way Fred had spun it, he and Susan were helping each other solve life's most difficult problems.

"The guy had my mother killed," Jason said later, "and he's up there talking about her like she was the love of his life."

Fred said Susan met Dawn in late 1998 and continued seeing her into 1999. They met, he said, at the water-pumping station in Poughkeepsie. Fred said he just happened to be working at the station one afternoon when Susan brought him lunch and Dawn happened to be driving into town to pay him back a few dollars he had loaned her. "And when Dawn came in, Susan was there. And I introduced her to Susan, and I introduced Susan to her, and went about my general work about the place. And Dawn and I went downstairs in the basement because I had to check one of the valves down there, and she gave me back the money that she owed me. And we went back upstairs, and I went on about my business. And her and Susan were talking for a while."

It was from that chance meeting, Fred suggested, that Susan and Dawn decided to hook up and begin a sexual affair, at first, without his knowledge.

As the DA had proven quite clearly already, however, not one piece of evidence existed that tied Dawn and Susan together outside of the relationship each had with Fred.

After Tepper asked Fred if he had, in any way, conspired with Dawn to murder Susan, Fred answered, in a raspy inflection, a simple, straightforward, shameless "No."

Those sitting in the courtroom looked at one another, not so much shocked, but perhaps more stunned by the confidence Fred had displayed in his swift response.

Jason Fassett shook his head slowly back and forth, whispering to himself, "F***ing liar . . . all you've ever done is lie, lie, lie."

To make sure the jury understood his client, Tepper asked the same question, but in another way: "Did you tell Dawn Silvernail that you wanted Susan Fassett dead?"

Without hesitation Fred replied forcefully, "Absolutely not!"

Fred seemed comfortable on the stand, answering

Tepper's questions quickly and tersely, without adding much additional information. He never once stopped to think about a question before blurting out what seemed like a well-rehearsed answer. The guy was cocky and unabashed, even now, as he sat and obviously told one lie after the next. What made Jason Fassett cringe was when Tepper asked Fred to talk about the night he received news of Susan's death—the moment after the telephone call from Special Agent James O'Connor. How Fred felt. What he thought.

It wasn't what Fred had said that made Jason's stomach turn, it was what Fred did before he spoke. He had the nerve to pause for an uncomfortable amount of time and ask Judge Dolan for a moment to "compose" himself, as if reliving that moment of the call had brought back such an overflow of emotional pain he couldn't speak about it immediately.

Fred's own wife had testified that Fred rolled over and went back to sleep after getting the news. Why such an emotional reaction now, sixteen months later?

Jason tensed up as Fred denied the accusations made against him by the DA's office. Tepper brought each one out through his careful line of questioning. If one had never read the newspapers or knew anything about the Fred-Susan-Dawn dynamic, he would think from listening to Fred that the guy barely knew Dawn and rarely saw Susan. When Tepper got into questioning Fred about the "alleged" sexual encounters between him, Susan and "supposedly" Dawn, Fred said he couldn't believe Dawn had actually told that story to the police.

It was Susan, he testified, who "told me about the lesbian affair. . . . I was flabbergasted when she told me."

A big surprise, in other words. Fred couldn't believe it.

Regarding the proposed location of the encounter Fred supposedly videotaped, the water-pumping station that

Dawn described to BCI investigators Jim Karic and Bill Gray, Fred laughed a bit as Tepper asked him, "Is this the type of place where you'd want to take off your clothes?"

"You wouldn't want to do that in *that* building," Fred answered with a bit of sarcasm, as if it were the last place on earth he'd ever have sex with a woman.

Inside his car with hookers, sure. But a water-pumping station?

No way!

As for the videotape allegation, Fred shook his head, shrugging it off, saying, "That just did not happen, sir. . . . I'm not really sure where she got that idea. . . . Susan Fassett was a *lady*. It was not something she did. If it had been suggested, well, her answer would have certainly, certainly, been no."

Tepper talked about the day Fred tried to commit suicide. He claimed one of the reasons for the attempt was because he had been "shocked, confused [and] scared to death" over losing "Susan . . . and I couldn't take the torment."

Tepper further asked Fred to describe that day.

"I went upstairs," he said, "got a gun, put it under my chin and squeezed the trigger."

He made no mention of being literally chased up the stairs by the sound of BCI converging on the house to serve a search warrant.

CHAPTER 64

Fred's world was full of denial and absurdity; he sat and explained a life to jurors that no one else who had taken the stand before him had agreed with in any way. It was as if Fred Andros had reinvented himself. Yes, for the past year, Fred had perhaps sat in his prison cell and scripted a conflicting chain of events that he wished had taken place. But now he was trying to sell those lies to the court and jury—and it wasn't working out so well.

Susan Fassett had spent a lot of time during the final months of her life trying to keep her weight down, getting her hair done as often as she could, her teeth capped and polished, and just doing her best to take care of herself and do the things she had always wanted to do. "She was just . . . physically probably feeling the healthiest and most beautiful she had probably felt in a long time. Unfortunately, it was this other person, Fred, who gave her what she needed in response to that," Jason Fassett later said.

The trial had changed Jason. Sitting there listening to Fred lie, and having his mother's life laid out in full view for the whole world to judge, and then splashed across the front pages of the local newspapers, made Jason tougher in one sense, but also more vulnerable and quiet in another. "I wear my heart on my sleeve now," Jason explained, "and I think it's more important not to hide things from those you love. I want people to know me and know who I am—and that wasn't the case before this all happened to me and my family."

No matter how the murder of his mother had changed him, the lies Fred Andros spewed on the witness stand stung Jason. He was twenty-two years old. He had grown out of that rebellious stage of his life that had gotten him into so much trouble when he was younger. There were things he understood a bit clearer now. Still, he couldn't comprehend why, for example, if Fred had loved his mother the way he claimed he had for all those years, he couldn't have worked it all out some other way? Fred had slept with Susan only days before her murder—testimony had brought that out. Apparently, they were at least talking about getting back together.

As Jason got himself a drink of water in the hall during a quick recess, he thought about how his life since his mother's murder had pretty much run on autopilot. The time, he realized, had flown by. That first October in 2000 was rough, he admitted. And every day since her death had been painful and depressing. But Jason was carrying on best he could. "It's hard," he said, "that specific day, October twenty-eighth. Kind of brings it all back for me every time."

Someone mentioned that court was back in session and Fred was getting ready to take the stand again, but this time it was Ned McLoughlin's turn to ask the questions.

Jason finished his water hurriedly and headed back into the courtroom. With any luck, McLoughlin could at least redeem part of Susan's memory that Fred had tried to destroy all over again.

CHAPTER 65

Fred didn't look as comfortable facing off against Ned McLoughlin as he had with his own lawyer. It was 3:30 P.M. when McLoughlin approached the front of the small courtroom and went to work on Fred. Looking at the clock, McLoughlin knew he had just about ninety minutes left to question Fred. The way to get him to trip up was to stick to the facts. Fred had been lying so much throughout the day that it was going to be difficult for him to keep track of what he had said.

McLoughlin started by asking Fred how much debt he was in near 1999, suggesting that Fred owed credit cards bills, home equity lines of credit and other loans in excess of $200,000.

"I—I don't think it was that high," Fred stammered, "but—"

The prosecutor ran through the list.

After a series of questions about a $400,000 garage Fred had built in back of his house, which was paid for, one source later told me, with stolen monies from the town and extorted monies from contractors, McLoughlin asked, "Did you have [Dawn's] home number?"

"Yes."

"Call her at home?"

"Once or twice."

"Fair to say the majority of your calls, though, were to page Dawn, put in the last digits of a pay phone and have her stand by, and you'd call her back?"

"Yes, that's what she suggested I do."

Fred had just testified on direct that Dawn and Susan met at the pumping station and on that day Dawn had paid him back money she had borrowed. McLoughlin wanted to clarify something for the jury that Fred himself had said.

"Did you tell (FBI Agent) Jim O'Connor (during that December 1999 interview) that Dawn drove down to borrow three hundred bucks because she had a car problem, and then she paid you back a couple of months later?"

"I don't recall that."

"You don't remember saying that to O'Connor?"

"No, I don't."

Fred wasn't going to admit to anything. In the scope of the trial, McLoughlin knew it wasn't Fred that would convince the jury to convict, but all of the other evidence the DA had presented to prove how much Fred had lied. For example, Fred's excuse for receiving several telephone calls from Dawn on the day of the murder was laughable. He told the jury Dawn had called him "hours before the murder" to explain how "angry she was at Susan for failing to return numerous telephone calls" from her throughout that day. She was so mad, in fact, she had "planned to visit Susan that night at the church." Fred was saying, indirectly, that Susan and Dawn were having a lover's quarrel and that he was in the middle—and now that spat had made Dawn upset enough to drive to the church and confront Susan. Still, where were the telephone records to prove Dawn had phoned Susan?

None existed.

Anybody in the courtroom who had followed the proceedings over the past few weeks was well aware that the evidence proved, without a doubt, that Susan and Dawn did not have a relationship outside of the three-way ménage à trois they were involved in with Fred.

The state asked, "When Investigator Art Boyko showed up at your house at somewhere near three-thirty in the morning," referring to the early-morning hours after Susan's murder, "you knew what it was that Dawn had said to you the previous afternoon?"

Indeed, she was heading over to the church to confront Susan.

"That's correct," Fred said.

"So you had a clue for BCI about the murder of Susan Fassett, didn't you?" McLoughlin suggested.

"I can't recall," Fred answered. And then he explained that his memory wasn't as sharp as it once was, ever since his suicide attempt. There were things that he had forgotten about and doctors told him it was because of the gunshot wound to his head.

At one point, McLoughlin asked Fred a simple question: "Did you ever consider the idea of telling Susan Fassett, 'Hey, I can't tell you why, but don't go to choir practice tonight'?" If what Fred had said earlier—that Dawn had expressed an interest in harming Susan—had any truth to it, why wouldn't he warn Susan about Dawn? After all, he said he loved Susan. Why would he allow his lover to be hurt without stepping in and doing something about it?

"No," Fred said.

McLoughlin took it one step further. "How about an anonymous call to the police station, then? Is that something you did?"

"No."

"Why couldn't you just page Agent O'Connor and say to him, 'I'm worried about the woman I love'?"

Fred said, "No."

Then came the questions regarding why Fred waited so long to tell authorities that Dawn had murdered Susan. If what he was saying was true, once he found out Susan had been shot, he had to believe that Dawn had done it. She'd expressed a desire, according to Fred, to confront Susan about not returning her phone calls. Moreover, Fred had not told the police or federal authorities until December 21, 1999, on that night in the U.S. Attorney's Office in White Plains when his feet were put to the flame. It was nearly two months before Fred spoke up, and that was only *after* he was poked and prodded and backed into a corner. Ned wanted to know why. If he had loved Susan so much and was so distraught over her death to the point of contemplating suicide, why not tell authorities right away who had committed the murder, or even who he *thought* had committed the murder?

After a long pause, Fred had the nerve to say that he was "afraid Dawn would implicate" him in the crime if he came forward and told anyone what she had done.

Regarding the calls Fred had made to Dawn throughout the day of the murder, McLoughlin wanted to know why Fred would telephone Dawn at her work so many times. "Didn't you make these calls?"

"How do I know?" Fred denied. "The telephone records could be mistaken."

What became clear as Ned McLoughlin walked Fred through every situation he had gotten himself into, and ultimately lied his way out of, was that Fred Andros was going to continue to lie—and there was no sense in confusing the jury more than they likely were already.

After the prosecution put on a total of twenty-nine witnesses over the course of eleven days of testimony,

Noel Tepper was confident that two witnesses and Fred's testimony would suffice. Ned McLoughlin had spent the following morning, February 21, 2001, asking Fred a series of questions before Fred Andros was let off the hook and was sitting once again in front of the judge, next to Tepper.

And then the defense rested its case at three-thirty that same afternoon.

CHAPTER 66

Noel Tepper argued that the case against his client, Fred Andros, was fairly straightforward, as far as the jury should be concerned. As he gave his summation before the jury on the morning of February 22, 2001, Tepper kept it pretty simple. He called Dawn "a murderess and a liar." He said she shouldn't be believed. Nor should she be trusted in any manner whatsoever.

"If Dawn was willing to murder," Tepper said at one point, "I will have to assume she was willing to lie also—and it's pretty clear she *did* lie a number of times, *under oath*."

All great points.

In the end, Tepper went on for about two hours, finally saying, "If you think Dawn lied, you have every right to disregard her testimony."

And if Dawn's story was tossed out, what, really, was left?

It came down to a few important things, DA Ned McLoughlin suggested during the opening moments of his summation. "Common sense that you bring as regular citizens to this process," he encouraged, "to determine what is and what is not, according to your own life experience and your own sense. And it's also about accountability, how we hold someone responsible for something we say they did."

Ned McLoughlin spoke of a man, a former prosecutor, who would leave an empty chair beside him during murder trials to remind jurors of the victim. Concerning his victim, Susan Fassett, McLoughlin said Fred had committed the "ultimate larceny. . . . [Susan's] life, her future, has been taken from her. Her future as a mother, future as a wife, has been stolen. Someone took it. And the name on this indictment, ladies and gentlemen, is not Dawn Silvernail. It's Fred Andros. That's who is charged here. That's who, despite other suggestions, you need to examine based on the grand jury charge."

Dawn had admitted her role and agreed to plead guilty already—don't make the case about Dawn at this stage, he implored.

This murder, McLoughlin suggested, was all about Fred Andros.

The jury didn't rush to judgment—although, the verdict would still come in rather quickly. After the first day of deliberations, jurors retired for the night and decided to come back the following day for more discussion. Senior court reporter Thomas Loguidice was ordered to read back certain sections of testimony for jurors and then they quickly went back into deliberations.

Awhile later, at about 11:30 A.M., the jury was back in the courtroom asking to hear the charges against Fred read once again back to them.

For the remainder of the afternoon, until about 3:58 P.M., jurors hacked it out and then announced that they had reached a verdict.

Fred Andros was found unanimously guilty on both counts: murder and conspiracy. Fred dropped his head and sighed, while one of his daughters, who had been supporting her father most every day, fell down and lapsed into great tears of anguish and melancholy, while the jury was polled.

The judge set a sentencing date for March 14, 2001, when Jason Fassett, who had been forced to sit in silence throughout the trial, would have his day in court to speak up for his mother and tell Fred Andros exactly what he thought of him.

CHAPTER 67

On March 14, 2001, Ned McLoughlin addressed the court regarding a notification that, God forbid, if Fred Andros was ever let out of prison for any reason, an immediate notice be given to the Fassett family. Jef Fassett wanted to know the moment his wife's killer—if ever—was walking the streets a free man.

"The court will take care of that," the judge said.

McLoughlin had a letter in his hand written by Mary Ann Taber, Susan's sister, that he slowly read into the record. Then Susan's mother, Helen, approached the front of the courtroom and began to read from a statement she had prepared. *"Fred Andros, it's hard for me to find words to describe how I feel about you. I had never seen you until you walked into the courtroom. You can't imagine the awful thoughts that came into my mind when I saw you. I have never had such thoughts about anyone in my life before. You were the person [responsible] for the death of my daughter."*

Helen spoke about the mistakes her daughter had made in life. She talked about how much her family would miss Susan, ending, *"I now pray that you spend the rest of your life in prison,"* adding that she was *"sorry"* Fred's family had to go through such a *"difficult time"* on his account.

Helen and Mary Ann were simple, God-fearing

women, much like Susan. They didn't need a litany of words to describe the pain they felt—and would continue to feel. It was clear in the few words spoken by Helen and Mary Ann's letters that the depth of Susan's death was just beginning for them. (Sadly, Mary Ann would soon die of brain cancer and Helen from old age.)

Jef Fassett read from a statement, noting how much Fred had taken away not only from him or even his sons, but the little world they all lived inside the Poughkeepsie region. The many different people Susan had helped would no longer benefit from her loving and caring nature.

And that in itself was a crime, a damn shame.

"You claimed to love Susan," Jef said sternly, with emotion, *"but you've never had any concept of what love is, other than the love of yourself."*

Jef called Fred a *"predator of women,"* adding how Susan's one *"fatal mistake was that she tried to discard you first and your answer was to orchestrate her death as a punishment for her defiance."*

Jason Fassett was not an angry kid. He was not some revenge-filled, bitter murder victim's son who was hell-bent on showing his rage to the one man who had caused his mother's death. But then Jason never expected how he was going to feel while standing in front of Fred, talking about his mother and how Fred had manipulated and conned and then killed her without one measly smidgen of remorse or guilt.

"I sat in back of you every day in this courtroom with a million thoughts racing through my head," Jason said, *"all boiling down to how could this be my life?"*

The courtroom was mesmerized by Jason's sincerity. He was mad as hell—sure he was—but he had also been closer to his mother than anyone else on the planet. Damn it, he missed her.

"From the day that this happened," Jason continued, *"I knew that you did this. As much as I wanted to not believe it and as much as I told myself this cannot be real, not even you were capable of it, I knew the truth."*

As Jason spoke, he began to feel a sense of empowerment building, as though through talking about it, some sort of redemption would greet him when he finished. So he went with his feelings, saying at one point, "I knew that only one person could actually be pathetic and desperate enough to hurt my mother. And as you know, better than anyone, Fred, it wasn't your wife or my father, or even Bill Paroli or the f***ing Loch Ness Monster, or whoever else you want to come up with next." (All people—save for "Nessie"—Fred Andros had at one time accused of possibly being responsible for Susan's murder.) "It was you! You did this. You planned my mother's death. And you got some worthless Andros pawn to do the dirty work for you."

Near the end of what was turning into a long bashing of Fred's character and a rebirth, if you will, of Susan's value to the community and her family, Jason said, *"The two emotions I know—I love my mother and I hate you. Every person you took my mother away from hates you. There is half a room full of people here that hate you!"*

Concluding, Jason spoke of a *"higher court"* that would ultimately judge Fred, adding, *"My mother will have her justice, and you will suffer for all eternity."*

Little did anyone know on that day, as they all sat and listened to this heartbroken kid talk about his mother, that "eternity" would come for Fred a lot sooner than he or anyone who knew him might have expected. And that chance encounter with Susan (if one is subject to believe in a life after death) was—as the courtroom sat and listened to the judge sentence sixty-one-year-old Fred Andros to the maximum penalty of twenty-five years to life on one count, and eight-and-a-third to twenty-five years on a second count—right around the corner for Fred Andros.

CHAPTER 68

Dawn Silvernail was sentenced on March 16. As expected, Dawn was given eighteen years to life, a sentence of which she would likely serve the former end. Dawn was entirely remorseful and apologetic for her crimes during her sentencing hearing, and quite convincing about her wish to change what were "six seconds" that ended Susan Fassett's life.

Jason Fassett spoke once again, promising upfront that he would watch his language this time. In many ways, Jason had the same message for Dawn that he'd had for Fred. During one point, he said, *"From a place in my heart that I imagine I only have because of the compassionate person my mother was, I hope to one day forgive you."* Concluding a few moments later, he said, *"I hope that nothing I said was meant to hurt anyone from the Andros family or the Silvernail family because they are all victims of this just like my family. And I don't want them to have any more hurt or pain."*

After several legal matters were discussed, Dawn took to the floor to add whatever bit of understanding she could to the tragedy. It was, essentially, the first time she had spoken in public about the case.

She admitted killing Susan.

That she had "nothing against" Susan.

And that she murdered Susan "because I was coerced by another person, who has been duly dealt with."

Further along, she added, "I know that I have done a terrible thing and I know that I have to atone for it. . . ."

Directed specifically toward Jason Fassett, Dawn said, "Sorry wasn't enough."

She knew there wasn't anything she could say to make things better.

She would "never forget Susan."

She was sorry for putting her family and their needs before everyone else's.

Finally, in conclusion, "God will deal with me."

Fred Andros passed his time in prison not adapting too well to what was a regimented environment—if you kept your mouth shut and minded your own business. His health declined rapidly. Clinton Correctional Facility in Dannemora, New York, wasn't the most agreeable place for a guy like Fred to spend the remainder of his natural life, but what could he do? This was now his home. Some of the state's most hardened criminals were housed at Clinton, and Fred would have to manage best he could.

For the next twenty months after his sentencing, Fred led a rather mundane, apathetic life behind bars. It wasn't until the quiet night of November 29, 2002, that Fred Andros's life of lies caught up with him.

He retreated to his cell that night after dinner, feeling a bit light-headed, dizzy and lethargic. He needed to lie down and get a handle on himself. Maybe his blood sugar was low? Maybe he was getting the flu?

Whatever happened next, only Fred Andros knows, because as he sat on his cell mattress, holding on to his head, Fred had what some later described as a "massive" heart attack. Soon after, he was dead.

One would think the Fassett family would entertain a bit of relief in knowing that Susan's killer had met death himself. But Jason Fassett wasn't one to cheer at another person's misfortune—no matter who he was or what he did. Still, Jason said, he was certain Fred had gone to his grave being the one thing nobody wanted to be when confronting his Maker: a liar. "He lied to himself and everybody around him," Jason reflected. "Without coming clean. No remorse. No repenting. I'm not saying you need to be absolved, or anything like that. Or even 'saved' to go to heaven. It's not that. I just think a heart attack or something that dramatic, a death with no fore-warning, for example, is born out of the lifestyle people create through things like lying. Making themselves sick by doing bad things."

Jason is entirely convinced that Fred Andros believed in his mind that he'd done nothing wrong. And that's where the true depravity of who Fred was comes into play for Jason. "As far as everyone else around him is concerned, Fred Andros was God. But his whole life was a lie. A damn lie. And inside, I know in my heart that Fred Andros *knew* that he was a liar as he went into cardiac arrest and died alone inside that cold and lonely prison cell."

EPILOGUE

"What to call Fred?" Dawn Silvernail said to me one afternoon as our interviews wound down and I asked her for a closing comment about the man she claims put her behind bars. "A dead man?" She laughed, adding, "Seriously, though. Fred got out of doing his time in his prison."

Dawn has a "really good job," she said. She lives on the honor floor of Bedford Hills Correctional Facility for Women in New York, not too far down I-84, from where she murdered Susan Fassett. The honor floor has its perks. Her life, although she is in prison, revolves around a reclusive sort of simplicity she appreciates, like the luxury of having a small television in her cell. Her one lot in life, she claims, is having to relive those "six seconds" when she took Susan's life, over and over again, every day.

"I won't call myself a 'model inmate,' but so far I've been pretty good.

"It sounds like I'm being flip about this, but I'm really not. People—inmates—have attitudes and say things off the top of their mouths. I have told several people, I am in here because the situation that happened surrounding me is something that I made happen, if you can comprehend what I mean. I am in here for taking a gun and shooting somebody. I'm not in here because I'm a liar or a thief. All I ever wanted to do was tell the truth . . ." Dawn explains.

Dawn was asked in prison once what she would ask for if granted three wishes.

"My three wishes are simple. That today was October 28, 1999. That Susan Fassett was still alive. And my husband [Ed Silvernail] still loved me." She has had one trailer visit with Big Ed. As of this writing, they are still married, though more on paper than in heart. (Big Ed refused to talk to me, saying he did not want to contribute to the hell the Fassett family has been through already.) Dawn cried as she began to talk about Ed and what she did to him. "But no matter what I do, I cannot put the bullets back in the gun and undo what I did."

In that, Dawn said she is content with paying for her crimes—and deserves the time she was given.

After all was said and done, the hardest part of everything Dawn had to face, she said, was looking back on the reality that she actually took a human life. Why not kill Fred?—this was always a question many asked, including me. In answering that, Dawn made a point to say that being brought up Catholic, she was taught that *any* life is precious.

"One of the hardest things I have to face every day is that I *took* a life—and that there's no real way for me to repay that, to give a life back."

There was one time in the prison when a civilian was working in the courtyard and the guy went into cardiac arrest. Dawn was standing on the opposite side of a locked glass door, watching the guy struggle to breathe. She'd been trained in CPR and knew how to react.

The guy went down, grabbing at his chest.

"I was forced to have to stand there in that doorway and watch an officer and another civilian try to resuscitate this man," she said, "knowing full well that I had adequate training to be able to help, and knowing that because I was an inmate, I couldn't touch this guy."

That scene bothered Dawn for weeks after and, arguably, still does.

"Here was my chance," she said, "to give a life back and the prison wouldn't *let* me. This, I felt, would have been my shot to try to help make things right."

During the fall of 2007, Jason Fassett asked me to set up a meeting between him and Dawn. He wanted to sit in front of Dawn and just look at her, he said. He wanted to ask her several personal questions—I didn't ask and did not want to know—and see for himself what her reaction would be.

I asked Dawn one day on the telephone if she'd be willing to do this.

"You mean that?" she said through tears. "There is nothing more I would ever want. You mean Jason wants to meet me?"

At first, I was a bit worried about setting up such a meeting. Was Jason ready for this? Is it something that I should get involved in? I felt Jason was still suffering and struggling with his mother's death. I didn't want to be a part of contributing to that pain any more than this book likely would.

I called Jason. "She said she'd meet you," I told him.

It was his decision. I was the messenger. I couldn't just walk away with that information and never present the opportunity to him.

"Yeah, I want to do that," he told me. He was working out of state at the time.

One of the last times we spoke, Dawn asked me about

the meeting. She wanted to know if I had spoken to Jason yet.

I told her Jason wanted to come up and speak with her at the prison.

She cried.

Personally, I think the meeting would begin the process of mending Jason's broken heart. Susan was a pious woman. She believed in Christ. She would, I'm convinced, want Jason to forgive Dawn. If not for Dawn's sake, then for the sake of Jason letting go and moving on.

As of this writing, however, Jason and Dawn have not met.

I went back and spoke to Jason Fassett after finishing the book. As we spoke, he said something that had a profound effect on me.

"Going through and [talking about this through our interviews]," he explained, "it still seems like it might be a 'story' to me. It's hard to really, truly accept my mom is dead sometimes, even now."

At that point, Jason began to talk about his mother again. He wanted to be sure I had the proper, complete picture of who she was. "She had this warm smile that said, 'I know what you've done and I love you, anyway.'"

Susan knew that she was not the only sinner in her circle of friends and family. But she never judged. She never once thought a person was beyond reproach and repair.

"The honest truth," Jason went on, "is that she was a *good* person. This ordeal with Fred is the *one* really negative event in her life."

It does not, nor should it, define Susan Fassett, or who she was as a human being, Jason made perfectly clear.

"This was more than just a crazy murder in a small town," he explained. "It was Susan Fassett. I've heard *so* many people say, 'Not our Susan.' She was *so* important to *so* many people in different aspects. . . . Being a loyal wife was the only area she fell short in, and it's the one that cost her *everything*. What's terrible about it is, she was only trying to be happy. She wasn't selfish. She just never could have imagined the trouble or hardships her actions would cause."

For Jason, the story of his mother's life and death has, he admitted, caused him to reevaluate his entire life and what it means to live a healthy, truly happy life. "There are just so many lessons I've learned from this. I may just never be able to accept the price I had to pay to learn them. On some days, I can, when I'm feeling happy and positive about the person I've become. But on other days, none of it seems worth it, when my mom's not here to see it all with me."

Jason was quite open about what it meant to him to be able to talk about this tragedy with me.

"It helps that I know I'm talking to someone who understands," he concluded, "and cares about 'what life is like now,' after all the newspapers and reporters have long forgotten. . . . I loved my mom very much. Tell her story well."

ACKNOWLEDGMENTS

Art Boyko, Thomas Martin, Dr. Michael Baden, Jim Karic and any other police officer from the New York State Police who helped me get closer to the truth deserves my gratitude. Without fine law enforcement officers coming forward and agreeing to interviews, my job would be much more difficult. I am indebted to those officers who gave me their time.

Jim O'Neil was the perfect gentleman and helped me in more ways than he knows. Gaby Monet, one of Michael Baden's producers at HBO, once told me there was a great book in this story. Well, Gaby, you were right, and I appreciate you helping me out where you could.

I used trial transcripts, thousands of pages of court documents, letters, police reports, videotapes, interviews with many of the people involved conducted by the New York State Police and the FBI, along with nearly one hundred hours of interviews I conducted myself with dozens of the people involved in this case. I greatly appreciate everyone who helped me with that part of this book.

Jason Fassett was open and honest with me and I appreciate his time, sincerity and willingness to help me explore his mother's entire life so she would be remembered as more than just a victim of murder. Likewise, I'm glad Dawn Silvernail decided to talk to me. Through those interviews, I was introduced to someone I didn't think existed: a killer with a conscience.

Finally, I dedicated this book to my wonderful editor at Kensington Publishing Corp., Michaela Hamilton, the "Duchess of Darkness." This is the ninth book Michaela and I have worked on together. It has been a pleasure and, at the same time, an honor to be able to work with Michaela.

I know I forgot someone.

If so, sorry.

Curtain.

UPDATE 2014

SMALL TOWNS, BIG CRIMES: THE MYTH OF MURDER

When I think about writing this book, I recall driving through Northwestern Connecticut on Route 44, up through the Peoples State Forest toward Mohawk Mountain (a picturesque drive everyone should be lucky enough to take once in his or her life), finally reaching the New York border at the small town of Millerton, population in the 2010 census a whopping 958 souls.

I was heading to Pleasant Valley, New York, the scene of Susan Fassett's murder. I had scheduled my first interview for the book with Jason Fassett. I was a bit apprehensive and not much looking forward to this particular meeting. On the phone, days before I left, Jason seemed, understandably so, still torn up and feeling the effects of his mother's terribly violent murder, even over a decade later. I hated like hell to have to ask him to dredge it all up again. There were embarrassing aspects of this case. It was going to be a difficult interview. Sitting and talking to victims' family members is an essential part of my research. I am humbled and grateful every time someone allows me into his home to tell me the story of a loved one's life lost to the hand of a murderer.

As I looked back recently on that drive to Pleasant Valley and my role in the world of crime and murder, a thought occurred to me: *What have we—in this country—made murder out to be?* These types of "big" questions enter my mind frequently these days. *Am I going about my work in a manner that reflects who I am and who the victim of a particular crime was?*

As a lifelong New Englander, I saw the mountainous landscape in and around Pleasant Valley as comparable to the small farming community I live in. Just a mile from my home, there's a town gazebo and green. We have a first selectman, as opposed to a mayor. We go to church bazaars, take hayrides, and see cows and chickens roaming about town. We (including myself) bounce around town in pickup trucks. The word "hayseed" comes to mind more than bucolic, and there's a bit of redneck in all of us. There's even a branch of the Amish here in town.

I love the country life. I value seeing my neighbors at local events. A school assembly takes place and you literally know everyone. There's a certain comfort in that. The center of town has that same New England charm made famous by Normal Rockwell in his popular paintings. During the Christmas season, with snow on the ground, lights on the trees, my town reminds me of Bedford Falls, the fictional town in *It's a Wonderful Life*. I am lucky, grateful, and realize that this simple life I have been given is a gift. I never forget the fact that I am blessed.

Pleasant Valley was all of this to the people I met there while working on this case—and quite possibly more. And with that serene, almost surreal picture of rural bliss in your head, tarnish it now with the idea that out of this simple community emerges the story of a local woman everyone knows having a sexual tryst with another woman and a scurvy troll of a man whom everybody also knows (and most hate). The end result, as you have just read, is the murder of one woman by the other in the parking lot of the local church.

It feels made-up. It has the same familiar, over-the-top ring of a tawdry Hollywood script. The crime itself, the aftermath, along with the sinister and salacious secrets exposed, are quite literally unbelievable. And yet it is true.

This sort of crime would devastate a small town—and certainly did here. Residents suddenly realized that no matter where you live, no matter how well you think you know the person standing next to you in line at the local market, no matter how sequestered you think you are from big-city crime, if evil wants to enter your community, it will happen with a blow that knocks everyone back into reality. No matter where you live, if someone wants you dead, watch out: you are likely going to wind up on a slab in a morgue somewhere.

It's not surprising that when you look at the top Internet searches for any year, "scandal" and "crime" dominate. Crime television, moreover, has become an absolute obsession.

I look at high-profile cases, such as Jodi Arias, Casey Anthony, Natalee Holloway, even the plight and plague of a Lindsay Lohan or Paris Hilton, in addition to our utter fascination with celebrity and all things reality TV, and I cannot help but see how these high-profile celebrity cases and crime obsessions *unfairly* reflect the reality of American crime/culture today.

The Jodi Arias case, with all of its hype and wall-to-wall coverage, is not what the average American murder is composed of, yet the Arias case and those like it exemplify perfectly our prejudices. You see, we promote cases like Arias's trial because she was pretty, took nude selfies, committed the ultimate act of bloody murder, and stared at everyone as though she were an innocent "good" girl. (Sadly, I have a strong feeling some actually bought into it!) Watching television, trolling online, and reading the news, you'd guess that Jodi Arias and those like her make up a majority of American murderers.

Wrong.

The ugly truth is, we have an obsession in this country with the train wreck of celebrity life (*we* turned Jodi Arias and Casey Anthony into celebrities), and the media's hunger for big ratings to stuff these stories (and reality stars) down our throats until we vomit—be it a blond, blue-eyed college student missing and presumed murdered; a young mother whose child winds up dead in the trunk of her car; an Elizabeth Taylor wannabe, popping pills and drinking and trashing hotel rooms; a somewhat pretty woman who photographed herself naked and decided to butcher a good man and then became a superstar during her trial; or, more recently, a homophobic, racist, bearded reality TV star.

These cases and celebrities do not teach us *anything* about the real world of murder or how crime and celebrity affects, essentially, the world (the community) we actually live in. Watching television, reading the news, you'd think the South is full of redneck, backwoods people who do stupid things. You'd think the murder rate in this country has skyrocketed beyond comprehension. You'd think most murder cases come in pretty little packages. Ask yourself this, however: When was the last time a trial with minorities at the center was analyzed or publicized by the same wall-to-wall coverage as the Jodi Arias or Casey Anthony case received?

Even more shockingly, in fact, the murder rate in the

United States has plummeted by 50 percent—yes, half—over the past two decades. Since 1981, according to the Centers for Disease Control and Prevention (CDC), the homicide rate for ten- to twenty-four-year-olds is the lowest it has ever been, just 7.5 per 100,000.

In other words, when it comes to murder, celebrity, and realty TV, things aren't always what they seem.

While I don't have the actual data, I would guess that the media's coverage of murder (and celebrity) has gone up 2,000 percent or more. Our access to stories about celebrity and crime today is unheralded and endless. We feed on this stuff all day, every day—and a majority of what satisfies our hunger for it all is not a reflection of who we are.

And that, to me, is a sad, sad fact.

The Fassett case is a textbook example of what constitutes crime today in our communities. This is a case, like most, with not so television-friendly faces. There's no gorgeous Jodi Arias or girl-next-door Casey Anthony at the center. No blond, blue-eyed, curvaceous starlet. Here we have real people! Within all of its scandal and raunchy sex, the Fassett case explains more about us as a culture than any of the high-profile cases we have come to identify as synonymous with murder in America. The murder of Susan Fassett and all of its Lifetime Television elements, its murder-in-a-small-town convolutions, the lesbianism, that frumpy, scrub of a man, Fred Andros, embody the fact that throughout the ages, the motives for murder have never wavered or changed, not in the slightest.

People kill people—and will continue to—for three main reasons: love, money, and revenge. Everything beyond these three is a subcategory branching from each. The Fassett case points clearly to the sad and ominous fact that anyone, at any time, can be the victim of a murder. The snow-globe-style perfection of small-town

America, which we think exists, is often tinged with our weaknesses and fallibilities.

People are people.

We all have faults.

We all have desires and fantasies.

We all have *secrets.*

Susan was gunned down, lest we forget, in the parking lot of a church as she came from choir practice. She was married to a local police officer. She was having sex with a female, while the man with whom she was cheating on her husband videotaped it all.

Remember, things aren't always what they seem.

Something akin to this story is going on in your town right now. It might not involve murder, but it is certainly causing great pain and loss for those involved.

There is never culpability, of course, on the victim's part, however much the news and television talking-head pundits (many of these do not have the slightest clue as to what it is they are talking about) want to play the blame-the-victim game. But we blame the victim, every time we make the perpetrator the star of our newscasts and media conversations. The murder victim is never at fault for anything, for any reason.

We all have temptations and decisions to make based on the people we interact with on a daily basis. The fact remains—and will remain for as long as we exist (and is the reason why true crime as a genre on television and in the news has blown up)—that we do not know our neighbors, some of our closest friends, or even our own family members as well as we *think* we do. And this, after we realize it, scares the hell out of us. The idea that someone we thought we knew all those years could commit an act of evil and harbor secrets we never saw coming makes us feel vulnerable, weak-minded, stupid, and violated.

I need to make this point very, very clear: Murder is no

game. It is not just fodder for nightly television viewing. Murder is not some sort of ratings-grab. Murder is not a sporting event we can analyze and talk about as if we are speaking of made-up characters. Murder is final. It affects lives (and communities) *forever.* And you cannot just go on television or speak to the media and say whatever you want about a perpetrator or victim. It's disingenuous and feeds into the overhyped and sensationalized image of what murder has become in this country.

Entertainment.

Dawn Silvernail continues to proclaim remorse for murdering Susan Fassett. Dawn says she still sees Susan in her dreams and thinks about what she has done to the Fassett family and the Pleasant Valley community every day. She is sorry. I heard from several of Dawn's former cellies that she is a paradigm of a model prisoner.

This is all great. But no matter what Dawn says or does now, we can never forget that she is a murderer. She took a gun and shot a woman. She needs to pay the price for that evil act and allow justice its course.

Jason Fassett is doing well, I'm told, and now lives in the Southwest.

Jef Fassett has moved on and remarried and lives a quiet life. Jef is, of course, a victim in this story, too. He can never, *ever* be viewed as a villain.

A close family member of Fred Andros's contacted me after the book came out and verified for me that all I had written about him was accurate to a tee. This person was close to Fred at one point, but had stepped away from him as the years passed because Fred's life had become such a maddening reflection of what was wrong in the world.

This leads me to my final point. A true, real "bad guy"

like Fred Andros resonates with us because we have come to believe (and hope) that in every human being there is an inherent drive to do and be good—that all of us have a natural instinct to care for one another. You know the feeling: We all want to give as much money as we can to the soup kitchen, promising ourselves time and again that if we hit Lotto we'll donate heaps of cash to all those people who need it. We also want to see the good in everyone. We believe, more importantly, that those we choose as friends and neighbors could never do what people like Fred Andros did—that those close to us could never hurt us. We've all seen the neighbor on the local news report saying something to the effect of: "He was a nice guy. I don't understand how this happened." (They said this about John Wayne Gacy, lest we forget!)

What we don't see is that evil is transparent, yet full of trickery. Some people in this world, whom we have to come to terms with as a community, are careless and remorseless monsters. Some are sociopaths bent on going through life taking and taking and taking (as we currently see in Washington, DC, but choose to do nothing about). They sleep, eat, and breathe darkness and narcissism. Ice runs through their veins. They don't have hearts. They do not care about you, me, or the world. They care about one thing: themselves. They have a psychopathic gene, which allows them to wear a mask of sanity and walk around as though they are our friends, loving and caring for people the same as we do.

I am here to tell you, after staring these types of people in the eyes, after sitting and speaking with men who have killed dozens and do not give a damn about those lives and their loved ones, to watch out for the sociopath— because all of you reading this right now, well, the sad truth is, you have one or two in your life as we speak.

You just don't know it.

—*M. William Phelps*

CHAPTER 1

To feel that sun on his back for the first time as a free man: *Oh, how warm and liberating.*

He took a breath. A deep one.

In through the nose, out through the mouth.

Life on the outside. It had a ring to it.

On September 4, 2001, a glorious Tuesday afternoon, exactly one week before terrorists would attack New York and the world would change forever, eighteen-year-old Kyle Hulbert found himself standing in court. Not the criminal kind, but probate. Today Kyle was set to be released.

"He's turned eighteen," Kyle's social worker explained to the judge.

Kyle sat quietly, listening; his eyes, like his mind, darted back and forth, a million miles a second. "He's not showing any signs of psychosis. We want to have him released. Declare him an adult."

Emancipation.

Kyle said the word to himself.

Emancipation.

It sounded so historical and unassociated with his life. Yet here he was.

The state spoke, claiming its position was that they didn't think Kyle was well enough to leave the facility just yet.

The judge heard the evidence and sat back to think about it.

Kyle stood and thought, *Come on . . . let me go.*

"Release him," the judge uttered.

Kyle had been a ward of the state.

Not anymore.

Funny, he didn't feel that much different when the doors of the courthouse closed behind him and Kyle found himself exiting the courthouse now his own "man," breathing that fresh Virginia air into his lungs as a free young adult for the first time. It was a day he had looked forward to over the past year, especially. With all of the problems Kyle had gotten himself into at the foster homes where he'd lived, school, and within his community, Kyle viewed this day as a new beginning. Here he was now walking out the door an independent man, dependent upon nobody but himself.

"They gave me a bus ticket," Kyle said of the court, "and cut me loose."

Stepping onto the concrete outside the courthouse, looking back one last time, Kyle considered what was in front of him. This was it. He *was* on his own. He'd have to fend for himself from this point forward. Think for himself. Feed and clothe himself.

Survive.

More important (or maybe *most* important), he'd have to medicate himself. It was up to Kyle now. No one would be asking if he had taken his meds. Or handing him a little paper cup with the day's rations inside, making sure he swallowed every last bit. It would be Kyle's decision. His alone. The state had given him a three-month supply of the psychiatric prescriptions he needed to feel right; yet it was going to be up to Kyle to go to the pharmacy, actually pick up the drugs and then ingest each pill.

Every. Single. Day.

"I didn't stay on them very long," Kyle explained. "It's a bad cycle. A minor manic phase will set in and I'll forget to take the medication."

And then the catch-22 effect would occur: Because Kyle was not on his meds, he didn't feel he needed them.

Kyle didn't realize, but he was a boy in a man's body. Truly. The state of Virginia, however, under its coveted laws, claimed he was old enough (and well enough) now to make adult decisions on his own. Tall, skinny—"lanky and scrawny" is what they'd call him. Dark black hair, silken and slick, like oil. Kyle had a gaunt look to him. Chiseled and bulimic-like weight-loss facial features: pointed cheekbones, sunken eyes, and the somewhat terribly transparent, cerebral wiriness of a hyped-up meth addict—although Kyle claimed he never dabbled in the drug. He didn't need to. Kyle was amped-up enough already by what were voices and characters stirring in his head like a thousand whispers. This, mind you, even with a dozen years of psychiatric treatment and medications behind him.

Kyle had what some may view as a strange look on life.

His birthday, for example, was not a day like most: cake and ice cream and feeling special. Kyle never did feel special—not in the traditional sense that a kid wearing a pointed cardboard birthday hat tethered by a too-tight rubber band pinching his neckline, ready to blow out candles with his family and friends surrounding him, did. Kyle called it—the day he was born, that is—his "hatching day," as if he had emerged from a cocoon, slimy and gooey and ready to take on the world, born out of some sort of metamorphosis. And yet, as he thought about it walking toward the bus stop on that emancipation day, on his own for this first time—no counselor over his shoulder, no psychiatrist telling him what he should do or how he should think anymore— this was Kyle's *true* hatching day. His rebirth. A time for Kyle to take on life by himself and make decisions based on the tools he had been given.

"I am constantly struggling with a question," Kyle observed. "Psychology teaches us that a person's personality and psychological makeup is a composite of past experiences . . . and I am suffering from a complex network of fantastical memories of things that never actually happened."

Despite his often volatile and strange behavior while in mental hospitals and in both group and foster homes, along with Kyle's biological father's request that he be continually detained and treated, the state had to cut Kyle loose. In fact, Kyle's father, who had given up custody of Kyle when Kyle was twelve ("I was too much to handle . . ."), had always kept in contact. As Kyle said, "He kept tabs on me and my entire life, and he knew about my behavioral problems. And he knew, which is why he fought against me being emancipated, that letting me off the leash was not a good idea at the time, because it was *not* going to end well. In fact, he told them, 'You let Kyle out and he is going to kill somebody.'"

The judge decided, however, it was time. Kyle Hulbert was eighteen. And Kyle, as it were, was not going to argue with being given a free pass on life.

"Kyle Hulbert," a law enforcement source later analyzed, "has been, since he was six years old, in and out of mental institutions. Kyle's world includes a number of darker characters . . . demons or presences . . . that live in his head."

And now this "man" was free to roam the world and do what he wished. Thus, on September 4, 2001, Kyle found himself on the street, walking, with literally nowhere to go.

No home.

No friends.

No family.

There was a certain "high," Kyle recalled, about being freed from the structured, routine life inside an institution. It felt good. It felt right. It felt redemptive.

"I was happy that I was free! No more leashes. No more having to worry about institutions. I was . . . free. Those are the only three words that I can say describe how I was feeling."

Kyle had been told to have a plan. And he did. Kyle said his "plan" on this day, as he walked down the street in front of the courthouse toward the bus stop, was to go and find a girl he could "fuck senseless."

After that, well, whatever came his way, he would roll with it.

CHAPTER 2

Kyle had what he called "half-baked" plans as he broke from those ward-of-the-state chains holding him down. Just out and free to do what he wanted, Kyle thought about going to college, taking up study, maybe a career of some sort. That thought came and went rather quickly, however, as Kyle realized he had to find some money to live off of first. Moreover, a lifelong dream of his to become a published writer would have to take a backseat to surviving on his own.

"My main concern was filling out the Social Security paperwork and getting that going," he said. "I had already been approved for it."

Odd, the government had approved him for mental disability and there were funds set up and headed his way, come December. Yet he was deemed "sane" enough to leave the institution and fend for himself on his own.

It didn't make sense.

Kyle said he was told by the state: "Because of your mental health, you are going to have a hard time holding down a job."

It was the reason why they approved him for financial aid.

"They had already seen how I handled jobs in the past," Kyle explained. "I got fired from each job I ever had."

There was not a doctor or therapist who spoke to Kyle over the years who did not know that demons whispered to this young man, that he saw things "others couldn't or wouldn't," and that the world spinning out of control inside Kyle Hulbert's head was not a place where happily-ever-after resided. Kyle had talked about having "dreams or visions of the apocalypse." Those "voices" inside his head would eventually (in totality) go by the name of "the 6." A lot of this, Kyle realized, sounded foolish. Imaginary. Something from a person who should be locked up. Most would respond by saying he was crazy. This sort of make-believe world he lived in as a five-year-old kid became an everyday part of his life as Kyle grew into his teens. He believed it was as real as the pet dragon he saw regularly and explained was as real as "one of my cats."

"I cannot identify the first [memory]," he said many years later, talking about that moment in childhood when these different visions and thoughts inside his head began, "and you must understand that one of the aspects of psychosis is an inability to distinguish 'reality' from 'fantasy.'"

To him, that chaos going on inside his adolescent mind—the dreams, hallucinations, and voices—were his absolute reality. It all seemed "perfectly natural . . . even if they weren't."

It did not take long for Kyle to become aware that he thought differently than the other kids around him and "there was something wrong" inside him. He knew that if he approached the other kids, talked to them about what he saw and heard, he would be shunned and ostracized, bullied, and likely beaten up, definitely laughed at. So he kept most of these things to himself, at least at first.

The voices and visions did not scare him, he said later. Some kids might be frightened by what he saw; but to him, it was a world he embraced. A secret he came to love.

There was one day—Kyle was six years old—when he had what he recalled was his first "hallucination." It is a term Kyle needed to put in quotes, he said later, because hallucination was not the best way to describe what he saw. Hallucination was merely "the quickest and most efficient way" of explaining what happened. People could comprehend what a hallucination is—yet he considered what happened to him to be real—even to this day.

Another way to describe it, he reconciled, was to use the word "magic."

Inside his head, Kyle lived within a world of his own, literally. This was *his* world. He didn't create it, he claimed. Or ask for it to appear before him. It wasn't like that at all. It just happened. One day it wasn't there and then the next, well, it was—and the most important part of this for Kyle as he talked through it years later was that to him it wasn't a fantasy, or some type of dream. It wasn't something that came and went: The bogeyman underneath the bed. The monster in the closet. The imaginary friend you sit with and share tea with as a child.

This was his life. His world.

There was one major issue—of the many that would begin to accumulate—for Kyle as he sat years later and looked back on everything that had happened.

"The biggest problem I have encountered—and one we will have to address—is that I have a great deal of memory that conflicts with things I *know* to be true. . . . Consider everything I tell you to be as 'true' as I 'know' it all to be, and any inconsistencies are entirely unintended."

This statement, so incredibly honest and sincere, would come back to haunt Kyle Hulbert as he grew into an adult, and some of what he "saw" and "heard" would indeed become reality, however interspersed with brutal violence, blood, murder, and carnage it would soon be.